National Corporate Law in a Globalised Market

CORPORATIONS, GLOBALISATION AND THE LAW

Series Editor: Janet Dine, *Director, Centre for Commercial Law Studies, Queen Mary College, University of London, UK*

This new and uniquely positioned monograph series aims to draw together high-quality research work from established and younger scholars on what is an intriguing and under-researched area of the law. The books will offer insights into a variety of legal issues that concern corporations operating on the global stage, including interaction with the WTO, international financial institutions and nation states, in both developing and developed countries. Whilst the underlying foundation of the series will be that of company law, broadly defined, authors are encouraged to take an approach that draws on the work of other social sciences, such as politics, economics and development studies, and to offer an international or comparative perspective where appropriate. Specific topics to be considered will include corporate governance, corporate responsibility, taxation and criminal liability, amongst others. The series will undoubtedly offer an important contribution to legal thinking and to the wider globalization debate.

Titles in the series include:

Company Law in the New Europe
The EU *Acquis*, Comparative Methodology and Model Law
Janet Dine, Marios Koutsias and Michael Blecher

EU Corporate Law and EU Company Tax Law
Luca Cerioni

Corporate Governance and China's H-Share Market
Alice de Jonge

Corporate Rescue Law – An Anglo-American Perspective
Gerard McCormack

Multinational Enterprises and Tort Liabilities
An Interdisciplinary and Comparative Examination
Muzaffer Eroglu

Perspectives on Corporate Social Responsibility
Edited by Nina Boeger, Rachel Murray and Charlotte Villiers

Corporate Governance in the 21st Century
Japan's Gradual Transformation
Edited by Luke Nottage, Leon Wolff and Kent Anderson

National Corporate Law in a Globalised Market
The UK Experience in Perspective
David Milman

National Corporate Law in a Globalised Market

The UK Experience in Perspective

David Milman

Lancaster University, UK

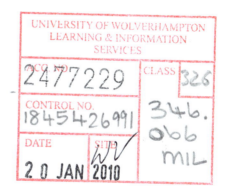
CORPORATIONS, GLOBALISATION AND THE LAW

Edward Elgar
Cheltenham, UK • Northampton, MA, USA

Published by
Edward Elgar Publishing Limited
The Lypiatts
15 Lansdown Road
Cheltenham
Glos GL50 2JA
UK

Edward Elgar Publishing, Inc.
William Pratt House
9 Dewey Court
Northampton
Massachusetts 01060
USA

A catalogue record for this book
is available from the British Library

Library of Congress Control Number: 2009930861

Mixed Sources
Product group from well-managed
forests and other controlled sources
www.fsc.org Cert no. SA-COC-1565
© 1996 Forest Stewardship Council

ISBN 978 1 84542 699 6

Typeset by Cambrian Typesetters, Camberley, Surrey
Printed and bound in Great Britain by MPG Books Group, UK

This book is dedicated to the memory of Professor R.R. Pennington
(1927–2008)

Contents

Abbreviations used for law reports and periodicals

ABLR	Australian Business Law Review
AC	Appeal Cases
ACLR	Australian Corporate Law Reports
ACSR	Australian Corporate and Securities Reports
All ER	All England Law Reports
ALR	Australian Law Reports
Am Jo of Comp Law	American Journal of Comparative Law
Am Jo of Int Law	American Journal of International Law
Anglo-Am L Rev	Anglo-American Law Review
App Cas	Appeal Cases
Aust Jo of Corp Law	Australian Journal of Corporate Law
B of Eng Quart Bull	Bank of England Quarterly Bulletin
BCC	British Company Cases
BCLC	Butterworths Company Law Cases
BJIBFL	British Journal of International Banking and Financial Law
BPIR	Bankruptcy and Personal Insolvency Reports
Bus L R	Business Law Review
Calif L Rev	California Law Review
Camb L Rev	Cambrian Law Review
CFILR	Company Financial and Insolvency Law Review
Ch	Chancery
Ch App	Chancery Appeals
CJQ	Civil Justice Quarterly
CLJ	Cambridge Law Journal
CLP	Current Legal Problems
CLR	Commonwealth Law Reports
CLWR	Common Law World Review
CMLR	Common Market Law Reports
CMLRev	Common Market Law Review

Co Law	The Company Lawyer
Col J of Transnat Law	Columbia Journal of Transnational Law
Col L Rev	Columbia Law Review
Conv	Conveyancer and Property Lawyer
Cornell J of Int Law	Cornell Journal of International law
Cornell L Rev	Cornell Law Review
Corp Gov	Corporate Governance
CSLJ	Corporate and Securities Law Journal
CUP	Cambridge University Press
DLR	Dominion Law Reports
EBLR	European Business Law Review
EBOLR	European Business Organisations Law Review
Econ Hist R	Economic History Review
ECR	European Cases Reports
EHRR	European Human Rights Reports
ELJ	European Law Journal
ELR	European Law Review
ER	English Reports
EWCA Civ	England and Wales Court of Appeal Civil Division (neutral citation)
EWCA Crim	England and Wales Court of Appeal Criminal Division (neutral citation)
EWHC	England and Wales High Court (neutral citation)
Exch	Exchequer Cases
FCR	Federal Cases Reports
Fed L Rev	Federal Law Review
Griff L Rev	Griffith Law Review
Harv L Rev	Harvard Law Review
Hist Res	Historical Research
HL Cas	House of Lords Cases
ICCLR	International Company and Commercial Law Review
ICJ Rep	International Court of Justice Reports
ICLQ	International and Comparative Law Quarterly

IFLRev	International Financial Law Review
IIR	International Insolvency Review
IJLMA	International Journal of Law and Management
IL & P	Insolvency Law and Practice
ILRM	Irish Law Reports Monthly
Ins Intell	Insolvency Intelligence
Ins Law	Insolvency Lawyer
Int Insolv Rev	International Insolvency Review
Int Jo of Disc and Gov	International Journal of Disclosure and Governance
Int Rev of Law and Econ	International Review of Law and Economics
IR	Irish Reports
Ir Jur	Irish Jurist
JAL	Journal of African Law
JBL	Journal of Business Law
JCLS	Journal of Corporate Law Studies
JIBLR	Journal of International Banking Law
JLS	Journal of Law and Society
Jo of Comp Econ	Journal of Comparative Economics
Jo of Econ Hist	Journal of Economic History
Jo of Fin	Journal of Finance
Jo of Fin Econ	Journal of Financial Economics
Jo of Fin Reg and Comp	Journal of Financial Regulation and Compliance
Jo of Int Econ Law	Journal of International Economic Law
Jo of Law Econ and Org	Journal of Law, Economics, and Organization
J of Leg Studs	Journal of Legal Studies
Jo of Leg Hist	Journal of Legal History
Jo of Law and Soc	Journal of Law and Society
Jo of Pol Econ	Journal of Political Economy
JWTL	Journal of World Trade Law
KB	King's Bench
Law and Cont Prob	Law and Contemporary Problems
Law Teach	Law Teacher
Leg Hist	Legal History
Leg Studs	Legal Studies
Liv L Rev	Liverpool Law Review

Lloyds Rep	Lloyds Law Reports
LMCLQ	Lloyds Maritime and Commercial Law Quarterly
LQR	Law Quarterly Review
Mal L Rev	Malaya Law Review
Manag Law	Managerial Law
Melb Univ L Rev	Melbourne University Law Review
MJ of Euro and Comp Law	Maastricht Journal of European and Comparative Law
MLR	Modern Law Review
NI	Northern Irish Reports
NILQ	Northern Ireland Legal Quarterly
NLJ	New Law Journal
NSWCA	New South Wales Court of Appeal
NSWLR	New South Wales Law Reports
NwULRev	Northwestern University Law Review
NZLR	New Zealand Law Reports
NZULR	New Zealand Universities Law Review
OFT	Office of Fair Trading
OJLS	Oxford Journal of Legal Studies
Ottawa L Rev	Ottawa Law Review
OUP	Oxford University Press
Ox Univ Comm LJ	Oxford University Commonwealth Law Journal
PCC	Palmers Company Cases
P & CR	Property and Compensation Reports
PL	Public Law
Pen L Rev	Pennsylvania Law Review
QB	Queen's Bench
RabelsZ	Rabel Journal of Comparative and International Private Law
RALQ	Receivers, Administrators and Liquidators Quarterly
Recov	Recovery
SALJ	South African Law Journal

SASR	South Australian State Reports
SC	Session Cases
SJ	Solicitors Journal
SLT	Scots Law Times
SMCLN	Sweet and Maxwell's Company Law Newsletter
Stan L Rev	Stanford Law Review
STC	Simons Tax Cases
Stat L Rev	Statute Law Review
Syd L Rev	Sydney Law Review
Th Inq Law	Theoretical Inquiries in Law
Trin Coll L Rev	Trinity College Law Review
Tul L Rev	Tulane Law Review
UKHL	House of Lords (neutral citation)
UKPC	United Kingdom Privy Council (neutral citation)
Univ Chic L Rev	University of Chicago Law Review
Univ Penn L Rev	University of Pennsylvania Law Review
US	US Supreme Court Reports
WLR	Weekly Law Reports

Table of cases

EUROPEAN COURT OF HUMAN RIGHTS

Table of legislation

Delegated Legislation

Preface

I am grateful for the opportunity to write this monograph as it enables me to tie together diverse streams of consciousness acquired over the past 30 years of teaching corporate law. When I entered academe as a lecturer in 1978, my focus on Company Law (as the subject was then designated) was essentially parochial. This was no fault of my teachers at the Faculty of Law at the University of Birmingham, who included the visionary Professor Robert Pennington, a scholar all too well aware of how membership of the EEC would change the shape of our national corporate law model. The problem was that for less perceptive individuals like myself, at this stage of evolution in the subject, even the EEC input appeared fairly peripheral. My belated appreciation of a much wider perspective on corporate law came about through a variety of factors. First and foremost, from the mid 1980s I became involved in teaching LL.M. candidates at the University of Manchester on a postgraduate course entitled Corporations in International Business Law. This gave me the opportunity (greatly aided by the insights of generations of students from a range of overseas jurisdictions) to reflect upon the comparative nature of the subject. Why do different jurisdictions adhere to certain basic corporate principles, whilst adopting a diversity of approach in other areas of Company Law? Are there universal core principles of Company Law? Is there an ideal model of Company Law to be located on planet Earth? Will globalisation lead to a state of convergence in Corporate Law?

Subsequently, I became wedded to the already well-established idea that for instructional purposes, the UK system of corporate law might be viewed as a *commodity* to be sold to the international business community, and that in the interests of boosting the invisible earnings of UK plc, it was necessary to develop a product that was commercially competitive. I was not alone in drawing this apparently mercenary conclusion. A perusal of the first publication in the UK Company Law Review (1998–2001) library, *Modern Company Law for a Competitive Economy*, will unearth the following statements from Margaret Beckett, the then Secretary of State for Trade and Industry:

> An up-to-date company law framework, based on principles of consistency, predictability and transparency, is particularly important in the context of a glob-

alised economy, in terms both of competing for inward investment, and producing internationally competitive companies. (para 3.8)

Later she states:

> In today's increasingly globalised economy, the national framework of company law cannot be considered in isolation. It represents part of the nation's basic infrastructure. This can best be seen in relation to business mobility. Naturally many reasons affect the decisions of internationally mobile businesses as to the country in which to locate, and it is worth emphasising that the UK scores extremely highly in general in this area; surveys repeatedly confirm that a wealth of features make the UK an excellent place in which to do business. But the security and predictability of the business environment is a key element. The Government is determined to ensure that the nation's framework of company law does not through increasing obsolescence become a disincentive to establishing business in the UK. (para 4.4)

Similar sentiments are also apparent in the terms of reference for the Company Law Review – see second bullet point in para 5.1 of those terms. The Irish Company Law Review Group, which produced its First Report in 2001 and consolidated recommendations for reform in 2007, adopted a similar perspective when embarking upon its reform study.

If we want concrete examples of how businesses are prepared to relocate to exploit more favourable corporate laws found in other jurisdictions, I would point to the migration of German businesses to the UK to use our private company format, with its lack of a minimum share capital requirement. Similarly, distressed German firms have been keen to move their base to this country prior to a declaration of insolvency, so as to be entitled to use the company voluntary arrangement model. Both of these phenomena will be discussed in this work.

My awareness of the diversity in national corporate systems, already whetted by interaction with my LL.M. students, was sharpened when I was asked in 1999 by the Company Law Review to lead a team of academics from the Centre for Law and Business at the University of Manchester to produce a study of national corporate law regimes in the EU. This study was made available on the Company Law Review website and is mentioned in the Final Report (see p. 7).

Having moved to Lancaster University in 2005 I was exposed to a new way of looking at the subject of corporate law. Heavy emphasis was given to the social and cultural foundations of corporate law. Whilst not entirely comfortable with an approach exclusively based on such perceptions, I did find a number of insights gleaned from this tradition particularly useful. My conversations with Philip Lawton undoubtedly opened my eyes to a perspective on Company Law that until that stage I had not fully appreciated.

I have taken liberties when defining the parameters of *corporate law*. In particular, I have included reference to the limited liability partnership where this is deemed appropriate. 'Corporate law' for the purposes of this study encompasses both private companies and public undertakings. The regulation of financial services and corporate insolvency fall within the catchment area. In order to complete this study it has proved necessary to trespass into related fields, such as private international law, though I claim no expertise in that subject.

The project seeks to analyse how a national system of corporate law responds to global trends. My primary goal is to focus on English law, but in order to understand actual and potential developments in that jurisdiction, the experience of other corporate systems can prove enlightening. Although the focus is on factors impelling change in corporate law, it must not be imagined that it is uniquely affected by globalisation; other substantive legal regimes have also felt the pressure of the new world order, most notably fiscal law, competition law and employment law.

The timing of this publication is not ideal. After sitting on the excellent work of the Company Law Review for several years, the government eventually produced a Bill in 2005. That was designated the Company Law Reform Bill. Although most of its reforming provisions were welcomed, many commentators observed that, if enacted, this would leave UK corporate law in a mess, in that most of the Companies Act 1985 would remain in force albeit in amended form. Certainly, the law would not be available in a user-friendly fashion. The government took this criticism on board and the Bill changed its nature to part reform part consolidation. In the process it became the lengthiest Bill on record. The Bill was finally enacted in November 2006 as the Companies Act 2006. However, because of the substantial transitional problems, its full and final implementation has been delayed until October 2009. This book will therefore be published in the period of interregnum, which is hardly ideal. I have attempted to include in an Appendix the latest state of play on implementation, but the position changes regularly here, depending on the latest ministerial announcement.

One other timing issue deserves mention. In the final months of writing up, the world financial system went into meltdown. This has caused a reappraisal of many articles of faith. The idea that free markets are the solution to every regulatory issue is no longer seriously contended. The state clearly has a role to play where markets fail. That is as true in corporate law as in every other regulatory regime.

In completing this monograph, I have been assisted by many individuals and a variety of organisations. Particular thanks go to John Birds, David Burdette, Blanaid Clarke, Phil Lawton, Geoff Morse, Sol Picciotto, David Sugarman, Adrian Walters and Gary Wilson. Former colleagues at the Centre for Law and Business at the University of Manchester have collectively afforded me a rich vein of insights. Several academics at the Nottingham Law School, where I held a Visiting Professorial Fellowship in 2008, were most helpful. Gratitude is to be extended to all such parties. Responsibility lies firmly at my door.

Generally, the law in England and Wales is stated as it stood at 31 December 2008, though some later developments have been included at proof stage.

David Milman
Centre for Law and Society,
Lancaster University,
December 2008

---

[1]　*Modern Company Law for a Competitive Economy* (March 1998).

1. Introduction

No man is an island (John Donne, Meditation XVII, Devotions Upon Emergent Occasions)

1 AIM OF THE TEXT

This book seeks to examine whether, and, if so, to what extent, UK Company Law has been affected by those processes of globalisation that have increasingly had a bearing on the course of our modern lives. This evaluation will involve both a study of the characteristics of modern UK corporate law and some comparison with the models adopted in other jurisdictions to regulate companies. The reasons for this mutation, if indeed any such metamorphosis has occurred, will also require analysis. Finally, it will be necessary to speculate on where this process will lead to in the medium term.

Globalisation is a phenomenon that has become widely discussed in popular discourse in the past two decades.[1] Although not a new concept, it arouses fierce emotions depending upon one's political perspective. Its influence has been felt in many areas of national law, particularly revenue law, employment law and trade law. Clearly, it rests heavily upon the convergence of *economies* and *markets*. However, it is a much wider manifestation than that. It is no exaggeration to state that it involves the global/regional bonding of *cultures* and *societies*. The convergence of legal cultures through transnational legal measures forms part of the equation and hence part of our study.

Very often, of course, globalisation involves a combination of economic and legal integratory forces; the emergence of the European 'Project' encompassing both EU law and the fundamental protections afforded by the European Convention on Human Rights and Fundamental Freedoms (hereafter 'ECHR') best testifies to that phenomenon. In that context, let us offer

---

[1] There is a vast literature on the phenomenon of globalisation and its merits/demerits – see, for example, J. Stiglitz, *Globalization and its Discontents* (2001) (Penguin/Allen Lane) and his follow-up text *Making Globalization Work* (2006) (Penguin/Allen Lane). R. Cranston, chapter 1 in S. Worthington (ed) *Commercial Law and Commercial Practice* (2003) (Hart Publishing) is also recommended. Note also W. Twining, *Globalisation and Legal Theory* (2002) (Butterworths).

one example of how globalisation in this wider sense has worked change on UK corporate law. In the 1980s, a headline financial scandal was the so-called 'Guinness Affair'[2] in which the shares in a party to a contested takeover (a public company) were allegedly propped up by illegal means in order to promote their attractiveness as an exchange for shares in the target company. When this alleged abuse came to light, the Department of Trade and Industry conducted an investigation[3] which resulted in the prosecution of certain leading City figures. That prosecution rested heavily upon evidence gleaned from interrogations by DTI inspectors, which were carried out without the benefit of the interviewee enjoying 'the right of silence'.[4] After convictions were obtained, one of the defendants, Ernest Saunders, challenged his conviction by arguing that to base a prosecution largely on compelled evidence involved an infringement of his civil rights under the European Convention on Human Rights, in particular Art 6 ECHR. The right to remain silent was cited as being allegedly infringed. The European Court of Human Rights, having concurred with this contention,[5] the offending statutory provisions in the Companies Act 1985 had to be changed[6] to reflect this new perception. Thus, 'how' this form

---

[2]   For an insider's account, see J. Guinness, *Requiem for a Family Business* (1997) (Pan Books). Also see G. McCormack (1994) 15 Co Law 40.

[3]   The DTI Investigation was carried out under the aegis of what is now the Companies Act (CA) 1985, ss. 432(2) and 442 (both provisions are largely unaffected by the Companies Act 2006).

[4]   The English courts had denied the existence of such a right in DTI investigations – *Re London United Investment plc* [1992] BCLC 285.

[5]   *Saunders v UK* [1997] BCC 872. Followed in *IJL* [2002] BCC 380. Notwithstanding any breach of ECHR rights (which were compensatable) the convictions could not be said to be unsafe – *R v Lyons* [2002] 3 WLR 1562.

[6]   See now Companies Act 1985, s. 434(5A), s. 434(5B), s. 447 (all largely unaffected by the Companies Act 2006). For comment on these enforced changes, see R. Mitchell and M. Stockdale (2002) 23 Co Law 232. In this context, one could also cite *Davies v UK* (42007/98) [2005] BCC 401, where the European Court of Human Rights ruled that excessive delay in prosecuting director disqualification proceedings might breach ECHR. See also *DC, HS and AD v UK* [2000] BCC 710. In *Eastaway v UK* (74976/01) [2006] 2 BCLC 361, excessive delay in disqualification processes was again held by the Strasbourg court to infringe Art 6, but in *Re Blackspur Group (No. 4)* [2006] 2 BCLC 489, the English courts made the point that a breach of Art 6 did not necessarily undermine any resulting disqualification. Having said that, these rulings have had an impact and may well explain why the undertakings procedure is used so extensively these days. The ruling of the ECHR in *GJ v Luxembourg* [2000] BPIR 1021 that protracted delay in completing liquidation may breach Art 6 is also beginning to exercise the minds of practitioners. Not all ECHR challenges have proved as successful – witness *Fayed v UK* (1994) 18 EHRR 393, where it was held that rights under Art 6 were not affected by the process of investigation itself, as the investigation process did not determine rights.

of legal globalisation has worked change is exemplified in one particular respect.

When evaluating the 'why?' question, *two* reasons become apparent immediately. Firstly, European harmonisation processes have *forced* corporate law change on the UK (and in fairness on the other 26 EU Member States). Secondly, our understanding of (and respect for) different cultures has increased immeasurably over the past 30 years. This is partly due to the power of the media, the popularity of foreign travel, the rise of the internet, but also as a result of a growing willingness to engage in commerce across foreign borders on an arm's length basis (as opposed to crude imperialistic exploitation). Potentially profitable markets have to be tapped, no matter where located. That willingness has been boosted by technological advances, particularly with regard to communications methods, transport innovations and money transfer systems. This trend towards opening up our perspective on global commercial life in turn has given impetus to comparative studies of law. It is fair to say that no self-respecting law reform body would produce a report for the adaptation of its national corporate law without recourse to some comparative analysis. During the course of the following study, other influences will become evident.

2 COMPANY LAW IN SOCIETY

Most developed jurisdictions find room for a legal institution known as Company (or Corporate[7]) Law, with the pivotal foundation being the artificial legal person known as the company. This is not surprising because even so-called primitive jurisdictions would feel at home with the idea of an artificial entity (such as a temple or an idol) being treated as a legal person. The company has become *the* prime exemplar of an artificial legal person existing in modern society. Hundreds of millions of such 'persons' now inhabit the globe. They provide the main employment prospects for much of the world's population of natural persons, and some corporations are so large as to rival (and even supplant) many national governments of developing countries in terms of their economic muscle.[8] The company has become the pivotal

---

[7]   As far as I am concerned, these terms are interchangeable. The fact that this branch of law is more usually labelled as 'Corporate' rather than 'Company' is an indicator of a growing US influence on discourse – see Chapter 9 below.

[8]   For instance, Janet Dine, quoting published data, tells us in *Company Law* (6th edition, 2007) (Palgrave Macmillan) at 353 that 51 of the top 100 economies in the world are operated by corporations rather than by nation states. Having said that, it is sometimes easy to overstate the case for the power of multinationals – see S. Wheeler, *Corporations and The Third Way* (2002) (Hart) at 9–10.

economic player in Western-style capitalist societies. That socio-economic model now dominates the globe, but it is not above criticism.[9] Corporations are an everyday feature of modern life, but are not always regarded as fully fledged citizens (see, for example, their treatment under Indian constitutional law[10]). It is not part of this study to examine whether the corporation is a force for good or an instrument of the devil. This is a fruitless exercise often coloured by one's own political prejudices. We merely accept the corporation's ubiquity and recognise the corresponding need to regulate it.

In Chapter 3, we shall attempt to define the fundamental components necessary to make a Company Law model operate effectively.

3 CORPORATE LAW HISTORY

Companies have long been associated with commercial venturing in far-flung territories. The earliest form of company recognised in English law, the chartered company, was almost exclusively preoccupied with this sphere of commercial activity. One could cite here the Muscovy (or Russia) Company (1555), the Levant Company (1581), East India Company (1600), the Hudson's Bay Company (1670) and the Royal Africa Company (1672).[11] Many of these chartered companies lasted for hundreds of years; some are still with us today.[12] In 1688, the power to charter corporations passed effectively from the Crown to Parliament, but it was still exercised, with the British South Africa Company (1889) being a good example of the latter genre.

It should never be forgotten that one of the seminal events in the history of UK company law was tied up indirectly with the forces of 'mercantil-

---

[9]   The classic exposé was presented in A. Sampson's *The Seven Sisters* (1975) (Hodder and Stoughton). Note also P. Muchlinski, *Multinational Enterprises and the Law* (1979) (Blackwell). See also Joel Bakan, *The Corporation* (2004) (Constable), Noreen Hertz, *The Silent Takeover* (2002) (Arrow), Janet Dine, *International Trade and Human Rights* (2005) (CUP). There is an excellent selection of essays in M.K. Addo, *Human Rights Standards and Responsibilities of Transnational Corporations* (1999) (Kluwer). See also D. Kinley (2004) 25 Co Law 298. The piece by R. McCorquodale and P. Simons in (2007) 70 MLR 598 is also recommended.

[10]   In the UK, clearly little thought was given as to whether corporations qualified for protection under the Human Rights Act 1998.

[11]   For the advent of chartered companies, see chapter 2 in J. Micklethwait and A. Wooldridge, *The Company* (2003) (Weidenfeld and Nicholson), W.E. Minchinton in chapter 7 in T. Orhnial, *Limited Liability and the Corporation* (1982) (Croom Helm) and M.B. Likosky, *The Silicon Empire* (2005) (Ashgate) at 61–8. For an illuminating history of the Russia Company, see R. Griffith (1994) 15 Co Law 105.

[12]   See *DTI Annual Companies Report 2005–06* for further details.

ism',[13] in some senses a precursor to the modern phenomenon of globalisation, but in reality a crude vision of economic trade/global resources as a finite cake to be divided between those exerting the greatest political/military might. In effect we are talking about a zero-sum game in world trade. Developed in France in the 17th century, mercantilism expostulated that export trade was to be encouraged at all costs by opening up new markets through dubious means. In England, it is arguable that this philosophy set in train the events that ultimately led to the infamous South Sea Bubble Affair in 1720.[14] The origins of the company (which had been incorporated in 1711) that was later to achieve notoriety in that context lay in the desire to trade across national barriers, in particular the intention to dominate the slave trade with South America. The collapse of that company, which by that stage had redesigned itself into a domestic speculator in the National Debt, led to a dead hand being placed on the development of UK corporate law for over a century by the enactment of the Bubble Act[15] (with its draconian, but little used,[16] criminal enforcement procedure), a piece of legislation which remained on the statute book until 1825.[17]

General incorporation[18] was introduced in English law in 1844. The introduction a decade later of limited liability in English law was undoubtedly influenced by events elsewhere, as will become clear in Chapter 2.

In later times, the influence of transnational corporate venturing on the shape of English corporate law was apparent. Many of the great prospectus frauds in the late 19th century were carried out in the context of companies said to be operating in the more remote corners of the globe.[19] A general

---

[13] For discussion of this economic theory of mercantilism and its impact on English law see D. Hughes Parry (1931) 47 LQR 183 at 198. The theory itself clearly has its limitations and was at the time rejected by influential thinkers such as Adam Smith in *The Wealth of Nations* (1776) (Penguin Classics, 1968), where free trade was preferred.

[14] For studies of the Bubble, see Viscount Erleigh, *The South Sea Bubble* (1933) (Peter Davies Ltd), V. Cowles, *The Great Swindle* (1960) (Collins), M. Balen, *A Very English Deceit* (2002) (Fourth Estate) and R. Dale, *The First Crash: Lessons of the South Sea Bubble* (2004) (Princeton University Press). The periodical literature is also extensive: L.C.B. Gower (1952) 68 LQR 214, M. Patterson and D. Reiffen (1990) 50 Jo of Econ Hist 163, A. Santuari (1993) 14 Jo of Leg Hist 39.

[15] 6 Geo I c. 18.

[16] Prosecutions were rare – see the comments of LCJ Ellenborough in *R v Dodd* (1808) 9 East 516.

[17] 6 Geo IV c. 91.

[18] See H.N. Butler (1986) 6 Int Rev of Law and Econ 169.

[19] See R. Cranston, chapter 1 in S. Worthington, *Commercial Law and Commercial Practice* (2003) (Hart). On the fictional front, see A. Trollope, *The Way We Live Now* (1875) (OUP edition, 1982), where a central plot line involved a fraud connected with the incorporation of 'The South Central Pacific and Mexican Railway'.

perusal of the case law of the period throws up some delightful and exotic corporate names.[20] Public outcry at prospectus frauds led to corrective legislation in the form of the Directors Liability Act 1890. Another element in the jigsaw was the issue of foreign seizure of assets held by UK companies engaged in global commerce and in particular seizures effected in the wake of the Russian Revolution in 1917. This caused many difficulties for the English courts.[21]

Bringing us through to modern times, we can clearly see how the collapse of the US-based energy giant Enron in 2001 has shaped the development of corporate law not merely in the US (through the Sarbanes-Oxley Act 2001[22]), but also in many jurisdictions where Enron subsidiaries were incorporated and operated.[23] Foreign issuers in the US have been forced to comply with new tougher US standards on disclosure and corporate governance, thereby promoting a greater degree of convergence in these areas. In the UK, the Companies (Audit, Investigations and Community Enterprise) Act 2004 contained a number of elements influenced by a desire to combat an Enron-style fraud.[24] There is a growing consensus that there has been an overreaction to the Enron débâcle[25] and parallels have been drawn with the misguided Bubble Act. On a European level, the Parmalat scandal[26] will have compara-

---

[20]   See *Central Railway Co of Venezuela v Kisch* (1867) LR 2 HL 99, *Erlanger v New Sombrero Phosphate Co* (1878) 3 App Cas 1218, *Re Cape Breton Co* (1885) 29 Ch D 795, *Re Ambrose Lake Tin and Copper Mining Co* (1890) 14 Ch D 390, *Lagunas Nitrate Co v Lagunas Syndicate* [1899] 2 Ch 392. Generally, note *Re German Date Coffee Co* (1882) 20 Ch D 169, *Ooregum Gold Mining Co of India v Roper* [1892] AC 125, *Allen v Gold Reefs of West Africa* [1900] 1 Ch 656, *Moseley v Koffyfontein Mines* [1911] AC 409.

[21]   See, for example, *Re Baku Consolidated Oilfields* [1994] 1 BCLC 173.

[22]   On SOX see M.G. Lunt [2006] JBL 247, J. Friedland (2002) 23 Co Law 384 and E. Wymeersch (2003) 3 JCLS 283. The stringent requirements imposed by this Act on directors signing up to public share offers issued by their companies has led to a decline in placings in New York and a corresponding boost for the London market. For the impact on foreign issuers, see S. Harter-Bachmann (2006) 27 Co Law 35

[23]   For European reactions to Enron, see K.J. Hopt (2003) 3 JCLS 211. For the French response to Enron, see S. Hebert [2004] JBL 656.

[24]   See The Companies (Audit, Investigations and Community Enterprises) Act 2004, ss. 8 and 9 (CA 1985, ss. 389A, 389B) (provisions improving auditors' access to information and increasing the potential liability of directors for information provided to auditors) – replaced by CA 2006, ss. 499–501.

[25]   On Enron and its consequences, see P. Davies, chapter 8 in J. Lowry and L. Mistelis, *Commercial Law: Practice and Perspectives* (2006) (Butterworths), J. Armour and J.A. McCahery (eds), *After Enron: Reforming Corporate Governance and Capital Markets in Europe and the US* (2006) (Hart Publishing), W. Bratton (2002) 76 Tul L Lev 1275, S. Griffin [2003] Ins Law 214, T.R. Hurst (2006) 27 Co Law 41.

[26]   For background on the Parmalat collapse (which occurred in December

ble effect. It certainly appears to have influenced the adoption of EC Directive 2006/43 on Accounts.

Most recently of all, the sub-prime lending crisis in the US has caused perturbation throughout the financial sector in Western Europe, placing more than one banking corporation in jeopardy.[27] This has led to the nationalisation of one UK bank, the downgrading of many financial institutions and the rethinking of banking regulation in many countries. The ensuing credit crunch has spread from financial institutions to the retail and manufacturing sectors of many economies by restricting access to capital and through reduced consumer expenditure.

4   CORPORATE LAW 'FAMILIES'[28]

It is possible to produce an ethnography of corporate law systems. Legal scholars like Wood[29] have done much to open our eyes to this phenomenon and other academics have intervened in the debate. Here is my suggested preliminary breakdown:

4.1   Systems Based on English Law

This group consists of jurisdictions which formerly were part of the British Empire or territories that fell under the British mandate after the First World War (for example, Palestine[30]/Israel). Reflecting the massive extent of that political entity, one finds systems of corporate law dotted across the globe that are reassuringly familiar. This similarity arose out of the wholesale export of

---

2003), see A. Melis (2005) 13 Corp Gov: An International Review 478. The Parmalat case has not had a great impact in the UK, but it was problematical in Ireland hence the fiercely contested *Eurofoods* litigation – see Chapter 8.

[27]   On the implications of Northern Rock for the European Single Market, see C. Bamford (2007) 29 Co Law 65.

[28]   See J.H. Farrar and B.M. Hannigan, *Farrar's Company Law* (4th edition, 1998) (Butterworths) by at 748. Note also K. Pistor et al. (2003) 31 Jo of Compar Econ 676 and K. Pistor et al. (2003) 23 Univ of Penn Jo of Int Econ Law 791.

[29]   See *Maps of World Financial Law* (3rd edition, 1997) (Allen & Overy Global Law Maps), and P. Wood (2003) 24 Co Law 34 for an unusual classification. Geographers have shown scholarly interest in the distribution of governance models – see G.L. Clark and D. Wojcik, *Geography of Finance: Corporate Governance in a Global Marketplace* (2007) (OUP).

[30]   For a recent study that suggests that the transplantation of English company law into post-Ottoman Palestine was not as simple a process as it might appear to be, see R. Harris and M.Crystal – http://works.bepress.com/ron_harris/13. This article will appear in (2009) Th Inq Law.

UK statutory law (including the Companies Act) as part of a policy ultimately tied up with imperialism and bolstering the position of British traders.[31] One result, according to Gower, was that the Companies Act 1948 acquired the status of a Commonwealth statute![32] The application of common law principles had both a similar motivation and effect. Some of these imported legal standards were specifically retained by post-independence legislation to operate in default of new lawmaking. The Privy Council undoubtedly played its part in this process through the instrumentality of its Judicial Committee.[33] A survey of corporate law models found in Africa, the Indian subcontinent, Asia, the Caribbean and in the old dominions would produce strong evidence of the impact of the English corporate law model. In some of these countries, the model is more advanced than that operating in the home country, as some jurisdictions have been adept at implementing company law reform proposals more quickly than English law.[34] As that Empire has fragmented, so have these 'subordinate' jurisdictions looked for sources of inspiration other than English law, a process exacerbated by the move of English company law into the EU tradition. Typically, corporate systems based upon the increasingly dominant North American model have filled the void. This has been noticeable in the Pacific rim jurisdictions, especially in New Zealand and Australia. The Caribbean countries show a similar pattern. Israel moved in that direction in 1999.

---

[31]   On this, see R. McQueen (1995) 5 Aust Jo of Corp Law 187 and his more recent piece in (2008) 17 Griff L Rev 383. Note also R.S. Rungta, *The Rise of the Business Corporation in India* (1970) (CUP).

[32]   (1962) 4 Mal L Rev 36.

[33]   See, for example, *North West Transportation Co v Beatty* (1887) 12 App Cas 589 (shareholder voting obligations), *Natal Land v Pauline Colliery* [1904] AC 120 (pre-incorporation contracts), *Cook v Deeks* [1916] 1 AC 554 (fiduciary duties of directors), *Lee v Lee's Air Farming* [1961] AC 12 (corporate personality) *Howard Smith v Ampol Petroleum* [1974] AC 821 (directors' duties on a takeover), *Taupo Totara v Rowe* [1978] AC 537 (directors' payoffs), *Downsview Nominees v First City Corporation* [1993] AC 295 (liability of receivers in negligence), *Agnew v IRC (Brumark)* [2001] UKPC 28 (fixed or floating charge?), *Citco Banking Corp v Pusser's Ltd* [2007] UKPC 13 (alteration of articles), *Gamlestaden* [2007] UKPC 26 (unfair prejudice jurisdiction), *Benichou v Mauritius Commercial Bank* [2007] UKPC 36 (floating charge crystallisation). Most former British colonies have discarded the Privy Council and we are left with a number of small independent Commonwealth countries plus a few Crown dependencies. Canada ceased sending cases to the Privy Council in 1949. Malaysia followed suit in 1985, as did Australia in the following year. In more recent years, Singapore (1994), Hong Kong (1997) and New Zealand (2003) have gone down the route of deciding not to send appeals to the Privy Council.

[34]   The prime example here is Ghana, which for many years had one of the most advanced corporate law models in the Commonwealth. Jamaica implemented the recommendations of the Jenkins Committee (1962) in 1965, some time before the UK legislated – see S.J. Leacock [1975] JBL 252.

4.2 US-inspired Models

Originally a British colony, the USA became an imperialist power in the old sense of the concept (witness its conquest of the Philippines[35] and other Spanish colonies) and that political status enabled its models of corporate law to penetrate the furthest corners of the globe from the Caribbean[36] across the Pacific. The military victory of the US over Japan in 1945 also had profound effects upon Japanese corporate law.[37] In more modern times, the overwhelming economic power of the USA (and US-based multinationals) has led to an even wider dissemination of US corporate law influence. Thus, today, much of the Caribbean and many Central/South American states now take their corporate law lead from the US.[38] The influence has spread to Canada, New Zealand and other Pacific rim jurisdictions. Even within Continental Europe (where latent hostility to US cultural dominance is strong), it is not uncommon to find corporate law concepts and reforms being inspired by American ideas. The idea of a group of companies is indisputably American in origin and is now used as a primary business vehicle across the developed world. Certainly, a perusal of reforms in the area of corporate rescue across many nations will find the pervasive influence of the iconic Chapter 11 of the US Bankruptcy Code.[39] The same could be said of the development of rules regulating insider trading/market abuse, the evolution of codes of corporate governance practice and the emergence of the corporate social responsibility philosophy. The role of US-based institutional investors (such as CalPERS, the Californian public service employees' retirement services pension fund) also cannot be underestimated in the spreading of US corporate law hegemony, as a significant percentage of its holdings are in foreign securities. US vulture funds dealing in distressed debt are making their presence felt in many economies (and legal systems). The media has also played its part by elevating to cult status certain American law corporate practices. Popular discourse in corporate law matters is dominated by 'Americanisms' – terms such as 'insider trading', 'Chinese walls', 'poison pills', 'raiders', 'greenmail', 'junk bonds', 'prepacks' and, most recent of all, 'sub-prime lending' are now universally recognised.

---

[35] For the Philippines, see P. Herrera-Davila (1981) 2 Co Law 139.

[36] For the Canadian influence in the Caribbean, see S.F. Goldson (2003) 24 Co Law 378.

[37] For a clear account of Japanese corporate law, see S. Bottomley in chapter 3 of R. Tomasic (ed.), *Company Law in East Asia* (1999) (Dartmouth).

[38] On Barbados, see J. Purvis (1983) 4 Co Law 280.

[39] This is certainly true of Germany, which reformed its law of corporate rescue in 1999 with Chapter 11 very much in mind.

4.3   Civil/Continental Law Jurisdictions

The paradigm here is France, which of course built up an impressive imperial portfolio in competition with the British Empire. The influence of French corporate law is found in the wider Europe,[40] Africa,[41] in certain parts of the Caribbean and South America, in South Asia and in Quebec. Louisiana corporate law has a strong French flavour to it. The Middle East is also an area where French corporate law ideals have penetrated. Other continental legal systems have left some imprint on global corporate law. The Dutch have shaped corporate law developments in their former colonies (such as Indonesia[42]) and also South Africa. The German influence is less marked across the globe, mainly because of the loss of its imperial territories in the wake of its defeat at the end of the First World War. Having said that, ideas can prove more robust than political entities and German corporate law influences can be detected in countries such as Cameroon[43] and Japan pre-1945. China has flirted with the two-tier board model. Within Central Europe there is a strong and continuing German law influence, with Austrian Company Law being the prime manifestation. The new accession Member States, based in Eastern Europe with their transitional economies, will naturally look to Germany for inspiration because of the geographical proximity of this economic powerhouse. A perusal of the enterprise laws in the now defunct state of Yugoslavia will attest to that.[44] Rather like English law, this continental tradition is under threat from the American hegemony. Argentina moved very much into the Anglo-Saxon camp with its corporate law reforms in 1983 and China appears to be heading in the same direction.

4.4   Other Families

This residual category is diverse. One could certainly assert that there is now an EU family of corporate law spanning some 27 jurisdictions. That 'family' is best viewed as second generation, drawing upon traditions from the discrete categories outlined above. The US influence on EU law is clearly present (particularly in the area of business rescue), though until recently there has been a marked reluctance to concede the fact.

---

40   There is a definite French corporate law influence in Turkey (see M. Yavasi (2000) 21 Co Law 225) and Greece.

41   For the Ivory Coast, see V.B. Dumonteil and J.J. Bartagna (1984) 5 Co Law 47.

42   See A.I. Pulle (1996) 17 Co Law 122.

43   Cameroon was a former German colony transferred to a French mandate.

44   See J. Dine, M. Koutsias and M. Blecher, *Company Law in the New Europe* (2007) (Edward Elgar) for discussion of the Yugoslav Enterprise Law 1996.

There is also a dwindling band of jurisdictions that locate a system of corporate law (if they have one) within a strong socialist tradition. At present, these countries, led by China, Russia and various non-EU Eastern European states, are very much in the market for importing corporate law models. The process of change here has been remarkable,[45] though the net effect on diversity has been negative.

The Islamic view on corporate law is interesting. Although usury is banned by the Sharia, there is no fundamental objection to the idea of a company with separate legal personality nor to the economic consequence of limited liability. Corporate law systems in Egypt, Jordan and Saudi Arabia have much in common with Western models. There is a growing and accessible body of literature on corporate law systems in these traditions.[46]

Other jurisdictions are difficult to fit into any model – South Africa is perhaps the best example of this genus.[47] Although the impact of Roman/Dutch law generally was marked in pre-Boer War days, the corporate law system was for many years influenced by English law. Influence must not be read as dominance; witness the South African hostility to the floating charge for proof of that qualification. Increasingly, in recent years this jurisdiction has moved towards the orbit of US corporate law. This has caused problems in certain areas (such as business rescue), where the US influence is at odds with underlying cultural traditions.

5 UNITARY AND FEDERAL MODELS

In categorising systems of corporate law, the political structure of jurisdictions can create difficulties. In a unitary state, the relevant corporate law applies generally. However, many large modern states are organised constitutionally along federal lines. The obvious example is the USA, but the same problem

---

[45] On corporate law developments in Russia, see W.G. Frenkel (1996) 7 ICCLR 175, S. Lucas and Y. Maltsev (1996) 45 ICLQ 365, O. Markova (1998) 8 ICCLR 334. Note also the essay by K. Pistor, chapter 9 in J. Sachs and K. Pistor (eds), *The Rule of Law and Economic Reform in Russia* (1997) (Westview Press). More generally, the work of R. Dragneva (ed.), *Investor Protection in the CIS: Legal Reform and Voluntary Harmonization* (2007) (Martinus Nijhoff) is recommended.

[46] See, for example, the pieces by L.M. Al-Rimawi, looking at corporate law in various Arab countries, in particular Jordan – (1998) 19 Co Law 28, (1998) 19 Co Law 89, (1998) 9 EBLR 30.

[47] For South African Company Law and its history, see S. Girvin (1992) 13 Jo of Leg Hist 63 and J.J. du Plessis (1993) 14 Co Law 224. Sri Lanka also has a Roman-Dutch law heritage in its Company Law model – see D. Jayasuriya (2008) 29 Co Law 250.

arises in major corporate law players such as Canada and Australia. In these countries, corporate law is restricted by internal 'state' boundaries. This has the potential to generate much confusion and economic dislocation. 'Uniform'[48] companies legislation seems to be the preferred solution, but constiutional difficulties abound. Thus, in Australia in 1990, a bizarre legal power battle over the soul of corporate law was played out. In *NSW v The Commonwealth*,[49] the High Court of Australia confirmed that the Commonwealth of Australia lacked the constitutional power to enact a manda-tory statute governing corporations. A pragmatic settlement then had to be brokered which involved the states themselves opting into a new Uniform model statute.[50]

The solutions to the problem of federal states here are varied. One way out is to make corporate law the exclusive subject of federal legislation, but polit-ical sensitivities need to be borne in mind. Another, more subtle, model is to start from the premise that corporate law is the province of the local states, but to provide a standard model into which such states can contract. This is now the favoured approach. One could note here the Model Business Corporations Act[51] in the US and the Canadian Business Corporations Act[52] as exemplars of this methodology. This was also the solution worked out in Australia in the wake of the constitutional litigation mentioned above. In addition, one could identify certain strategic areas of corporate law that are to be governed by federal law: for example, the Securities and Exchange Acts and more recently the Sarbanes-Oxley Act 2001 in the USA.[53] The US Bankruptcy Code of 1978 also exemplifies the federal perspective.

6   THE PICTURE IN THE UK AND BRITISH ISLES

The United Kingdom presents an interesting conundrum. Although, superfi-cially, we have a unitary political entity, the forces of devolution are growing.

---

48   See R.W. Parsons [1962] JBL 235.
49   (1990) 169 CLR 482.
50   For discussion, see R. McQueen (1990) 19 Fed L Rev 245.
51   For information on the MBCA, which was produced by the American Bar Association in 1950, see the ABA website.
52   On the Model Business Corporations Act and the Canadian Business Corporations Act 1975, see L. Getz (1971) 5 Ottawa L Rev 154. The changes in Canada can be traced back to the Dickerson Report of 1971.
53   On Sarbanes-Oxley, see M.G. Lunt [2006] JBL 249, J. Friedland (2002) 23 Co Law 384. Part 1 of this Act boosts the powers of supervisory bodies and upgrades direc-tors' responsibilities.

Indeed, in the realm of corporate law, we have always had several distinct systems operating alongside each other for some 150 years. Thus corporate law is administered in England and Wales separately from the regimes operating in Scotland and Northern Ireland. Each of the latter jurisdictions has its own Companies Registry, based in Edinburgh and Belfast respectively. The significance of this multiplicity of company law administrative units was reflected by the extraordinary case of *Re Baby Moon (UK) Ltd*,[54] where it was held by Harman J that an English company, which had erroneously located its registered office to Scotland, could be wound up in England as the English jurisdiction applied, but leave would need to be granted by the English courts to serve the petition out of the jurisdiction at its registered office.

Although the administration of UK corporate law is devolved, the fundamental substantive core has much in common. Many of the provisions of the Companies Act 1985 apply automatically in Scotland, though that Act did contain discrete provisions designed solely for Scotland (for example, Part XVIII on floating charges). These provisions have since been superseded by Part 2 of the Bankruptcy and Distress (Scotland) Act 2007 (ss. 37–49). The same is, however, still true of the Insolvency Act 1986 – one could note here the different approaches taken towards preferences in ss. 239 and 242 respectively. Section 239 requires the person giving the alleged preference to be influenced by a desire to prefer; no such motivation requirement is found in s. 242, which focuses on the effect of the alleged preference. Under the Scotland Act 1998, company law is a reserved matter outside the competence of the Scottish Parliament and therefore notwithstanding the fact of devolution, the power to legislate in company law matters is reserved by Westminster.[55] Notwithstanding these trends towards a harmonised approach, the courts of the two jurisdictions have in the past indicated a propensity for divergence and there is no reason to doubt that this healthy diversity of judicial attitudes will continue and become more marked in the future.[56]

The position is somewhat different for Northern Ireland,[57] which had its own statutory code prescribed by the Companies Order (Northern Ireland)

---

54   (1984) 1 BCC 99, 298. The distinct nature of the two systems is also apparent on reading *Arthur Little v Ableco Finance* [2003] Ch 217, though that case illustrates how blurred the boundaries can become. Note also *Re Brownridge Plastics Ltd* (unreported) (2005), where the question before Hart J was the appropriate court to file notice with when putting a Scottish company into administration.

55   Under the Scotland Act 1998.

56   See, for example, the difference of opinion reflected in *Dimbula Valley (Ceylon) Tea Co v Laurie* [1961] Ch 353 and *ex parte Westburn Sugar Refineries* [1951] AC 625 (on dividend payments), and *Jesner v Jarrad Properties* [1993] BCLC 1032 and *Re Guidezone Ltd* [2000] 2 BCLC 321 (unfair prejudice jurisdiction).

57   Under CA 1985, s. 745, Northern Ireland generally fell outwith the scope of the Companies Act.

1986 (SI 1986/1032, NI 6) (as amended), which usually mirrors legislation enacted by the Westminster Parliament. There can, however, be a significant time lag, which may work to the disadvantage of Northern Irish businesses. That position is likely to change as s. 1284 of the Companies Act 2006 is now largely fully implemented (with effect from October 2008), in that Northern Ireland will be covered by the Companies Acts. This principle is further developed by ss. 1285–7 of the Companies Act 2006. This change has been brought about to enable businesses in the Province to get the immediate benefit of corporate law reforms enacted in Great Britain.[58] This is particularly important where deregulation is now often the prime mover behind company law reform.

We must not forget other territories within the British Isles but technically outside the UK (and the EU). The Crown Dependency of the Isle of Man has its own distinct corporate law 'brand' (based upon the 1931 Companies Act[59]), as does Jersey[60] and Guernsey.[61] These jurisdictions can be quite flexible as they compete for offshore business, the main driver of their respective economies. The Companies Acts do not for the most part apply to the Channel Islands or the Isle of Man, apart from Part 28 of Companies Act 2006, which regulates takeovers. This exception is justified because the jurisdiction of the Takeover Panel used to extend to a comparable degree. Other constituencies of the Channel Islands, such as Sark, do not appear to have any discrete corporate regulations.[62]

---

[58]   See the summer 2005 consultation carried out by Angela Smith MP acting on behalf of the Department of Enterprise, Trade and Investment in Northern Ireland.

[59]   For Isle of Man Company Law, see J. Bates, *The Isle of Man Companies Act 1992* (1992) (Sweet & Maxwell). The basic legislation is the 1931 Act as amended. Note the Isle of Man Companies Act 2006, which was driven by the need to attract offshore business – see (2007) 28 Co Law 46. As a result of the 2006 Act, companies incorporated under the 1931 regime can re-register and take advantage of new facilities (such as corporate directors and deregulated share capital maintenance rules). Foreign companies can simply continue their personality by adopting the 2006 Act. Protected cell companies are envisaged by Part VII of the 2006 Act.

[60]   A major source of Jersey Company Law is the Companies (Jersey) Law 1991 as amended.

[61]   See the Companies (Guernsey) Law 1994 as amended. For aspects of Company Law in Guernsey, see A. Walters and A. Sarchet (1997) 18 Co Law 219 (protected cell company novelty). See also G. Moss [2001] 14 Ins Intell 73 and the news item noted in (2006) 27 Co Law 21 which refers to the Protected Cell Companies Regulations 2005. See N. Carey and A. Sarchet (2006) 27 Co Law 252 generally. The protected cell idea has been adopted in jurisdictions such as Bermuda and the Cayman Islands.

[62]   On this lacuna and its implications for English law see *Official Receiver v Vass* [1999] BCC 516.

7 HARMONISATION OF CORPORATE LAW

7.1 The EEC Programme

Since 1972 the UK has been locked into the EEC Company Law harmonisation project.[63] That project is carried out largely through the medium of directives authorised under Art 44(3)(g) of the EEC Treaty. That article forms part of the regulatory matrix concerned with achieving the goal of freedom of establishment. This right of establishment is protected by Art 43 of the Treaty and the philosophy behind it is reinforced by the European Charter on Fundamental Rights (Art 16). The prohibition on new incorporation taxes also reflects the same mindset.[64] Without a doubt, this harmonisation process has proved to be the prime driver behind company law reform in the UK for the past 35 years. That programme has advanced on many fronts and has experienced the full range of ups and downs, with these setbacks often related to general political problems within Europe rather than being due to inherent problems with the proposed harmonisation measure. Looking at the picture today, we can see the influence of harmonisation in most fields of corporate law through adopted directives in the following fields:

- incorporation and disclosure (First Directive 1968/151);[65]
- share capital (Second Directive 1977/91 as amended by Directive 2006/68);
- company contracts (First Directive 1968/151);
- company accounts and audits (Fourth Directive 1978/660, Seventh Directive 1983/349, Eighth Directive 1984/253) (soon to be replaced by Directive 2006/43) and Accounts Modernisation Directive (2003/51). The International Accounting Standards Regulation 2002/1606 completes the picture;
- branches (Eleventh Directive 1989/666);

---

63   There is an impressive literature base here – J. Dine (1988) 13 ELR 322, V. Edwards [2000] CFILR 342, C. Barnard (2000) 25 ELRRev 57, P. Cabral and P. Cunha (2000) 25 ELRRev 157, M. Andenas (2006) 27 Co Law 1, R. Drury [2005] JBL 709, T.C. Hartley (2005) 54 ICLQ 813, E. Werlauff (1992) 17 ELR 207, M. Andenas, K. Hopt and E. Wymeersch, *Free Movement of Companies in EC Law* (2003) (OUP).

64   See EC Council Directive (1969/335), *Fantask (C188/95)* [1998] 1 CMLR 473 and *Modelo (C56/98)* [2001] STC 1043.

65   For contemporary comment, see G.A. Zaphirou [1968] JBL 280. A good insight into the thinking behind this Directive might also be gleaned from *Ubbink Isolatie* (136/87) [1990] BCC 255 – see F. Wooldridge (1990) 11 Co Law 62. The First Directive was amended by Directive 2003/58.

- single member companies (12th Directive 1989/667) (implemented via SI 1992/1699);
- admission of securities to listing, prospectuses (Admissions Directive 1979/279, Listing Particulars Directive 1980/390, Public Offers Directive 1989/298 and Investment Services Directive 1993/22 and new Prospectus Directive 2003/71);
- takeovers (Takeover Directive 2004/25/EC);
- mergers, scissions and cross-border mergers (Third Directive 1978/855, Sixth Directive 1982/891 and Tenth Directive 2005/56);[66]
- disclosure of major shareholdings and disclosure of information by issuers (Directive 1999/627, Transparency Directive 2004/109);
- insider trading and market abuse (Insider Trading Directive 1989/592[67] and Market Abuse Directive 2003/6);
- shareholder voting rights in listed companies (Shareholder Rights Directive 2007/36).

For the future the most likely possibilities for Company Law Harmonisation Directives relate to small businesses.[68] The proposal for a Draft Fourteenth Directive on relocation of registered office has now encountered problems and it is not clear whether it will ever come to fruition (see below Chapter 9 for consideration of this issue).

The harmonisation programme has also spawned new corporate entities ranging from the European Economic Interest Grouping (EEIG Regulation 1985/2137[69]), through the 'single member company' (Twelfth Directive 1989/667) to the European Company or Societas Europea (Regulation 2001/2157[70] and Directive 2001/86). More specialised organisational structures were harmonised with regard to Open Ended Investment Companies

---

[66]   Implemented in this country by SI 2007/2974. On the Directive see F. Wooldridge (2006) 27 Co Law 309.

[67]   Considered by the ECJ in *Ipourgos Ikonomikon v Georgakis (C391/04)* [2007] 2 BCLC 692.

[68]   See [2008] 235 SMCLN 1 for details of the proposed statute for a European Private Company (SPE).

[69]   Introduced into English law by SI 1989/638 – see S. Israel (1989) 9 Co Law 14, S. Keegan [1991] JBL 457. At the last count, there were only 186 EEIGs with their principal place of establishment in Great Britain. The EEIG was modelled upon the French GIE – see B. Bott and W. Rosener [1970] JBL 313.

[70]   Official figures for 2005/6 disclose one SE registered in Great Britain. On the SE, see M. Vasseur [1964] JBL 358 and [1965] JBL 73, P. Sanders [1968] JBL 184, J. Wouters (2000) 37 CMLRev 257, V. Edwards (2003) 40 CMLRev 443, F. Wooldridge (2004) 25 Co Law 121, L. Cerioni (2004) 25 Co Law 228 and 259, J Schmidt (2006) 27 Co Law 99, M.C. di Luigi (2008) 19 ICCLR 58.

(UCITS Directive 1985/611[71]). The belated adoption of European Works Councils (see Directives 1994/45 and 1997/54) in this country can also be viewed as a consequence of this harmonisation strategy.[72]

If harmonisation is viewed in these terms, the areas where no progress has been achieved stand out. In particular, the failure to address the issue of how to regulate groups of companies, which was the subject of the draft Ninth Directive,[73] is obvious. Little has been done until recently in the area of shareholder rights, an issue which was addressed in the Draft Fifth Directive.[74] Private companies have attracted little attention until recent times. Most notably, there has been virtually no harmonisation of the substantive rules governing corporate insolvency law, though some worthwhile advances on the procedural front have been achieved through the medium of the EC Regulation on Insolvency Proceedings (1346/2000) (to be discussed in Chapter 8).

Why was company law harmonisation seen as such a significant element in the EC programme? The answer lies in that other cherished EC goal, namely freedom of establishment, as demanded by Art 43 of the EEC Treaty. If businesses were to be given the freedom to operate and relocate across Europe it was vital to create a level playing field in terms of regulation.[75] The view was taken that every effort should be made to avoid the possibility of a 'race to the bottom' or Delaware syndrome[76] developing on the European side of the Atlantic. A Delaware syndrome involves companies incorporating in certain states, not in order to extend market operations in that state, but rather to exploit laxities (or, depending on one's point of view, attractions) in the local corporate law regime. States feel compelled to play this game to secure economic advantage over their neighbours. The European Court of Justice (ECJ) ruling in *Centros*[77] has shown that freedom of establishment has

---

71   Implemented by SI 1996/2827 – see M. Thomas (1998) 19 Co Law 26.
72   Introduced into the UK by SI 1999/3323. On works councils generally, see S. Wheeler (1997) 24 JLS 44.
73   For comment on the Draft Ninth Directive, see F. Wooldridge [1982] JBL 182.
74   On the Draft Fifth Directive, see M. Clough (1982) 3 Co Law 109, J. Welch (1983) 8 ELR 83, J.J. du Plessis and J. Dine [1997] JBL 23.
75   See M. Andenas, K. Hopt and E. Wymeersch, *Free Movement of Companies in EC Law* (2003) (OUP) and V. Edwards, *EC Company Law* (1999) (OUP). Note also M. Gelter (2005) 5 JCLS 247.
76   The Delaware syndrome is well-documented and fiercely debated – W. Cary [1974] 83 YLJ 663, R Drury [1998] 57 CLJ 165 and (2005) 5 JCLS 1, L.A. Bebchuk (1992) 105 Harv LR 1435, R.K. Winter (1989) 89 Col L Rev 1526, M. Roe (2003) 117 Harv LR 588, J. Dean [2003] 14 ICCLR 196, P. Omar [2002] 13 ICCLR 445 and [2005] 16 ICCLR 17.
77   Case C212/97 [2000] 2 WLR 1048. See V. Edwards [2000] CFILR 342. For a fuller discussion, see Chapter 7.

outpaced company law harmonisation. Other factors have conspired to reinforce the importance of corporate law harmonisation, namely the drive towards a single capital market; we could note here Art 294 (ex 221) of the Treaty, which seeks to prevent barriers being established to prevent free movement of capital. This in effect has created a right to invest in the shares of companies incorporated in other Member States without fear of discrimination.[78] The economic and political need to encourage cross-border corporate activity has also been a harmonisation driver.

It is important to reiterate that the programme has been driven entirely by formal measures emanating from the EU institutions. Constitutionally, the European Court of Justice has no residual power to introduce harmonisation through the back door. Witness the case of *Cooperative Rabobank v Minderhoud* (C104/96),[79] where an attempt to argue that all of the rules governing irregular company contracts should be harmonised along the lines of promoting sanctity of transaction was decisively rejected by the European Court of Justice. This type of deficient company contract (where one of the parties was subject to a conflict of interest) was not specifically addressed by the First Directive and therefore the Court of Justice was impotent when it came to applying its mantra of security of transaction to that particular scenario. However, as will become apparent later in this volume, the European Court of Justice through its rulings can promote harmonisation indirectly. Indeed, it has played a pivotal role through the development of the concept of 'direct effect' with regard to both Treaty provisions[80] and directives.[81] The evolution of the concept of 'state liability' also is entirely attributable to ECJ jurisprudence.[82] The Court of Justice has decisively rejected arguments by Member States that their non-implementation of Company Law Harmonisation Directives can be justified by a similar degree of inactivity by other Member States.[83]

The harmonisation programme is constantly evolving. There is a greater recognition of the attractions of 'subsidiarity'.[84] The Winter Study Group,[85]

---

[78]   See, for example, *Factortame* (C221/89) [1991] ECR I-3905, *Manninnen* (C319/02) [2005] 2 WLR 670.

[79]   [1998] 1 WLR 1025.

[80]   See *Reyners v Belgium* [1974] ECR 631, *Segers* (C79/85) [1987] 2 CMLR 247 for the direct effect of Treaty provisions in this context.

[81]   For the direct effect of directives, see *Karella v Minister of Industry* (C19 and 20/90) [1994] 1 BCLC 774.

[82]   See *Francovich (C6 and 9/90)* [1991] ECR I-5357.

[83]   *Ministère Public v Blanguernon* (C38/89) [1991] BCLC 635.

[84]   On subsidiarity, see Art 5(2) of the EC Treaty. See also K.J. Hopt [1999] 1 ICCLJ 41.

[85]   For discussion of the Winter Report from the High Level Group of Company

set up in the wake of the débâcle over the initial failure to adopt the Takeover Directive, has made some significant proposals for reform. Reforms in the area of corporate governance seem likely having been spurred on by the Parmalat affair.[86] Equally, existing harmonisation regimes may be revisited under the SLIM (Simplified Legislation for the Internal Market) initiative.[87] The Directive 2006/68, which introduces the possibility of deregulation of the notorious Second Directive,[88] is a perfect example of this new policy direction at work.

7.2 Other Harmonisation Schemes

Europe is not alone in this strategy of seeking to develop a harmonised system of corporate law. We have already seen how in federal jurisdictions, means have been developed via model laws to promote commonality. Looking further afield, in Africa there is the Organisation for the Harmonisation in Africa of Business Law (OHADA) scheme.[89] In the Caribbean, the CARI-COM project[90] has also achieved some success in bringing together corporate law systems, though the proximity of the US has had a greater impact. Indeed, the highly regarded Canadian model has attracted support in this region (the Barbados Companies Act 1982 being heavily derived from the Canadian Business Corporations Act).

At the truly global level, the United Nations Commission on International Trade Law (UNCITRAL) programme also deserves mention. Its Model Law on Cross-border Insolvency (1997)[91] has proved a significant measure, being adopted in a number of jurisdictions including the US, Japan and Great Britain (through the Cross-Border Insolvency Regulations (SI 2006/1030)). Northern

---

Law Experts on a Modern Regulatory Framework for Company Law in Europe (November 2002), see B. Pettet (2004) 57 CLP 393 and the editorial note in (2002) 23 Co Law 52.

[86] See abovenote 26.

[87] On Simplified Legislation for the Internal Market, see E. Ferran [2005] 6 EBOLR 93 at 96.

[88] See above.

[89] There are 16 countries in OHADA (which was established in 1993) and these are mainly French-speaking jurisdictions. For OHADA generally, see P. Omar [2000] Ins Law 257. The dominance of the French language has caused difficulties for Cameroon (which is bilingual) – see N. Enonchong [2007] 51 JAL 95.

[90] The activities of CARICOM are described at www.caricom.org. For its initiative in the field of Company Law, see B.M. Surya (1982) 3 Co Law 44. See also P. Maynard [1982] JBL 421, K.I.F. Kahn (1985) 6 Co Law 341.

[91] See Chapter 8 for full discussion. The complete text of the Model Law and the Cross-border Insolvency Regulations can be found in Volume 2 of L.S. Sealy and D. Milman, *Annotated Guide to Insolvency Legislation* (11th edition) (2008) (Sweet & Maxwell).

Ireland subsequently enacted the appropriate implementing measure via SR 2007/115 with effect from 12 April 2007.

8   LEGISLATIVE MEASURES

The UK Parliament has always kept one eye on commercial developments occurring in other jurisdictions in the area of business organisation structures, where those developments may threaten the economic stability of the UK. A perusal of the Parliamentary and public debates in the mid-19th century, when the possibility of limited liability companies being introduced into the UK was being considered, clearly attests to that concern.[92] This is certainly true if one scrutinises the deliberations of the Mercantile Law Commission[93] in 1854.

The formal introduction of the private limited company into English law in 1907 offers a good illustration of these convergence forces at work in the legislative process.[94] However, it should be noted that the private company had in reality been on the scene for a number of years prior to that date, as is clear from a perusal of the works of leading practitioners[95] and from judicial pronouncements.[96]

The Law Commissions in England/Wales and Scotland certainly undertake comparative research before making recommendations for the reform of UK company law.[97] Indeed it appears from s. 3(1)(f) of the Law Commissions Act 1965 that they have a statutory obligation to do so. This technique is most recently apparent when one looks at the policy deliberations leading to the introduction of Part 11 of the Companies Act 2006 (statutory derivative claims).

In more modern times, the introduction of the limited liability partnership in April 2001, via the agency of the Limited Liability Partnerships Act 2000,

---

[92]   Bouverie was concerned about businesses being incorporated in the US and France with limited liability and then trading in this country.

[93]   For discussion, see R.A. Bryer (1977) 50 Econ Hist Rev 37.

[94]   The advent of the private company is analysed in E. Manson (1910) 26 LQR 11. The GmbH was formally devised in Germany in 1892. By perverse coincidence, the European idea of the limited partnership was introduced into English law at the same time as the private company, but as an organisational structure it has proved unpopular when set against the virtues of the private company.

[95]   Sir Francis Palmer had noted the phenomenon in 1877 in his treatise *Private Companies and Syndicates*. For an account of Palmer's role in promoting the private company, see the Biographical Note in *Palmer's Company Law* (24th ed) (1987) (Stevens and Sons) at ix.

[96]   See *British Seamless Paper Box* (1881) 17 Ch D 467 at 478 per Cotton LJ and Lord Macnaghten in *Salomon v Salomon & Co Ltd* [1897] AC 22 at 48.

[97]   See, for example, *Shareholder Remedies* (1997) (LC 246) (Cmnd 3769).

shows how concerns that the UK was falling behind commercial competitors in the provision of business structures sought after by the professions, can lead to legislative reform. The Limited Liability Partnerships (LLP) emerged in the US in Texas in 1991 as a response by the professions to the burgeoning risks of professional liability litigation. The recent introduction of the LLP into Jersey[98] coupled with threats from major accountancy firms that they would 'go offshore' arguably proved a decisive factor in persuading the UK government to act. Since that legislation was enacted, several thousand firms (mainly professional firms) have changed their legal basis from that of partnership to that of limited liability partnership.[99] The legal model devised in Texas has in the space of a mere decade well and truly crossed a continent and ocean.

9 CONVERGENCE AND THE COURTS

We have already asserted that the European Court of Justice officially has no residual role to play in pursuing a harmonisation policy beyond the scope of measures formally agreed. At national level, however, the national Member State courts are obliged by Art 10 (ex 5) of EC Treaty to facilitate the implementation of directives.[100] More generally, they frequently take into account global trends when formulating jurisprudence. Certainly, in English law, the courts appear very sensitive to the notion that the health of the City of London is vital to the economic well-being of the country. Let us consider a few illustrations of these thought processes at work.

Historically, the work of Lord Mansfield[101] in the 18th century in seeking to attune English commercial law with continental traditions is important, though there is no direct impact on company law mainly because it was operating under

---

[98] Under the Limited Liability Partnerships (Jersey) Law 1997. See P. Morris and J. Stevenson (1997) 60 MLR 538. For the debate leading to the introduction of the LLP into English Law, see A. Griffiths [1998] CFILR 157, C. Bradley [2001] CLWR 330. On LLPs, see J. Freedman and V. Finch [1997] JBL 387, V. Finch and J. Freedman [2002] JBL 475, E. Deards [2003] JBL 435, M. Lower (2000) 22 Liv L Rev 89, S. Cross [2003] JBL 268. For the leading monograph see *Palmer's Limited Liability Partnership Law* (2002) (Sweet & Maxwell) edited by G. Morse et al.

[99] A perusal of the *Companies Annual Report for 2005/06* discloses some 16,699 LLPs registered in England and Wales. The irony is that the Companies Act 2006 now allows auditors to cap liability (see ss. 534 et seq.) – one wonders whether some of those firms that have rushed into the LLP may now have had second thoughts.

[100] See *Marleasing* (C106/89) [1990] ECR I-4135.

[101] Lord Mansfield was Lord Chief Justice 1756–88. Lord Mansfield had a role in devising the rule against fraudulent preferences, a staple of corporate insolvency law. On Lord Mansfield's influence generally, see C.H.S. Fifoot, *Lord Mansfield* (1936) (Clarendon Press).

the dead hand of the Bubble Act for the entirety of Lord Mansfield's tenure as Lord Chief Justice. What matters was that Lord Mansfield affected the environment in which company law later came to operate.

In *Re Scandinavian Bank*,[102] a case which we discuss in Chapter 4 below, Harman J gave the green light to UK public companies having shares denominated in foreign currencies. The Companies Act 2006 has confirmed this ruling by giving it a statutory imprimatur (see s. 542).

The issue in the test case of *Acatos & Hutcheson plc v Watson*[103] was whether there was a breach of the bar on companies acquiring their own shares in a scenario where a company acquires another company which just happens to own shares in the first company. After considering a range of factors, including the stance taken by the Australian courts,[104] Lightman J ruled that this situation (which was not uncommon in practice) should not be deemed a breach of company law. Again, the fact that to hold otherwise would be to frustrate takeovers in the City of London arguably influenced the process of forming the judgment.[105]

In *Re Maxwell Communications Corp (No. 2)*,[106] Vinelott J had to decide whether English law should permit a creditor to contractually assent to a deferred or subordination status on liquidation. At first sight, this would appear to offend against the fundamental principle of equality of treatment of non-secured creditors. In deciding this question in the affirmative, the judge was impressed by the fact that contractual subordination was permitted in a number of jurisdictions enjoying developed economies – namely South Africa, Switzerland and the USA. That survey again proved decisive in the final judgment. As Vinelott J stated: 'It would, I think, be a matter of grave concern if, at a time when insolvency increasingly has international ramifications, it were to be found that English law alone refused to give effect to a contractual subordination'.[107]

---

102   [1988] 1 Ch 87.
103   [1995] BCLC 456.
104   For the Australian jurisprudence, see *Dynason v JC Hutton Pty Ltd* (1935) ALR 419, *August Investments Pty Ltd v Poseidon Ltd and Samin Ltd* [1971] 2 SASR 71, *Trade Practices Commission v Australian Iron and Steel Pty Ltd* (1990) 22 FCR 305
105   Ibid at 451. Although the sentiment was not unequivocally expressed in the judgment, the case typifies the approach of the English courts towards takeover facilitation. Approving devices that frustrate takeovers would be a cardinal sin, because takeovers are major earners for a range of professional repeat players in the City of London.
106   [1994] 1 BCLC 1 – discussed by M. Fealy [1993] CLJ 396, R. Nolan [1995] JBL 485. See also *Re British and Commonwealth Holdings (No. 3)* [1992] BCLC 322.
107   [1994] 1 BCLC 1 at 20–21.

A different use of comparative legal material was at the heart of the House of Lords ruling in *Re BCCI (No. 8)*.[108] Here the House of Lords had to determine, amongst other things, whether a bank could take a charge over monies deposited with it by the chargor client, a so-called 'charge-back' arrangement. Millett J, as he then was, had indicated in *Re Charge Card Services*[109] that this outcome was a conceptual impossibility. Banking practitioners were disappointed with this analysis and the Legal Risks Review Committee expressed its concerns.[110] Subsequently, in *Re BCCI (No. 8)*,[111] Lord Hoffmann rejected the 'conceptual impossibility' thesis by pointing out that a number of legal systems based upon English law had explicitly legislated for charge-backs, thereby proving that the concept was a feasible legal option. This argument could have been countered by the retort that the need for legislation indicated a non-acceptance at common law, but that is not significant to our discussion here; comparative insights informed the conclusion.

This trend (which over the years admittedly has had its setbacks[112]) towards ensuring that English law is internationally competitive runs alongside a more established phenomenon reflecting the evolutionary processes of the common law. Although it is true to say that the English courts have always been prepared to give judicial notice to Commonwealth authorities, that willingness to be receptive to new ideas has become more marked in recent decades.[113] This is not exclusively a phenomenon only reflected in corporate law; it is much more pervasive. As far as corporate law is concerned, we could point to Commonwealth authorities playing a pivotal role in the emerging law of directors' duties to creditors.[114] Certainly, a perusal of the judgment of the

---

[108]   [1997] 3 WLR 909.

[109]   [1986] 3 WLR 697.

[110]   See Legal Risks Review Committee, *Reducing Uncertainty: The Way Forward* (1992) – reviewed by D. Capper (1993) 44 NILQ 71.

[111]   Supra.

[112]   Witness the SWAPS affair – *Westdeutsche Landesbank Girozentrale v Islington LBC* [1996] AC 669.

[113]   This phenomenon, whereby English courts are informed by Commonwealth jurisprudence, is a general practice and not restricted to corporate law. This practice of judicial borrowing is not restricted to common law judicial interaction – see B. Markesinis [2002] CLJ 386.

[114]   See, for example, *Kinsella v Russell Kinsella Pty Ltd* [1968] NSWLR 722, *Walker v Wimborne* (1976) 137 CLR 1, *Nicholson v Permakraft* [1985] 1 NZLR 242, *Jeffree v NSCC* (1989) 15 ACLR 217. The principle has subsequently been introduced into Ireland – *Re Frederick Inns Ltd* [1994] 1 ILRM 387. The literature mapping this development is impressive – R. Grantham [1991] JBL 1, D. Prentice (1990) 10 OJLS 265, A. Keay [2002] JBL 379, (2003) 66 MLR 665, [2005] CLJ 614, [2005] 18 Ins Intell 65. Professor Keay's work in this area is also expanded in A. Keay, *Company Directors' Responsibilities to Creditors* (2006) (Routledge-Cavendish).

Court of Appeal in *West Mercia Safetywear Ltd v Dodd*[115] would point to that influence. More recently, in *National Westminster Bank v Spectrum*,[116] the House of Lords sided with their judicial brethren from New Zealand[117] in deciding that a fixed charge over future book debts based upon the orthodox English *Siebe Gorman*[118] precedent created only a floating charge. Thirty years of City of London practice disappeared overnight, much to the angst of the banking community.

10 LEGAL AND OTHER COMMERCIAL TRANSPLANTS[119]

The process of national systems formally adopting (either by legislation, precedent or evolving social norm) corporate structures and concepts from other jurisdictions, although commonplace, is not without difficulty. Some imported concepts fit in easily alongside existing structures. Others are less successfully adopted. The difficulties of this practice were noted by Kahn-Freund,[120] who highlighted the importance of context when considering usage of comparative analysis and in particular, in evaluating whether a transplant could be viable.

On the positive side, one could cite the adoption of the informal rescue procedures known as the London Approach to a number of leading Asian economies.[121] The spread of the private company from its genesis in Germany (GmbH, 1892)[122] to its reception in England (1907) and France (SARL,

---

[115]   [1988] BCLC 250. See A. Keay [2002] JBL 379.

[116]   [2005] UKHL 41. See A. Berg [2006] JBL 22.

[117]   *Supercool Refrigeration v Hoverd Industries* [1994] 3 NZLR 300.

[118]   *Siebe Gorman & Co v Barclays Bank* [1979] 2 Lloyds Rep 142.

[119]   See A. Watson, *Legal Transplants: An Approach to Comparative Law* (2nd edition, 1993) (University of Georgia Press). See also his work in (1976) 92 LQR 79, [1978] 37 CLJ 313. Note also the essay by P. Legrand in chapter 2 of D. Nelken and J. Feest, *Adapting Legal Cultures* (2001) (Hart). For an outstanding review of 'reception' techniques in the British colonies, see B.H. Macpherson, *The Reception of English Law Abroad* (2007) (Supreme Court of Queensland Library). Note also R. McQueen (2008) 17 Griff L Rev 383. Scholars have also examined the economic efficiency of legal transplants in general – see N. Garoupa and A. Ogus (2006) 35 Jo of Leg Studs 339.

[120]   (1974) 37 MLR 1 (Chorley Lecture).

[121]   See N. Segal [2000] 13 Insolv Intell 17.

[122]   This was partly due to a reaction by the business community to over-regulation of public companies – see F. Fabricius [1970] JBL 229.

1925)[123] and finally to the Netherlands (BV, 1971)[124] offers another good illustration of how successful corporate models can migrate. On much the same theme, we could cite the emigration of unit trusts[125] from the US to the UK in the 1930s, a transition that eventually required a regulatory response.

On the other hand, a good illustration of the difficulties that can arise is provided by the story of the limited partnership in English law. This was a model that had been operated successfully on the Continent for many a year. Accordingly, it was introduced into English Law by the Limited Partnerships Act (LPA) 1907. It proved to be unpopular and even today there are only 13,426 limited partnerships registered in this country.[126] Compare this statistic to the 17,499 LLPs registered since 2001. Why has the limited partnership registered such a poor performance? The introduction of the private limited company into English law in the same year may offer some explanation in that apart from possible technical tax advantages, the limited partnership has little to offer entrepreneurs over and above that provided by the private company.

The attempt to transplant the South African rescue device of judicial management into Australia in 1961 (albeit under the guise of official management) was a resounding failure.[127] Another example of a failed transplant is illustrated by the fate of the two-tier board in France. This German corporate governance idea has never really taken off in France,[128] though it has been adopted successfully in the Netherlands.

Having noted the successes and failures, what one can conclude? As we noted above, there is much in Kahn-Freund's observation that failed transplant may not necessarily be attributed to inherent weaknesses in the trans-

---

[123] The GmbH model arrived in France through the back door. It had been used in Alsace and Lorraine and when these provinces were returned to France at the end of the First World War, this model was allowed to continue, thereby creating pressure to introduce it generally into France – for the fascinating story, see F. Wooldridge [1970] JBL 317.
[124] See P. Sanders [1973] JBL 194.
[125] See K.F. Sin, *The Legal Nature of the Unit Trust* (1997) (Clarendon Press) at 27–9.
[126] On the LPA 1907, see E. Berry [2005] JBL 70 at 85, J. Henning (2000) 21 Co Law 165, S. Sheikh (2002) 23 Co Law 179 and T Prime and G. Scanlan (2007) 28 Co Law 262. For current limited partnership registrations, see *DTI Annual Companies Report 2004–05*, where the figure of 12,377 is reported for Great Britain, with more than a third of these in Scotland (an interesting statistic). The limited partnership has enjoyed a significant boost in popularity in the past five years.
[127] For a critique of judicial management, see H. Rajak and J. Henning (1999) 116 SALJ 262. On the failure of official management in Australia, see J. Farrar [1976] JBL 214.
[128] For French resistance to the German model, see CLAB survey of national systems of European Corporate Law (1999).

plant but may owe more to underlying cultural differences.[129] There is a path-dependency[130] aspect to legal reform that is particularly relevant when contemplating transplants. It is a recognition of this problem that has led the EU to seek to harmonise not merely substantive company law, but also the social and economic environment in which it operates. But, even with this fair wind, transplants do not always succeed because culture is resilient.

11   THE COMPANY LAW REVIEW (1998–2001)[131]

For many years prior to 1997, the process of corporate law reform in the UK had been a disgrace.[132] Clive Schmitthoff famously described a former Companies Act as a 'repository of historical relics'.[133] In our preface, we noted how the Company Law Review process, which produced two White Papers[134] in response, was largely driven by a desire to ensure that UK corporate law was an internationally competitive model. There is nothing new in this concern.[135] The Irish Company Law Review Group stressed this as an

---

[129]   See T. Ruskola (2000) 52 Stan L Rev 1598. See P. Lawton [2007] 49 Manag Law 249 for discussion of how cultural aspects of the Chinese family firm might have an impact upon the enforcement of shareholder rights through standard substantive mechanisms.

[130]   For the convincing path dependency theory in corporate law, see M.J. Roe (1996) 109 HLR 641.

[131]   For the *Final Report* see URN 01/942 (2001). See J. Rickford, chapter 1 in J. de Lacy, *The Reform of UK Company Law* (2002) (Cavendish). Note also B. Pettet (1998) 19 Co Law 134 for an early appraisal of the project. See also M. Arden [2002] JBL 579. The UK was not alone in reflecting on the state of its company law. In France in 1998, the Marini Report covered similar ground – see A. Tunc in B. Rider (ed.), *The Realm of Company Law* (1998) (Kluwer) at 161–6, P. Omar (1998) 19 Co Law 62, (1999) 20 Co Law 310.

[132]   A compelling critique of the process of company law reform before 1998 is provided by L.C.B. Gower in (1980) 14 Law Teacher 111 at 115 and by J. Freedman, chapter 11 in F. Patfield (ed.) *Perspectives on Company Law (1)* (1995) (Kluwer).

[133]   [1960] JBL 151 at 151.

[134]   See *Modernising Company Law* (Cm 5553-I, 2002) and *Company Law Reform* (Cm 6456, 2005). For a reaction to the 2002 White Paper, see R. Goddard (2003) 66 MLR 402 and for comment on the 2005 follow-up, see C. Howell (2005) 26 Co Law 203.

[135]   See here the observations of Eve J in *Re Jewish Colonial Trust* [1908] 2 Ch 287 at 295, commenting upon the rationale behind the Companies (Memorandum of Association) Act 1890 which apparently was designed to enable English companies to change their objects to compete more effectively with foreign firms.

important consideration in its first report in December 2001.[136] The methodology of the UK Company Law Review is, however, interesting. The Steering Group was composed of individuals with a wide range of skills and perspectives. Extensive use was made of comparative research. The University of Manchester Centre for Law and Business survey of European national corporate law systems has already been mentioned.[137] In addition, the 1997 study by a team led by Cally Jordan of Company Law in Hong Kong[138] assisted in the process of forming reform proposals for the UK. Academics and practitioners on the Steering Group made use of their extensive knowledge of comparative corporate law models.

12 THE COMPANIES ACT 2006

This new legislation, which represents a potent brew of reform and consolidation contained within the longest Act in English law (all 1300 sections and 16 schedules at the time of initial enactment), does have considerable relevance to our study. Some of the deregulation/modernisation strategy favoured by the Company Law Review in order to make our system of corporate law more competitive is indeed introduced through that legislative mechanism. For example, the rules on share capital maintenance are loosened insofar as that is consistent with the EC Second Company Law Harmonisation Directive (1977/91). The 2006 Act remodels and simplifies the law of overseas companies (Part 34) and introduces a mechanism under which foreign disqualification orders can be recognised and enforced in the UK (Part 40). More of these matters later. In spite of these undoubted changes, much of the 2006 Act is familiar and it is not as radical a measure as has been claimed.[139]

The 2006 Act has been such a massive venture[140] that implementation has been staged over three years, with 1 October 2009 now being set as the final implementation date for all but a very few provisions. Whether that target is

---

[136] For discussion of this issue, see para 1.2 of the Report. The point was made that Ireland had updated other regulatory systems to cope with the globalised economy, but that companies regulation had lagged behind. The Irish Company Law Reform Group was established under s. 68 of the Company Law Enforcement Act 2001.

[137] Centre for Law and Business (University of Manchester). Noted in *Final Report* (URN 01/942) at p. 7

[138] For this 1997 report (which is available electronically) see C. Jordan [1997] IFLRev (July) 29.

[139] See J. Birds (2007) 49 Manag Law 13.

[140] For the background to the legislative passage, see P. Bovey (2008) 29 Stat L Rev 11.

met remains to be seen. Further details on the current state of play with regard to implementation can be found in Appendix 1.

13 DOES CORPORATE LAW MATTER?

One of the underlying themes in this work is that an effective national system of corporate law is a relevant consideration in terms of attracting transnational commerce. This assertion, which has its doubters in terms of general applicability,[141] is based in part on intuition. It is, however, supported by a more scientific body of scholarship.[142] John Dunning[143] has argued that a rational actor in the transnational sector would have regard to the local legal system before investing in that country. It is difficult to argue with that assertion, provided it is not taken too far. A group of scholars headed by La Porta[144] have reached similar conclusions when comparing levels of shareholder protection in a range of jurisdictions. This type of numerical analysis as a comparative tool is very much in vogue.[145] Studies by Perry[146] in Sri Lanka and other South Asian countries suggest that the local legal infrastructure is not the only major consideration taken into account before the decision to invest is made. There is no doubt that other significant considerations may enter the equation – such as language, political stability, robustness of critical institutions,[147]

---

[141] See B. Cheffins (2001) 30 Jo of Legal Studs 459, where the point was made that the development of corporate law regimes owes more to market forces than legal norms.

[142] For an excellent account of the 'law matters' thesis, see B. Cheffins (2001) 1 JCLS 71 at 76–7.

[143] J. Dunning, *Multinational Enterprises and the Global Economy* (1993) (Addison-Wesley).

[144] See R. La Porta, F. Lopez de-Silanes, A. Shliefer and R. Vishny (1998) 106 Jo of Pol Econ 1113, and the later work published in (1999) 54 Jo of Fin 471, (2000) 58 Jo of Fin Econ 3. For a review of the so-called 'LLSV' thesis with critique, see A. Pekmezovic [2007] ICCLR 97 and 147.

[145] For a compelling critique of this methodology, see M.M. Siems [2005] 16 ICCLR 300. An alternative 'leximetric' methodology is developed by P. Lele and M.M. Siems in (2007) 7 JCLS 17.

[146] A.J. Perry, *Legal Systems as a Determinant of FDI: Lessons from Sri Lanka* (2001) (Kluwer). See also her work in (2003) 23 Leg Studs 649, (2002) 29 Jo of Law and Soc 282 and (2000) 49 ICLQ 779.

[147] On the importance of institutions in a variety of senses, see K. Pistor (2002) 50 Am Jo of Comp Law 97. In this context, M. Whincop, *An Economic and Jurisprudential Genealogy of Corporate Law* (2001) (Ashgate) is worth reading. K.W. Dam would agree with La Porta that law matters – but what really matters is efficient legal institutions to enforce that law – see *The Law-growth Nexus: The Rule of Law and Economic Development* (2006) (Brookings Institute Press), especially at 230. In

transport facilities, availability of appropriate skilled workers, raw materials, available market, etc., but it would be difficult to persuade a lawyer that the legal system is irrelevant to the decision-making processes of investors and entrepreneurs.[148] Indeed, the whole experience of Delaware corporate law seems to suggest that it may be an important factor. It is vital to the economy of offshore jurisdictions which are constantly seeking to steal a march on each other in developing business-friendly corporate regimes. Even between main-stream jurisdictions, differentials in corporate law are felt – witness the influx of small European businesses into the UK, seeking to exploit our private company format. Even more recently, we have seen distressed businesses desperately seeking to relocate to the UK before insolvency proceedings are commenced, simply in order to take advantage of our flexible insolvency regimes. On the basis that law does matter but is not the only behavioural determinant, we will proceed with our study.

---

support of this argument, Dam cites the failed attempt to import the highly successful German bankruptcy law into Russia, a failure attributed to inefficient Russian legal institutions.

[148]   This point with regard to the positive impact of protection on investors is made by R. La Porta et al. (2002) 57 Jo of Fin 1147.

2. Comparing core regulatory strategies

1 REGULATING COMPANIES: JUSTIFICATION

There is a fierce intellectual debate under way here.[1] The orthodox view of companies is that they are creatures of the state, and, as they confer on their incorporators the considerable economic advantage of limited liability for the firm's debts, it is entirely appropriate that in the public interest they be heavily regulated. This has been the view traditionally taken in English law[2] and is a perspective that is shared in much of Continental Europe.[3] On this view, there is no constitutional entitlement or fundamental right guaranteeing incorporation.[4] Companies can be controlled at the point of entry by refusing the privilege of incorporation[5] or by removing corporate status through processes such as liquidation and dissolution. Companies can be wound up in the public interest under s. 124A of the Insolvency Act 1986, even though they may be solvent. Ultimately, companies can be taken into public ownership if this is deemed necessary to protect the state interest. The nationalisation of Northern

---

[1]　For illuminating overviews of the paradigm theories on the juristic nature of companies, see S. Bottomley [1990] 19 Fed L Rev 203 and S. Worthington (2001) 22 Co Law 258 at 263.

[2]　Companies are creatures of statute – *Daimler v Continental Tyre* [1916] 2 AC 307 per Lord Parker, *Butler v Broadhead* [1974] 2 All ER 401 per Templeman J. *Sovfracht* [1943] AC 203 discussed by A. Farnsworth (1944) 7 MLR 80.

[3]　For the European view that companies merely enjoy a concession from the state, see the work of Savigny.

[4]　Neither the ECHR nor the US Constitution recognises such a right as part of the broader notion of freedom of association. The point is also considered in *Private Motorists Provident Society v AG* [1983] IR 339, where Carroll J indicates that Art 40.6 of the Irish Constitution does not in itself guarantee a right to incorporate – for discussion, see T.B. Courtney, *The Law of Private Companies* (2nd edition 2002) (Butterworths) at para 1.050. In EU law, we have a formally recognised right of establishment (Art 43 EC Treaty) and in Art II-76 in the Draft Treaty on the European Constitution, the right to engage in business was given explicit recognition – but neither provision gives an explicit right to incorporate.

[5]　*Bowman v Secular Society Ltd* [1917] AC 406, *R v Registrar of Joint Stock Companies* [1931] 2 KB 197, *R v Registrar of Companies ex parte AG* [1991] BCLC 476.

Rock[6] in 2008 affirms this philosophy at work. In pragmatic terms, this perspective leads to the further proposition that company laws should be *mandatory*.[7] Thus, individuals who operate a business using the corporate form under the umbrella of limited liability are obliged to comply with corporate laws. This hypothesis is embodied in legislation,[8] is well documented in the literature [9] and has attracted considerable judicial support in the courts in the UK.[10] Within the parameters of this mindset, we can see extremes ranging from a benign mandatory view to a more draconian approach (such as that taken in India, where state control of companies is most apparent).

In more recent times, an alternative thesis (or more accurately collection of theses) has emerged. This alternative argument, which originated in North America, concentrates on the history of companies and argues that they arose through market evolution rather than by an act of state legislation.[11] It then proceeds to expound the view that companies are good for society because of the positive contribution that they make to the economy by reducing transaction costs in the contracting process. Companies are at the hub of a web of repeat contracts, encompassing shareholders, directors, creditors, employees and other stakeholders. Therefore there is no need to excessively regulate companies because the effect of such an approach would be to dilute the undoubted economic benefits flowing from freely operating companies. This approach has been espoused by the Chicago school of academics (such as Easterbrook and Fischel) in recent decades,[12] but the ideas underpinning it have a long intellectual ancestry. For instance, Professor Ballantine[13] was one of the originators of this latter perspective. He played a key role in drafting the corporate code for California in the 1930s, a fact well-reflected in its deregulatory tone. In an article written for the *California Law Review*, Ballantine stated:

---

6   For background, see R. Tomasic (2008) 29 Co Law 297 and (2008) 29 Co Law 330. Parallels exist in the US and Europe for emergency state bailouts for troubled financial institutions and other key economic players.
7   For discussion see M.A. Eisenberg (1989) 89 Col L Rev 1549 at 1461.
8   See, for example, the prohibition on directors excluding their duties – CA 1985, s. 310 (CA 2006, s. 232).
9   J. Gordon (1989) 89 Col L Rev 1549. In English law, Otto Kahn-Freund was a firm believer in greater regulation of limited companies – see (1944) 7 MLR 54.
10   *British Eagle v Air France* [1975] 1 WLR 758, *Re Peveril Gold Mines Ltd* [1898] 1 Ch 122, *Exeter City AFC v Football Conference* [2004] BCC 498.
11   See G.M. Anderson and R.D. Tollison (1983) 3 Int Rev of Law and Econ 107. For a rebuttal, see G.A. Mark, chapter 1 in F. Macmillan (ed.), *International Corporate Law Annual Volume 1* (2000) (Hart).
12   For further support for this flexible approach, see U. Procaccia (1987) 35 Am Jo of Comp Law 581.
13   See,·for instance, (1925) 14 Calif L Rev 12 and (1931) 19 Calif L Rev 465.

A serious dilemma in drafting a corporation law is to make it liberal enough to facilitate business transactions without undue formalities of checks and balances, of votes and consents of shareholders, and applications to courts, and, at the same time, not so lax that the management or the majority may manipulate the machinery to the prejudice of creditors or investors or the oppression of minority shareholders. The practical difficulty must always be remembered that with the freedom of admission of foreign corporations to do business in the state and the exemption of the internal organization and affairs of such corporations from local regulation, it is perfectly useless to impose drastic limitations and requirements that will simply have the effect of driving corporations from their home state to more hospitable shores.[14]

This theory also draws support from the complimentary perspective offered by Manne and others that there is limited need for harsh regulatory rules because the capital markets provide the necessary regulatory constraints upon abusive behaviour – the so-called market for corporate control theory.[15]

A further refinement of this approach has been to focus on the contractual basis[16] of companies as organisations. Academics[17] have argued that, as the key relationships within companies and between companies and the outside world are regulated by a nexus of contracts, it is best left to the contracting parties themselves to arrange their own private form of regulation to allocate risks between the contractors. Such a perspective is not restricted to ivory tower academics; it has been used, albeit in non-explicit fashion, by English judges to underpin iconic rulings of the House of Lords in *Bushell v Faith*[18] and *Russell v Northern Bank*.[19] This is a valuable perspective, but it ignores the impact of limited companies upon non-contracting parties (for example, the passer-by who is run over by one of the company's vehicles which is being

---

[14]   Ibid at 465. In more recent times, K. Pistor has stressed the importance of a system of company law allowing for innovation – (2003) 31 Jo of Comp Econ 676.

[15]   See H. Manne (1965) 73 Jo of Pol Econ 110, C. Bradley (1990) 50 MLR 171, A. Belcher (1997) 17 Leg Studs 22 at 28–9. Note also B. Clarke [2006] JBL 355 for a discussion of this concept in the context of EU takeover regulation.

[16]   For excellent explanations of the origins and impact of contractarianism, see M. Whincop (1999) 19 OJLS 19 at 27 et seq., P. Ireland (2003) 23 Leg Studs 453, B.R. Cheffins [2004] CLJ 456 at 481 et seq., J. Armour and M. Whincop (2007) 27 OJLS 429.

[17]   For discussion of this idea, see F. Easterbrook and D. Fischel (1989) 89 Col L Rev 1416 and their text, *The Economic Structure of Corporate Law* (1991) (Harvard University Press). See further L.A. Bebchuk (1989) 102 HLR 1883. A critique is provided by W. Bratton (1989) 74 Cornell L Rev 407. For an English perspective, see also J. Parkinson, chapter 7 in D. Feldman and F. Meisel (eds), *Corporate and Commercial Law: Modern Developments* (1996) (Lloyd's of London Press).

[18]   [1970] AC 1099. It may also explain the ruling of the ECJ in *Powell Duffryn plc v Petereit* (C214/89), The Times 15 April 1992.

[19]   [1992] 1 WLR 588. See E. Ferran [1994] CLJ 343 for in-depth analysis.

driven negligently) and underestimates the significance of inequalities of bargaining power and the impact of information asymmetries. It is not surprising, therefore, that powerful critics have emerged.[20]

Professor Romano's views[21] offer a different (but no less valid) analysis. Here we find a theory that law (and in particular corporate law) is essentially a product comprising not merely the bare legislation but also the underlying culture. That culture includes constitutional stability, availability of relevant expertise and a database of precedent. Delaware scores highly on all of these criteria. The nature of that product, which takes time to mature, can serve a role in influencing reincorporation decisions by firms.

These alternatives to the concession/mandatory theories have influenced corporate law reform debates in the UK. It is no surprise to note their influence on the 1985 White Paper, *Lifting the Burden* (Cmnd 9571), a key milestone in Thatcherite reforms. Certainly, the Companies Act 1989 reflected that influence in its measures on the written resolution procedure and the so-called elective regime for private companies.[22] Both the facilitation philosophy and the regulatory competition perspective were very much to the fore in the *Final Report* of the Company Law Review in 2001. We noted in our Preface how those approaches informed the terms of reference of the Company Law Review in 1998. It is hardly surprising therefore to find it in a prominent position in the *Final Report*.

> We start with the general principle that company law should be primarily enabling or facilitative – i.e. it should provide the means for those engaged in business and other corporate activity to arrange and manage their affairs in the way which they believe is most likely to lead to mutual success and effective productive activity.[23]

Again:

> Company law is also a factor in wider international competitiveness. Globalising markets provide real choice as to where to locate economic activity and which jurisdiction to adopt. Our company law needs to be internationally competitive, to ensure that we retain our existing companies and attract new ones.[24]

---

20   For a persuasive criticism of contractual perspectives, see D. Campbell in his piece in (1997) 7 Aust Jo of Corp Law 343 at 361, where Campbell refers to the 'nexus of metaphors'. Note also V. Brudney (1985) 85 Col L Rev 1403.

21   See *The Genius of American Corporate Law* (1993) (AEI Press) and her seminal article in (1985) 1 Jo of Law, Econ and Org 225.

22   See J. Birds (1990) 11 Co Law 142.

23   URN 01/942 (2001), para 1.10.

24   Ibid, para 1.13.

These comments were made within the past decade but now must be viewed in the light of the global financial crisis, which has placed all regulatory systems under strain, and may well lead to a general ratcheting up of corporate law regulation or even a bout of protectionism.

2   HOW TO REGULATE?

In spite of the existence of these alternative perspectives, not even the most hardened zealot would deny that *some* regulation of limited companies is necessary. There is considerable dispute, however, on both the most efficient mode of such regulation and on the most appropriate degree of regulation. Consensus favours a cocktail of regulatory devices.[25]

2.1   Regulation by Legislation

The use of primary legislation is the standard method of regulating companies across the globe. This should surprise no one, as legislation is in general the usual method of structuring the relationship between social actors in a modern democratic society. Gower was so supportive of a legislative foundation for Company Law that he argued for consolidation.[26] This is not overly adventurous, when one considers that Partnership Law and other key areas of Commercial Law were consolidated in the UK in the late 19th century.

Matters are, however, more complex when it comes to regulating companies. Unlike the examples mentioned above, there was no well-established fund of common law principles on which to draw.

There is another problem to overcome when legislating for companies: not all companies pose the same type of regulatory problem. In English law, the approach has been to use a single monolithic statute to cover both public and private companies.[27] In continental jurisdictions (for example, France and Germany), it is more common to find separate and explicit regimes created for both public and private companies. Some common law jurisdictions (such as South Africa[28]) have also gone down this route. The UK has resisted this trend, though increasingly there are signs of a rupture in our companies legislation, most notably in the share capital maintenance and accounts provi-

---

[25]   See also E. Ferran (2001) 1 JCLS 381.
[26]   See L.C.B. Gower (1962) 4 Mal L Rev 36.
[27]   R.R. Pennington noted this weakness in the system of English company law – see (1962) 25 MLR 703 at 704.
[28]   For the close company in South African law, see J.J. Henning in (2004) 25 Co Law 95.

sions.[29] Traditionally, this schizophrenic manifestation owes less to a domestic reappraisal and more to EU influences, which have been most apparent in this respect since the enactment of the Companies Act 1980.[30] Having said that, the governing philosophy at present is 'Think Small First'. This certainly was a dominant mantra for the Company Law Review[31] and its impact upon the Companies Act 2006 is readily apparent, particularly in the area of company accounts, where the base rules are designed for small companies, with variations being prescribed for their larger counterparts.[32] The fact that under s. 270, private companies are no longer required to have a company secretary also exemplifies this policy. It is a pity that this philosophy has not been followed through to the point of accepting the wisdom of discrete legislative regimes for public and private companies. In my opinion, this remains a serious structural weakness in UK corporate law.

Other jurisdictions use legislation to regulate groups of companies. Germany is the prime example, with its highly detailed group law dating back to 1965. Whether this is the best way forward is a moot point, but other European jurisdictions have followed suit, albeit with a greater degree of flexibility being permitted.[33]

Legislation should naturally be clear.[34] According to the eminent jurist Lon Fuller, this requirement is one of the critical litmus tests for legality. Gower lamented the failure in UK corporate law to comply with this aspect of lawmaking.[35] Certainly, whether UK Company Law, with its massive bulk and micro-regulation, satisfies this Fuller criterion is doubtful.[36] The Jenkins Committee (Cmnd 1749) also saw the problem some 40 years ago, but felt unable to offer constructive solutions. Thus, in paragraph 6 of its report, it conceded: 'We would gladly see a reduction in this unwieldy mass of legislation but have not found it possible to make suggestions contributing to that

---

[29]   See Companies Act 1985, Parts 5, 13 and 14 and now Companies Act 2006, Parts 17–20 and 23.

[30]   For a comparative overview of the philosophy as applied in a range of countries, see J.J. Henning (2003) 24 Co Law 353.

[31]   *Final Report* URN 01/942 (2001) para 1.53. The Irish have adopted this maxim – see Company Law Review Group First Report (2001), para 2.3.

[32]   See, for example the structure of Part 15 of CA 2006, which makes this point apparent.

[33]   See, for example, the position in Italy (outlined by F. Wooldridge in (2004) 25 Co Law 93) and Belgium (see F. Wooldridge (2007) 28 Co Law 154).

[34]   Lon Fuller, *The Morality of Law* (1964) (Yale University Press) rule 3 (out of eight).

[35]   (1980) 14 Law Teach 111 at 115.

[36]   D. Campbell (1997) 7 Aust Jo of Corp Law 343 at 344.

end'.[37] All commentators agree that retrospective legislation should be avoided because it is a denial of the basic idea of justice.[38]

Legislation may seek to micro-regulate or it may seek to lay down general working principles. Compare here the different legislative approaches towards proscribing insider dealing in the UK and US respectively. The UK approach has in the past been in favour of detailed statutory proscription, whereas the US has favoured a general ban, leaving the courts room to develop the prohibition on insider dealing in more customised fashion as changing circumstances may demand.[39]

Legislation can break new ground or it can eliminate injustices located in the common law.[40]

Where legislation is used as the primary regulatory tool, it must be *responsive* in a prompt fashion. Legislative reform processes moving at the speed of a tortoise benefit no one. Primary legislation can be enacted in an emergency – witness the Insolvency Act 1994, which completed its Parliamentary passage in a matter of a few weeks in order to address an inconvenient judicial ruling what was perceived to be a major/immediate threat to government policy on corporate rescue.[41] In 2008, the Banking (Special Provisions) Act nationalising the troubled bank Northern Rock completed its Parliamentary progress in three days![42] The slow progress of the legislative process that ended with the enactment of the Companies Act 2006 shows that this is very much the exception to the rule.

---

[37]   Cmnd 1749, para 6.

[38]   Recent examples of retrospective companies legislation include CA 1981, s. 39, replaced by Companies Consequential Provisions Act 1985, s. 12 (now CA 2006, s. 612), reversing *Shearer v Bercain Ltd* [1980] 3 All ER 295 and Insolvency Act 1994, reversing the Court of Appeal in *Paramount Airways* [1994] BCC 172 (which in fact was mitigated later by House of Lords on appeal in *Powdrill v Watson* [1995] 2 AC 394). Both of these examples show legislation aiding the business community in the wake of inconvenient judicial rulings.

[39]   For an overview of the US approach towards insider trading, see J.M. Naylor (1990) 11 Co Law 53 and 83.

[40]   The English reversal of *Houldsworth v City of Glasgow Bank* (1880) 5 App Cas 317 by CA 1989, s. 131 (CA 1985, s. 111A; CA 2006, s. 655) is a good example of legislation combating injustice. Unfortunately, this particular common law authority denying remedies to members continues to cause difficulties in some jurisdictions – see M. Sifris and A. Trichardt (2006) 27 Co Law 155. In *Sons of Gwalia v Margaretic* [2007] HCA 1, the High Court of Australia discussed its current status in that jurisdiction.

[41]   See above note 32.

[42]   For comment on this Northern Rock-inspired legislation, see R. Tomasic (2008) 29 Co Law 297 and (2008) 29 Co Law 330.

Although responsive legislation is a credit to the system, there is a downside. Too much reform of the law can produce uncertainty for users and attendant instability. Hardly an ideal recipe for a business community needing to engage in forward planning. This is a criticism that has been applied to company law reform[43] and certainly those practitioners struggling with the avalanche of change ushered in by the Companies Act 2006 might respond sympathetically to that criticism.

2.2 Delegated Legislation

One trend is all too apparent in the UK – the use of delegated legislation as a means of regulating companies. This approach, which has been self-evident for the past 20 years, was favoured by the Company Law Review.[44] Major reforms of primary legislation have been carried out by this method, for example, the introduction of treasury shares into English law in 2003.[45] The Company Law Reform Bill 2005 (as the Companies Act 2006 was initially designated) sought to progress this trend further through the medium of Company Law Reform Orders. Provisions catering for these were in the Bill as originally introduced (see Part 31). They were rejected in the House of Lords on constitutional grounds[46] and no attempt was made to resurrect them when the Bill returned to the Commons. That said, there is no doubting the reliance placed by the Companies Act 2006 on secondary legislation. A perusal of the sections contained in Part 34 on overseas companies (which lack the critical detail) would confirm that observation. Such delegated legislation may be subject to either the negative or the affirmative resolution procedure for Parliamentary approval (see CA 2006, ss. 1289 and 1290 for these alternatives).

2.3 Self-regulatory Codes, Professional Rules and Bureaucratic Processes

These are also of growing significance. This is partly due to the increased complexity of companies legislation, but the trend has also been boosted by constraints upon Parliamentary time.

A pattern emerges of self-regulatory contracts becoming increasingly 'legitimised'. The historical evolution of the Takeover Code provides the best

---

43 See S. Copp (2004) 25 Co Law 291.
44 Op. cit. note 23.
45 SI 2003/1116. For comment, see G. Morse [2004] JBL 303.
46 See C. Bamford (2006) 27 Co Law 161 for discussion.

example of this phenomenon at work. The Code emerged in the wake of certain financial scandals in the mid-1960s. Initially, it was purely a work of self-regulation.[47] Progressively, it became the subject of judicial recognition via cases such as *R v Takeover Panel ex parte Datafin plc*[48] where the Court of Appeal adopted a flexible and inventive approach which balanced the needs of justice against the needs of the market. The possibility of a limited form of judicial review of the Code was thus accepted.[49] This was built on by the courts, indicating that observance/non-observance of the Code was relevant to issues such as compliance with compulsory share acquisition procedures, fulfilment of directors' duties and whether a company should be wound up in the public interest.[50] The Takeover Panel was then given a legal 'home' under the auspices of the Financial Services and Markets Act 2000 regime.[51] With the adoption of the EC Takeovers Directive (2004/25/EC),[52] it became necessary to place it on an even firmer legal footing. Owing to the delay in enacting and then bringing into force the Companies Act 2006, it was necessary to introduce transitional measures to comply with EC obligations.[53] Full implementation came on 6 April 2007 when Part 28 of the 2006 Act was commenced. A perusal of the history of the evolution of the Takeover Code will thus show the move from contract-based regulation to statutory control. It will also show that once again, native law has been changed to cater for EU considerations, though the change here has less to do with substantive content and more to do with juristic basis. The fact that a takeover system can work well once put on a statutory footing is confirmed by reference to the positive experience of related jurisdictions.[54]

---

[47]   For the early history of the Takeover Panel and its Code, see A. Johnston, *The City Takeover Code* (1980) (Clarendon Press). See also A. Johnston [2007] CLJ 422.

[48]   *R v Takeover Panel ex parte Datafin plc* [1987] QB 815. See also *R v Takeover Panel ex parte Guinness plc* [1990] 1 QB 146.

[49]   For the use of judicial review in Australia, see G. Morse (2007) 22 NZULR 622, R. Halstead and S. Magee [2005] (14) SMCLN 1, [2005] (16) SMCLN 5 and [2005] (20) SMCLN 5.

[50]   *Re Chez Nico Restaurants Ltd* [1991] BCC 736, *Dunford and Elliott Ltd v Johnson and Firth Brown* [1977] 1 Lloyds Rep 505, *St Piran* [1981] 1 WLR 1300. As the Takeover Code was viewed as quasi law, matters of interpretation were for the judge and not the jury in criminal trials – see *R v Spens* [1991] 1 WLR 624.

[51]   Under the auspices of the FSMA 2000, the Financial Services Authority entered a concordat with the Takeover Panel in 2001.

[52]   See A. Johnston (2004) 25 Co Law 270.

[53]   See Takeovers Directive (Interim Implementation) Regulations 2006 (SI 2006/1183) superseded by Companies Act 2006, Part 28.

[54]   For example in Australia and Ireland – see B. Clarke, *Takeovers and Mergers Law in Ireland* (1999) (Round Hall Press).

Corporate governance codes, originally entirely self-regulatory, have been part of the topography since the Cadbury Code[55] of 1992. The courts have on occasions used these to inform their rulings.[56] Corporate governance rules necessary to implement European requirements can now be created under the auspices of the Financial Services Authority.[57] Again, the Companies Act 2006 further advances the process of according these formal legal recognition (see s. 1269).

Self-regulation can also be introduced via the professional rules governing key players – such as brokers, auditors and insolvency practitioners. The regulatory contribution of auditors is most obvious, but insolvency practitioners have an important role to play in blowing the whistle on unfit directors of insolvent companies. It is clear that the introduction of the whistleblowing obligation imposed on insolvency practitioners by s. 7(3) of the Company Directors Disqualification Act 1986 was the prime factor behind the explosion of disqualification cases in the 1990s. Cases came to the attention of the authorities in a way that previously did not happen. A similar strategy has commended itself in Ireland, where under s. 56 of the Company Law Enforcement Act 2001, a whistleblowing obligation has been imposed on all liquidators, no matter how appointed, to report after six months of the period of office to the authorities, such report to include reference to any suspected abusive managerial behaviour.

Finally, self-regulation operates in the realm of corporate rescue, and is best exemplified by the so-called London Approach.[58] This is essentially a set of *social norms* applied in the City of London to deal with major corporate distress where several banks are involved as creditors. As yet, there are no signs that these 'rules' have been marked down for formal legal recognition.

Bureaucratic processes can play a role in how the law is applied in practice. These practices may introduce discretion or may in effect offer extra-statutory

---

[55]   *Committee on Financial Aspects of Corporate Governance* (1992) (Gee). For comment, see A. Belcher [1995] JBL 321, J. Dine (1994) 15 Co Law 73. On the exporting of the Cadbury Code to overseas jurisdictions, see A. Dignam (2000) 21 Co Law 70. Germany developed a similar approach with its Cromme Code in 2001 (named after Dr Gerhard Cromme). An English translation of this Code, which has since been amended, is available on the internet.

[56]   In *Re Macro (Ipswich) Ltd* [1994] 2 BCLC 354 at 407, the Code was referred to by Arden J in the context of an s. 459 unfair prejudice petition citing alleged prolonged managerial behaviour.

[57]   Companies Act 2006, s. 1269.

[58]   See Pen Kent (1994) 33 Bank of Eng Quart Bull 110, R.E. Floyd (1995) 11 IL & P 82, C. Bird (1996) 12 IL & P 87, N. Segal [2000] 13 Ins Intell 17 and J. Armour and S. Deakin [2001] 1 JCLS 21.

concessions.[59] Practice manuals should be in the public domain according to Lightman J in *Re POW Trust Ltd.*[60]

2.4   A Residual Role for the Courts?

Although the regulation of companies is primarily founded in legislation, the courts do have a critical role to play.[61] One need look no further than the foundational House of Lords authority in *Salomon v Salomon & Co Ltd*[62] to appreciate the significance of the judicial input. By revisiting another House of Lords staple, *Ebrahimi v Westbourne Galleries Ltd,*[63] we find the courts intervening to combat conduct that was clearly unfair, but not apparently in breach of existing discrete provisions in companies legislation. The law on auditor liability is dominated by the Law Lords ruling *Caparo plc v Dickman,*[64] a case which in some senses undermines the legislative policy relating to the inherent value of the company audit. This is not the only example one could cite where the judges have placed a proverbial spanner in the works.[65] From a more helpful perspective, the need for legislation to curb over-use of the unfair prejudice remedy was taken away by the House of Lords in *O'Neill v Phillips.*[66] Consideration of the floating charge origins in English law will highlight the role of the courts in pivotal decisions ranging from *Re Panama, New Zealand and Australia Royal Mail Co,*[67] through *Illingworth v Houldsworth*[68] to *National Westminster Bank v Spectrum Plus Ltd.*[69] Although in English law the floating charge has certain features defined in legislation, it is indisputably a creature of common law and remains so. In Scotland, by way

---

[59]   For an example of what may be viewed as an extra-statutory concession in the corporate law field, see the Slavenburg file, which is discussed in Chapter 5 below.

[60]   [2004] BCC 268 at 275–6.

[61]   See D. Milman [1990] LMCLQ 401.

[62]   [1897] AC 22. See Lord Cooke's Hamlyn Lecture, *Turning Points of the Common Law* (1997) (Sweet and Maxwell) chapter 1.

[63]   [1973] AC 360.

[64]   [1990] 2 AC 605.

[65]   Witness *Brady v Brady* [1989] AC 755 (made redundant by the removal of the financial assistance bar from private companies by CA 2006) and *Re Leyland DAF* [2004] UKHL 9 (reversed by CA 2006, s. 1282 and Insolvency Amendment Rules 2008 (SI 2008/737)). The case of *Lewis v IRC (Re Floor Fourteen Ltd)* [2002] BCC 198 also cut across official policy and was quickly neutralised by Insolvency (Amendment) Rules (No. 2) 2002 (SI 2002/2712). Similarly, the negative effects of *Exeter CC v Bairstow* [2007] BCC 236 were mitigated by SI 2008/386.

[66]   [1999] 1 WLR 1092.

[67]   (1870) 5 Ch App 318.

[68]   [1904] AC 355.

[69]   *National Westminster Bank v Spectrum Plus Ltd* [2005] UKHL 41.

of contrast, it is a creature of statute,[70] with some judicial enlightenment (and in some cases obfuscation)[71] being added.

One negative aspect of the common law system is the stultifying effect of precedent – old authorities are retained past their sell-by date.[72]

Focusing on the theme of this monograph, the Court of Appeal ruling in *Romalpa*[73] provides a good example of how English law has been changed by the mere fact of the operation of cross-border commerce. Here, the English courts, in reviewing a Dutch metal trader's terms given to an English importer, effectively incorporated continental commercial practice on reservation of title to goods prior to full payment into English law and in so doing profoundly disrupted corporate insolvency practice in this country. However, although the validity of such clauses is within certain bounds accepted by the English courts, any attempt to exclude the operation of the English law of security interests is not permissible.[74] The experience of English law in accommodating reservation of title clauses within the parameters of the established regime for corporate insolvency law has been matched to a large extent in Ireland[75] and Australia.[76]

Common law can often anticipate later statutory reforms. This is a recurrent pattern in English law. In *Re Duomatic Ltd*,[77] the English courts allowed informal variation of corporate constitutions (that is, where no formal special resolution has been passed) in cases where unanimity could be established. A significant corpus of jurisprudence has developed[78] under this principle,

---

[70] The arrival of the floating charge in Scotland in 1961 was entirely the result of statutory intervention via Companies Floating Charges Act 1961, in that under Scottish common law, floating charges were not recognised – *Carse v Coppen* [1951] SC 233. It was an import from south of the border. Scottish floating charges are still governed by CA 1985, Part XVIII. Registration of charges in Scotland is regulated by CA 1985, ss. 410–24 and CA 2006, ss. 878–92. See now Bankruptcy and Diligence (Scotland) Act 2007, Part 2.

[71] See the furore over *Sharp v Thompson* [1998] BCC 115. The Scottish Law Commission Report No. 208 (2007) is recommending change – see SE/2007/242.

[72] A point made elegantly by the French academic A. Tunc (1982) 45 MLR 1 at 5.

[73] [1976] 1 WLR 676.

[74] See *Re Weldtech Ltd* [1991] BCLC 393. See Chapter 7 below.

[75] The Irish experience commenced with *Re Interview Ltd* [1975] IR 382, which is noted by D. Milman in (1978) 122 SJ 172. For an overview of title retention in Ireland, see J de Lacy (1987) 22 Ir Jur 212.

[76] See J de Lacy [2001] Ins Law 64 and K. Stock [2002] 15 Ins Intell 1.

[77] [1969] 2 Ch 365.

[78] For comment, see R. Grantham [1993] CLJ 245. For recent authorities applying this principle, see *Extrasure Travel Insurance v Scattergood* [2003] 1 BCLC 598. Compare *Domoney v Godinho* [2004] 2 BCLC 15.

which has been further advanced by the introduction of the written resolution procedure via statute.[79] There have been suggestions that the *Duomatic* principle is now so well established that it ought to be converted into a statutory rule. This was the view of the Company Law Review.[80] Those suggestions, however, have not met with official support and were rejected in both the 2002 and 2005 White Papers.[81] Certainly, the principle is not formally recognised in the Companies Act 2006.

3 REGULATORY TOOLS, BUREAUCRATIC EFFICIENCY AND SANCTIONS

Above we have touched upon alternative modes of regulation for use in the companies context. Once that issue is resolved, there are secondary questions that must be addressed.

Firstly, how can we ensure bureaucratic efficiency? The use of conclusive certificates of incorporation[82] and charge registration[83] may be noted here. These are designed to import a degree of finality should disputes arise. English law does not go so far as to adopt the continental idea of nullity of companies.[84]

How are the appropriate corporate regulations to be enforced? Should the law use civil sanctions, criminal law offences or other methods (such as administrative penalties)? Australia[85] has moved clearly in the direction of civil penalties and this approach has attracted favourable comment.[86] Ireland[87] seems firmly wedded to its corpus of criminal sanctions. The view that English law is coming round to is that there should be a basket of such different sanctions to achieve the optimum effect. This is a sensible compromise.

---

[79]   See CA 1989, s. 116, introducing s. 379A into CA 1985. Now CA 2006, ss. 288–300.

[80]   *Final Report* (URN 01/942).

[81]   See Cm 5553-I (*Modernising Company Law*) and Cm 6456 (*Company Law Reform*) respectively.

[82]   See CA 1985, s. 13(7) (CA 2006, s. 15(4)) and *Jubilee Cotton Mills v Lewis* [1924] AC 958.

[83]   See CA 1985, s. 401(2)(b) (CA 2006, s. 869) and *R v Registrar of Companies ex parte Central Bank of India* [1986] 2 WLR 177.

[84]   See R. Drury (1985) 48 MLR 644 for a lucid account of the concept of nullity of companies.

[85]   The Cooney Committee (1989) recommended this approach towards adoption of civil penalties and it was implemented in 1993.

[86]   On the suitability of civil penalties in Singapore, see P.-W. Lee [2006] CLWR 1.

[87]   On the Irish approach, see CLRG First Report (2001), para 8.2.4.

So, for instance, civil sanctions have been used in a variety of contexts where directors are in breach of duty. This might involve the setting aside of improper transactions regarded as voidable, exerting an 'account' or requiring monetary compensation to be paid. It is significant that the wrongful trading regulatory innovation (see Insolvency Act 1986, s. 214) fell exclusively under the civil law umbrella.[88]

The criminal law has been used to punish the more serious types of breach of companies regulation, for example fraudulent trading under CA 1985, s. 458 (now restated by CA 2006, s. 993, a provision which increases the maximum penalty to ten years' imprisonment). Successful prosecutions for fraudulent trading are rare, according to official figures. This reflects a general problem with regard to the real value of criminal law sanctions in this area.[89] As far as insider trading/market abuse is concerned, English law again has traditionally opted for criminal sanctions, but the failure of these has forced a rethink, with a move towards administrative penalties operated through the auspices of the Financial Services Authority being the result (see FSMA 2000, s. 123 here). Civil sanctions are also a possibility, to compensate victims of market abuse.[90]

An alternative is the use of civil penalties imposed by bureaucratic bodies. One such example is provided by s. 242A of the Companies Act 1985 (to be replaced by CA 2006, s. 453). This provision enables the registrar to levy a penalty upon a defaulting company, though that levy can only be enforced where the company fails to pay up, by the registrar applying to the county court. The scale of the levy was determined by regulation and enforcement policy was guided by an internal practice manual.[91] In *R (on the application of POW Trust) v Registrar of Companies*,[92] it was held by Lightman J that this penalty system was ECHR-compliant and that it did not infringe Art 6 or Art 1 of the First Protocol. Lightman J did, however, suggest that the practice manual be put into the public domain.

Finally, the state can resort to more subtle means. 'Naming and shaming', a device made more effective by the dissemination opportunities offered by the internet, is beginning to be used against unfit directors.[93]

---

[88]   Compare IA 1986, ss. 216 and 217, which operate both civil and criminal sanctions in tandem. The criminal offence specified in s. 217 is one of strict liability – *R v Cole* [1998] BCC 87.

[89]   See L. Linklater (2003) 24 Co Law 1. For evaluation of the role of criminal sanctions, see (2001) 1 JCLS 381 at 406.

[90]   See the episode recorded in (2006) 27 Co Law 51 for this remedy at work. For civil remedies in Singapore, see R. Chandran (2001) 22 Co Law 63.

[91]   For regulations under the 2006 Act see SI 2008/497.

[92]   [2004] BCC 268. On s. 242A civil penalties, see *Registrar of Companies v Radio-Tech Engineering Ltd* [2004] BCC 277.

[93]   Details of disqualified directors are often mounted on the BERR website.

Issues can arise as to timing where multiple sanctions are involved.[94] Should civil proceedings be allowed to continue where criminal prosecutions are afoot? Would a prosecution be compromised by an adverse civil finding? Should both types of proceeding be allowed to run concurrently? These issues continue to raise concerns.

There is also the issue of who regulates. Auditors have been the standard bulwark against infringement, but their performance in many a recent corporate collapse has been lamentable.[95] Inadequate auditing performance has led to professional sanctions being imposed. Increasingly, ways are being found of spreading the enforcement burden by engaging regulatory intervention by shareholders (CA 1985, s. 459; CA 2006, s. 994), companies themselves (CA 1985, s. 212; CA 2006, s. 793) and by other professional repeat players such as insolvency practitioners (CDDA 1986, s. 7(3)). This is a sound policy, reducing the burden of enforcement costs on the state, although the state cannot absolve itself of all responsibility.

Enforcement can be aided by involving the public at large. People are exhorted to blow the whistle on disqualified directors by ringing a hotline. If necessary, a system of payment of bounties to informers and whistleblowers might be deemed appropriate. The SEC operates such a regime in the USA under the Insider Trading and Securities Enforcement Act 1988, so as to encourage people to come forward and report insider trading.[96]

When considering appropriate enforcement mechanisms, the economic burden needs to be borne in mind. The burgeoning cost to the public exchequer (as indicated in National Audit Office reports[97]) was one of the reasons why the director disqualification order procedure had to change and effectively be largely replaced by a more consensual undertakings model based upon agreement between the accused director and the prosecuting authorities.[98] What we have here is officially sanctioned plea bargaining, albeit under another name.[99]

The Company Law Review paid considerable attention to the question of sanctions in its major study of UK corporate law. The conclusion

---

[94]   See the discussion of this problem of concurrent proceedings (criminal/civil/disciplinary) in the editorial in (1996) 17 Co Law 1.

[95]   One need look no further than the example of Enron here, where the consequences for the auditors were so severe as to lead to the break-up of the well-known audit firm involved.

[96]   See J.M. Naylor (1990) 11 Co Law 53 and 83.

[97]   See National Audit Office Reports – HCP 1993–94 No. 907 and HCP 1998–99 No. 424.

[98]   By Insolvency Act 2000, s. 6.

[99]   The practice had already been developed by the courts in cases such as *Re Carecraft Construction Ltd* [1994] 1 WLR 172.

reached[100] was that there should be no general move towards decriminalisation. Financial assistance in share acquisition, so long as it was prohibited in corporate law, should continue to attract a criminal sanction.[101] Indeed, in the area of fraudulent trading, the maximum penalty was recommended to be increased from seven to ten years' imprisonment.[102] The idea of greater use of administrative penalties only attracted an ambivalent response.[103]

4   CRITICAL REGULATORY GOALS

If we accept that companies have to be regulated, and we pass over the question of the manner of that regulation, we now should consider the critical points of reference for any regulatory regime governing limited liability companies. Drawing on the UK experience, it is possible to identify a number of central issues.

4.1   Effective and Customer-driven Incorporation Processes

This is a primary objective of any modern system of company law. Most pragmatists accept that companies (unlike partnerships) do not materialise out of thin air or alternatively through private contractual bargaining; there must be some form of bureaucratic incorporation procedure designated by law.

Prior to the Companies Act 2006, incorporation procedures in English law had remained largely unchanged since Victorian times. They were paper-based and cumbersome. Admittedly, there was some tinkering as to the minimum number of subscribing members,[104] but the fundamentals were stable. With the development of speedy incorporation models in other jurisdictions, the English procedures were increasingly seen as uncompetitive.[105] Under the 2006 Act, there have been changes to improve the position. For example, the traditional distinction between memorandum and articles of association is no longer maintained as an article of faith. The memorandum under the 2006 Act is but a pale shadow of its former self and, indeed, it is no longer treated as part of the constitution (see s. 17).

---

[100]   *Final Report* (URN 01/942), paras 15.4 and 15.20.

[101]   Ibid, para 15.18.

[102]   Ibid, para 15.7. It was also recommended that the offence here be extended to overseas companies – para 15.8.

[103]   Ibid, para 15.22.

[104]   Witness the arrival of the single-member company in 1992 via SI 1992/1699, implementing the 12th Company Law Harmonisation Directive (89/667).

[105]   But the UK procedures are more effective than those in Germany, which has been forced to respond in order to preserve the future of the GmbH – see F. Wooldridge (2007) 28 Co Law 381.

The incorporation process should also offer choice – that is, a menu of different corporate entities suitable for the diverse needs of a range of would-be incorporators. There is a world of difference between a large business set up to generate profits for a myriad of shareholders and a small venture designed to promote social good. English law has consistently broadened choice here, with the most recent addition being the community interest company introduced under the auspices of the Companies (Audit, Investigations and Community Enterprise) Act 2004. This legislative base remains intact, notwithstanding the enactment of the 2006 Act (for confirmation, see CA 2006, s. 6).

4.2   Protecting Creditors from Abuse of Limited Liability

Notwithstanding the complaints of some commentators,[106] this has always been a concern of policymakers in English law since 1855. The ultra vires rule was often justified by reference to this policy. The argument ran that creditors would not extend credit to a limited company without reference to its stated business objects and so to allow companies to engage in commerce beyond those parameters would threaten creditors.[107] Certainly, the cumbersome share capital maintenance regime is posited upon the need to protect the largely mythical 'guarantee fund' for unsecured creditors. In continental jurisdictions, this philosophy is taken a step further by requiring mandatory transfers of distributable profits to reserves. The weaknesses in the general capital maintenance strategy have for many years been exposed[108] but the straitjacket imposed by the Second Company Law Harmonisation Directive (1977/91) has barred major reform. The Companies Act 2006 has squeezed every last drop of 'wiggle room' out of the situation; further change depends on European movement. This movement has manifested itself through Amending Directive (2006/68),[109] which becomes operational in April 2008. This will give

---

[106]   Some 60 years ago Kahn-Freund argued that traditionally English law had given greater emphasis to protecting shareholders than creditors – at the time of writing, that comment might not have been an inaccurate assertion, but it does not fully reflect the position today.

[107]   See *Ashbury Carriage v Riche* (1875) LR 7 HL 653 at 667 per Lord Cairns. This was a curious rationale when one considers that unsecured creditors could not invoke the rule to stop a company acting ultra vires.

[108]   See J. Armour (2000) 63 MLR 355.

[109]   For background, see E. Ferran [2005] 6 EBOLR 93. Under this Amending Direction, the protection available to creditors on a reduction of share capital has been watered down by switching the burden of proof onto creditors wishing to challenge a share capital reduction – see the Companies (Reduction of Capital) (Creditor Protection) Regulations 2008 (SI 2008/719).

Member States the option to deregulate share capital maintenance rules for public companies in a number of areas, including financial assistance, share capital reduction procedures and issue of shares for non-cash consideration. US-influenced corporate jurisdictions (including Canada, New Zealand and Singapore[110]) have now discarded share capital maintenance in favour of solvency-based regimes and the imposition of fiduciary duties upon directors. This strategy appears to work well and the aforementioned EU reform should be viewed in positive terms. The Isle of Man in its 2006 Companies Act has also gone down this well-trodden route of deregulation.

A basic tool designed to ensure that there is public confidence in the system of companies regulation is the so-called disclosure philosophy.[111] It is no surprise that it was the subject matter of the First EU Company Law Harmonisation Directive (68/151) (since amended by Directive 2003/58). Thus, the constitution of a company should be open to public inspection, as should details of its directors, and information should be available as to its balance sheet and accounts. Compliance rates are not perfect – the official estimates suggest something in the region of 84 per cent in 2005/6. The flip side of disclosure is that the public are deemed to have notice of these public documents[112] and this has in the past[113] and can continue to work to their disadvantage in some instances.[114] This disclosure strategy, which has impacted beyond the creditor protection sphere,[115] has been called into question in recent years in the UK, with abuse of open access to corporate information by animal rights activists minded to attack the homes of directors of companies whose businesses they disapprove of. Some corrective legislation geared to offering protection through a system of 'service addresses' has therefore been required.[116]

Another established control tool is the DTI investigation, which is often cited as being a quid pro quo for access to limited liability.[117] There are significant

---

[110]   H. Tijo (2006) 21 BJIBFL 316.

[111]   For an account see L.S. Sealy (1981) 2 Co Law 51.

[112]   *Ernest v Nicholls* (1857) 6 HL Cas 401.

[113]   *Re Jon Beauforte (London) Ltd* [1953] Ch 131.

[114]   In the area of charge registration, the public are deemed to have notice of the fact that a charge is registered – but not of its contents, according to *Wilson v Kelland* [1910] 2 Ch 306.

[115]   For example, it is now accepted that public companies have a right to know who their shareholders are – first introduced into English law in CA 1981. See now CA 2006, Part 22.

[116]   See The Companies (Particulars of Usual Residential Address) (Compliance Orders) Regulations 2002 (SI 2002/912), CA 1985, s. 723B and for the future CA 2006, s. 165 with regulations made thereunder.

[117]   See *Norwest Holst Ltd v Secretary of State* [1978] Ch 201.

doubts about the real value of these procedures, which often take an aeon to produce a report. A wag has compared the formal DTI investigation to being more like an archaeological dig than a post mortem! At best, they provide useful empirical material for future reform of the law. It is curious that the statutory provisions on DTI investigations are not consolidated in the Companies Act 2006, but remain stranded in the 1985 legislation. It seems likely that they will be relocated into a discrete statute at some future date.

With heightened concerns about the effectiveness of these old protective mechanisms, new strategies have emerged to ensure that the privilege of limited liability is not misused. So, for example, the director disqualification regime has in recent years taken centre stage as a means of protecting the public from continued abuse of limited liability. Director disqualification for unfit directors essentially dates back to the Insolvency Act 1976. The rules were substantially upgraded in the Company Directors Disqualification Act 1986 and then, because of the success of the regime and the consequential cost to the public purse, were later deregulated in the Insolvency Act 2000 with the introduction of the contract-based undertakings procedure. This approach based upon barring unfit entrepreneurs from future access to limited liability companies has been adopted in various jurisdictions, with local variations. In Ireland, for example, there are what are known as director restriction orders.[118] With the increased usage of this strategy across the globe, Part 40 of the Companies Act 2006 has introduced a new mechanism to give effect to foreign disqualifications in the UK – this will be discussed in Chapter 6.

In English law,[119] apart from denying the use of limited liability companies to undesirables, increasingly ways and means have been sought to enable out-of-pocket creditors (and those acting for them) to pursue the personal wealth of directors. In 1929, fraudulent trading was criminalised and also made a civil wrong.[120] The advent of wrongful trading liability, being treated exclusively as a civil wrong via the enactment of s. 214 of the

---

[118] See CA 1990 (Ireland), s. 150. A helpful general review of the mechanisms used to control errant directors in Ireland is provided by N. Fitzgerald in (2004) 20 IL & P 108. The key cases dealing with restriction orders are *Robinson v Frost* [1999] 2 ILRM 169, *Luby v McMahon* [2003] 1 IR 133, *Fennel v Frost* [2003] 1 IR 80. For comment, see A. Leyden (2006) 9 Trin Coll L Rev 147 and A. O'Neill (2007) 28 Co Law 116.

[119] Ireland introduced the notion of reckless trading in 1990 via s. 138 of the CA 1990 (which became s. 297A of CA 1963). In so doing, the Irish drew heavily upon the South African model in CA (SA) 1973, s. 424. For reckless trading in Ireland, see H. Linnane (1995) 16 Co Law 26, 319. Australia employs a similar concept via CA 2001, ss. 588G and 588H, as does New Zealand under the auspices of CA 1993, s.135 – see S.M. Watson [1998] JBL 495.

[120] This was recommended by the Greene Committee (Cm 1926).

Insolvency Act 1986[121] is a good reflection of the new strategy, though it has to be conceded that it has not been a resounding success.[122] This disappointment is in sharp contrast to the satisfaction of policymakers with the disqualification mechanism. The differential is almost entirely due to the fact that wrongful trading requires private litigation finance, whereas the public purse can fund disqualification. The courts in England have tended to increase the risk of directors being held liable for corporate debts.[123]

The position here is fluid. In the wake of the high-profile Farepak collapse,[124] the government is again looking at imposed trust devices to protect consumers who pay in advance for goods which are never delivered because the supplier becomes insolvent.[125] In the meantime, it has introduced a statutory reserve fund for unsecured creditors out of floating charge realisations.[126]

Creditors themselves are taking matters into their own hands by exploiting provisions imposing personal liability on directors. This has been happening for some time in the area of incorrectly labelled company cheques,[127] but more recently, major creditors like the HMRC have utilised the potential of s. 216 of the Insolvency Act 1986[128] and s. 15 of the Company Directors Disqualification Act 1986 to this end.[129] These opportunistic developments on

---

[121]   Interestingly, in Zambia, wrongful trading is both a civil wrong and a crime under the Zambian Companies Act 1994 – see K.K. Mwenda (2008) 8 Ox Univ Comm LJ 93.

[122]   See D. Milman [2004] JBL 493.

[123]   In Germany, a similar trend has emerged under which shareholders in the GmbH are being made personally liable for corporate obligations – see M. Shillig (2006) 27 Co Law 348.

[124]   See the preliminary ruling of Mann J in *Re Farepak Food and Gifts Ltd* [2006] EWHC 3272 (Ch), [2007] 2 BCLC 1.

[125]   See The Times March 2007. This is not a new issue – it was acknowledged to be a problem in the 1980s and research was undertaken – see A. Ogus and C.K. Rowley, *Prepayments and Insolvency* (1984) (OFT).

[126]   Insolvency Act 1986, s. 176A, inserted by Enterprise Act 2002. Attempts by secured creditors to access this fund have been rebuffed – see *Re Permacelle Finesse Ltd* [2008] BCC 208 and *Re Airbase (UK) Ltd* [2008] BCC 213 – discussed by A. Walters in (2008) 29 Co Law 129. This statutory fund is likely to prove more useful than the obsolete reserve capital mechanism (CA 1985, s. 120), which was abolished by the Companies Act 2006.

[127]   CA 1985, s. 349. As far as the CA 2006 is concerned, it is not clear if this rule will be reproduced.

[128]   *IRC v Nash* [2004] BCC 150, *IRC v Walsh* [2005] EWCA Civ 1291, *HMRC v Benton-Diggins* [2006] 2 BCLC 255, *HMRC v Yousef* [2008] EWHC 423 (Ch), [2008] BPIR 1491. Debt factors taking an assignment of a corporate debt can also exploit this provision – *First Independent Factors and Finance Ltd v Mountford* [2008] BPIR 515.

[129]   *IR v McEntaggart* [2006] BPIR 750.

the ground might suggest the need for a rethink on core strategy.[130] Undoubtedly, they should be a cause for concern for company directors.

Creditor protection may be self-executing, with the institution of security being the prime mechanism to achieve this goal. Historically, English law has always been pro-creditor. Witness the continued usage of the unique remedy of administrative receivership,[131] though its potential has been substantially curtailed by the Enterprise Act 2002. Other jurisdictions, such as the US and France, are pro-debtor – that is, in the present context, they are more inclined to bolster the position of the borrowing company. However, socio-economic as well as cultural factors come into play. It may be the case that in developing economies thirsty for inward investment, a pro-creditor strategy is the sensible option in the medium term.

4.3 Limiting Unauthorised Trading

Clearly, this is related to the aforementioned creditor protection policy. The ultra vires rule sought to restrict companies' trading operations to those delineated in their objects clause.[132] The argument goes that investors have put their money into a company simply in order for it to pursue its specified business objectives. This idea justifies the winding of companies for failure of substratum.[133] In many cases, this assumption is a fallacy; investors invest in successful businesses and are fairly unconcerned about how that success is achieved. Accordingly, the ultra vires control mechanism was doomed to failure, though English law was slower than many jurisdictions to recognise that reality.[134] Even within the enactment of the Companies Act 2006, traces of it still linger.[135]

The rules governing contracts made by directors exceeding authority appear to undermine the general restriction on unauthorised trading. From the earliest days of modern English company law, the courts have been inclined to uphold such contracts with the well-known ruling in *Turquand's* case[136] oper-

---

[130]   See D. Milman [2008] 21 Ins Intell 25.

[131]   See I. Macdonald and D. Moujalli [2001] 14 Ins Intell 76.

[132]   *Ashbury Carriage v Riche* (1875) LR 7 HL 653. For history, see B. Pettet (1997) 50 CLP 279.

[133]   *Re German Date Coffee Co* (1882) 20 Ch D 169.

[134]   See H. Rajak [1995] 26 Camb L Rev 9.

[135]   See CA 2006, s. 42, for example on charitable companies.

[136]   (1856) 6 E & B 327 followed by the High Court of Australia in *Northside Developments v Registrar General* (1990) 170 CLR 146. For a fascinating historical account of the collapse of the Royal British Bank and of the fate of the leading figures involved, see J. Taylor (2005) 78 Hist Res 230. See also the account given by G. Wilson and S. Wilson in (2001) 1 JCLS 211 at 222–3.

ating the so-called indoor management rule exemplifying that philosophy. A comparable approach was manifested in modern times by the Court of Appeal in *Freeman and Lockyer v Buckhurst Park Properties.*[137] This approach has been transported throughout the Commonwealth jurisdictions via the processes of the common law.[138] Fortunately, it is consistent with the EU philosophy of sanctity of contract, as exemplified by Art 9 of the First Company Law Harmonisation Directive (1968/151). The Companies Act 2006, s. 40 continues this trend by increasing the chances of unauthorised contracts being enforced by third parties through its amendment of CA 1985, s. 35A. This amendment in effect makes protection available to an outsider, where the transaction was approved by only some of the directors (as opposed to the whole board).

Taking an overview here, the fundamental problem has been to get the balance right between restricting improper use of shareholder funds, whilst at the same time not increasing the transaction costs of counterparties dealing with companies by requiring them to make burdensome inquiries as to whether appropriate internal procedures have been complied with. The trend in recent years across the globe has been to move towards security of transaction, at the cost of allowing breaches of organisational integrity to occur.

4.4 Curbing Misuse of Managerial Powers

There are echoes of this policy in the rules discussed above, but the issue is much wider. What we are talking about here ties in with concerns about corporate governance. Since Berle and Means published their classic thesis[139] in 1932, the problem of how to monitor agents who run companies has been a dominant theme in corporate law discourse, though it must be pointed out that the common law had begun to tackle this problem from the late 19th century by applying equitable principles. Companies are artificial persons who necessarily rely upon fiduciary agents (that is, directors) to undertake transactions on their behalf. It is therefore essential to have in place rules which prevent such agents from abusing their position. The general rules of agency law have to be modified to reflect the peculiarities of the corporate context. A key question is the extent to which these rules can be relaxed by shareholders themselves – issues of ex post facto ratification come to the fore here. For a long

---

137 [1964] 1 QB 480.
138 For an account, see D. Milman and A. Evans (1985) 6 Co Law 68. See *Crabtree Vickers Pty v Australia Direct Mail Advertising* (1975) 133 CLR 72. Note also D.A. Obadina (1997) 18 Co Law 45 and 76.
139 A.A. Berle and G.C. Means, *The Modern Corporation and Private Property* (1932) (Macmillan).

time, the basic rule on ratification has been that shareholders can ratify and in any vote held to consider the propriety of directors' conduct, the shares held by the alleged wrongdoer(s) can be voted upon,[140] but this has now been modified by s. 239 of the Companies Act 2006 to ensure that only independent shareholders can in future ratify.

4.5   Protecting Shareholders

The shareholder is the central player in the modern limited liability company. Without the shareholder's capital, the company would be starved of equity funds and would be forced into the clutches of bankers. All systems of corporate law must therefore have in place mechanisms to protect the shareholder interest in order to encourage investment.

All shareholders in the same class should be treated equitably. This fundamental is one of the General Principles in the Takeover Code (see General Principle 1).

There is an expectation, but not a formal requirement, that all shares should carry votes. The Jenkins Committee set its face against compulsion here, though there was significant dissent on the point.[141] The exercise of voting rights should be protected legally[142] and should be facilitated – for example, by permitting proxy votes to be used.[143]

At the most basic level, shareholders should be protected from expropriation of their economic interest in the company, as reflected by their shareholding. The courts will scrutinise carefully attempts to alter articles to introduce such a facility.[144] The Companies Act 1985, Part XIIIA did embody an expropriation facility (s. 429, now restated in CA 2006, s. 979) in the event of a hostile takeover bid, but the bid must be genuine for that mechanism to be engaged, as the House of Lords pointed out in *Blue Metal Industries v Dilley*.[145] Art 1 of the First Protocol of European Convention on Human

---

[140]   *North West Transportation Co v Beatty* (1887) 12 App Cas 589 – reversed by CA 2006, s. 239(3). But the Companies Act 2006 does not allow for ratification in circumstances where this was not available at common law – *Franbar Holdings Ltd v Patel* [2008] EWHC 1534 (Ch), [2008] BCC 885.

[141]   Cmnd 1749, para 137.

[142]   A shareholder has a personal right to vote – such a right can be enforced without the obstacle of the rule in *Foss v Harbottle* (1843) 2 Hare 461 – see *Pender v Lushington* (1877) 6 Ch D 70.

[143]   On the story of how proxy voting was accepted by English law, see V. Edgtton (2000) 21 Co Law 294.

[144]   See B. Hannigan [2007] JBL 471.

[145]   [1970] AC 827. The existence of s. 430C (CA 2006, s. 986) also exemplifies the protective approach.

Rights and Fundamental Freedoms will protect shareholders' property rights, but that protection is not absolute.[146]

Such protective mechanisms may take the form of substantive rights (for example, the right to demand an EGM[147]). These rights may be seen as inalienable.[148] Alternatively, organisational structures may need to be adopted to protect shareholders – the German two-tier board structure manifests this approach.[149] Here we have a management board overseen by a supervisory board manned by representatives of various stakeholder groups. Litigation procedures must also be taken account of where a legal system relies upon substantive rights to be enforced via the courts as part of its shareholder protection strategy. The possibilities afforded by alternative dispute resolution mechanisms should be carefully evaluated, though the jurisdiction of the courts cannot always be excluded.[150]

The CA 2006 will have enhanced shareholder protection as a central and visible strategy. The statutory derivative claim procedure,[151] unashamedly borrowed from Canada, is introduced into English law via ss. 260–64. Moreover, shareholder rights will be capable of entrenchment in the constitution (CA 2006, s. 22).

Attempts have been made by academics, such as La Porta et al.,[152] to classify just how supportive jurisdictions are towards minority shareholders by reference to the apparent strength of substantive law. This metric approach is interesting, but can only be effective if local cultural variations are fully accounted for. A comparison of paper shareholder rights is of limited value if those notional rights cannot be enforced due to cultural factors or difficulties with the local legal system (for example, the disincentive cost of shareholder litigation).[153]

---

[146] See *Lithgow v UK* (1986) 8 EHRR 329.

[147] EGMs as such will disappear under CA 2006 – all shareholder gatherings will be designated as 'meetings' without formal distinctions.

[148] See *Re Peveril Gold Mines* [1898] 1 Ch 122, *Exeter City AFC v Football Conference* [2004] BCC 498. There is no guaranteed right to vote in spite of a recommendation from the dissenters on the Jenkins Committee (Cmnd 1749). Voteless shares, however, are unlikely to appeal to listing authorities.

[149] See the articles by J. Shearman in [1995] JBL 517 and (1997) 18 Co Law 123. For corporate governance perspectives in France, see S. Hebert [2004] JBL 656.

[150] Sri Lanka has introduced via Companies Act 2007 (No. 7) an innovative ADR facility for shareholder disputes – see D. Jayasuriya (2008) 29 Co Law 250. In English law, an ADR facility cannot exclude the jurisdiction of the courts where a statutory right of access has been granted.

[151] See A. Keay and J. Loughrey (2008) 124 LQR 469.

[152] See chapter 1, note 144.

[153] See the discussion in Chapter 1, at p. 28 above.

4.6   Effective Termination Procedures

Companies in principle enjoy a right of perpetual succession, which is completely separate from the continued survival of shareholders – but many companies do in fact die; companies on average have a life span that is more tenuous than the domestic cat.[154] Sometimes death is imposed by a private actor (for example, by a creditor 'pulling the plug' via a hostile winding-up petition under s. 122 of the Insolvency Act 1986): in other cases, death is triggered by bureaucratic action (for example, by striking off the register under s. 652 of CA 1985 (see now CA 2006, s. 1000) or winding up in the public interest under s. 124A of the Insolvency Act 1986). Also, it may be self-inflicted in the form of a shareholder resolution to wind up the company voluntarily under s. 84 of the Insolvency Act 1986 or by a shareholder petitioning for winding up on the just and equitable ground under s. 122(1)(g) of the Insolvency Act 1986. To extend the metaphor, suicide may be a rational act in the world of companies.

Legal systems need to develop appropriate mechanisms to cater for this downside of corporate life. Those mechanisms need to ensure that the interests of all stakeholders are adequately protected when the existence of a company is terminated. The public interest needs protection in exercising this jurisdiction. But, equally, such mechanisms need to be cost effective. These two goals can on occasions come into conflict. The deregulatory trend is apparent via the introduction of the voluntary striking-off procedure for private companies (introduced in 1994), which has been extended to public companies by the Companies Act 2006 (s. 1003).

Finally, measures should be available to undo the dissolution process where that has operated unfairly. The current provisions in CA 1985 will be remodelled by ss. 1024–8 of CA 2006, with a view to enhancing the options for administrative restoration where the involvement of the court is not required.

4.7   Rehabilitation

This is a new goal widely embraced by modern corporate systems across the globe.[155]

Until the 1970s, little was heard of this trend, though English law has had in place reconstruction procedures since the start of the 20th century. South Africa, which did not recognise the floating charge, had been operating a

---

[154]   It has been estimated that the average life span of a UK company is now a mere 8.6 years (DTI Annual Report 2004/05, table A5).
[155]   See D. Milman, chapter 17 in J. de Lacy (ed.), *The Reform of UK Company Law* (2003) (Cavendish).

model called judicial management[156] since 1926, with mixed success. The global business rescue lobby received a major kickstart with the reforms embodied in the US Bankruptcy Code of 1978 and particularly the revitalisation of the Chapter 11 procedure. In English law, the issue was taken on board by the Cork Committee (1977–82).[157] In the great reforms of 1985–6 two new corporate rescue regimes, the Company Voluntary Arrangements (CVA) and the administration order mechanism, arrived on the scene. Across the globe, other jurisdictions felt the need to respond to corporate distress. Continental jurisdictions upgraded their rescue models in the 1990s.[158] Ireland introduced its court examiner procedure in the Companies (Amendment) Act 1990, partly in response to the sudden economic pressures placed on its native beef industry by the UN embargo on trade with Iraq after its invasion of Kuwait.[159] Australia introduced its highly successful voluntary administration procedure in 1993.[160] Asian jurisdictions rushed to introduce corporate rescue procedures in the wake of the 1997 financial crisis.[161] This is borne out by the experience of countries such as South Korea, Indonesia and Thailand.

What has happened in most of these jurisdictions is that they have now moved to second-generation business rescue models. That is certainly true of the UK, which has tweaked the CVA regime (via the Insolvency Act 2000) and completely restructured the administration model via the Enterprise Act 2002. The new administration model has gone from strength to strength, soaking up cases that previously would have been disposed of via administrative receivership or creditors' voluntary liquidation. Ireland also exemplifies a similar pattern of evolution, in its court examinership rehabilitation tool.[162] Even the iconic Chapter 11 procedure in the US has required a facelift.[163]

---

[156] On judicial management, see J. Henning, chapter 19 in H. Rajak, *Insolvency Law, Theory and Practice* (1993) (Sweet & Maxwell).

[157] Cmnd 8558.

[158] So, for instance, Germany has adopted a Chapter 11 variant – see E. Ehlers, chapter 4 in *Corporate Rescue: An Overview of Recent Developments from Selected Countries in Europe* edited by K.G. Broc and R. Parry (2004) (Kluwer). For corporate rescue reforms in Belgium in 1997, see M. Vanmeenen (2006) 27 Co Law 381.

[159] See G. McCormack, chapter 17 in Rajak (op. cit. note 156), A Campbell and C. Garrett [1996] (February) Ins Law 12.

[160] For voluntary administration in Australia, see chapter 6 in A. Keay, *Insolvency: Personal and Corporate Law and Practice* (3rd edition, 1998) (John Libbey).

[161] See R. Tomasic (ed.), *Insolvency Law in East Asia* (2006) (Ashgate) for a review of developments in insolvency law in Asia.

[162] For the Irish second-stage reforms to the examiner process, see C. Curran [2003] 16 Ins Intell 7.

[163] Even Chapter 11 has undergone change – so, for instance, in 2005 it was revised to speed it up and reduce costs – see G. Lee and J. Bannister [2005] 21 SMCLN 1.

The rescue bandwagon has seemed inexorable in all corners of the globe. One reason for its popularity is that it appeals to the diverse needs of politicians and practitioners. Awkward questions, however, remain. Has it worked? Statistics in the UK seem to suggest a negative answer[164] but powerful lobbies with vested interests are not always swayed by inconvenient data. So much credibility has been invested in the corporate rescue idea that it is difficult to see it being ditched. If anything, governmental interventions in the market to prop up key players in a range of economies suggest that there is still considerable vigour in the idea.

4.8 Developing a User-friendly Regime

Company law is inevitably complex. This is particularly true of UK company law, with its massive legislative base. The Jenkins Committee noted this deficiency way back in 1962, but, as we saw in a passage quoted above,[165] was unable to provide a solution. No such remedy has been found in the years since then and the malady has grown worse.

This problem of legislative overload has been commented on unfavourably in more recent times by Sealy.[166] English law (and, to a greater extent, Australia[167]) has opted for the micro-regulation of companies. US-based systems (for example, Canada[168]) prefer a more fluid and overarching matrix of general principles, with flexibility being reserved to the courts. The problem is how to balance certainty with flexibility; confusing masses of detail do not always offer certainty and certainly do not promote transparency. But leaving matters to be resolved by litigation is not an efficient solution. The problem is particularly acute for directors. Do they understand what is expected of them? Probably not. Directors of large enterprises have ready access to legal expertise, but that is less true of the director of the small private concern. The

---

[164]   See Insolvency Service seminar, 12 February 2008, unveiling its evaluation study.

[165]   See above at 35, where a quotation is drawn from Cmnd 1749, para 6.

[166]   *Company Law and Commercial Reality* (1984) (Sweet & Maxwell). See also E. Jacobs (1990) 11 Co Law 215 for an Anglo-Canadian comparison.

[167]   At the last count, the Australian Corporations Act had at least 1471 sections. In fairness, the problem has been recognised in Australia and since 1992 a simplification process has been under way producing reforms – see V. Mitchell (1999) 20 Co Law 98, G.P. Stapledon [1999] CFILR 114 and P. Darvas (2000) 21 Co Law 101. But see I. Ramsay (1992) 14 Syd L Rev 474 (an excellent explanation of why companies legislation is bound to be detailed and complex).

[168]   The Canadian Business Corporations Act (CBCA) 1985 has 268 sections. For background to the CBCA see *Partnerships and Business Corporations* (edited by J.S. Ziegel et al.) (2nd edition, 1989) (Carswell) at 99–103. New Zealand, whose 1993 Act boasts a mere 397 sections, has adopted a similar approach.

policy now is 'Think Small First'. The Companies Act 2006 tries to improve the position by restating common law rules in accessible statutory form. The best example of this is to be found in the new rules on directors' duties (ss. 171–7). These provisions seek to lay out general standards of behaviour, without stifling the possibility of organic development in the future through the common law.

When considering this question, it is important to bear in mind the potential diversity of users. Professional groups (such as credit reference agencies) may be users and may be entitled to expect clarity.[169]

Offshore jurisdictions place a high priority on the needs of international users. Witness the recent reforms of Company Law in the Isle of Man.[170]

4.9 Adapting to New Technologies

Any system of corporate regulation should make the best of emerging technologies.[171] The legislative challenge is immense here because the pace of technological change will always outstrip legislative reform.[172] English company law has for generations operated a paper-based system in terms of provisions for communication between stakeholders and the holding of information. That has been replaced in many fields via orders made under the Electronic Communications Act 2000,[173] and, most recently, the Companies Act 2006, which does much to move our system into the digital age. So, for instance, ss. 527–31 of the 2006 Act make provision for shareholders in listed companies to have their concerns about the audit process mounted on a company website. Documents related to company meetings can be communicated electronically (s. 333). Poll results can also be mounted on a website (s. 341). Although these moves are progressive, we do not appear to have gone as far as jurisdictions like Delaware, Canada and Australia in permitting virtual shareholder meetings, using modern remote but instantaneous communication techniques.[174] Germany has also recently introduced reforms designed to

---

[169] So, for instance, mechanisms used to check corporate files with regard to the usage of the new administration model are not working – see J. Harris (2006) 27 Co Law 321. See also (2006) 27 Co Law 305.

[170] For this development in the Isle of Man, see (2007) 28 Co Law 46.

[171] See U. Noack (1998) 9 EBLR 100.

[172] A point made by C.P. Rutledge (2000) 21 Co Law 62.

[173] See Companies Act 1985 (Electronic Communications) Order 2000 (SI 2000/3373). The courts have also shown a willingness to adapt company law to new technologies – *PNC Telecom plc v Thomas* [2004] 1 BCLC 88.

[174] For an excellent review from a Nigerian perspective, see I.O. Bolodeoku (2007) 36 CLWR 106. For Australia, see Corporations Law, s. 250B. In the Isle of Man, electronic/telephonic shareholder and board meetings are permitted by ss. 67(4) and

exploit websites as communication tools.[175] The issue was raised in the Company Law Review consultative document, 'General Meetings and Shareholder Communications', in October 1999 (at paras 39–40), but does not appear to have progressed beyond that stage in English law. That may not matter, as a new EU Directive (2007/36) will open up the usage of technology as a communication tool in the context of listed companies.[176]

4.10   Maintaining Effective and Reputed Capital Markets

In this respect English law has kept up with the field. The UK Stock Exchange has proved its competitive edge over the years, though it did require major revision via the Big Bang[177] in the 1980s. That revolution was designed to introduce greater competitive forces into the London securities markets. The advent of paperless shares is an important move in ensuring that market transactions can be carried out effectively in a digital age. The Financial Services Authority (which replaced the Securities and Investments Board in 1997) is charged with this important responsibility and as such, has wide powers delegated to it.

The EU has recognised the need for effective capital markets – hence the Lamfalussy initiative.[178] The importance of this goal for all systems is exemplified by the push to curtail abusive market activities like insider trading[179] and cold calling.[180] The General Principles of the Takeover Code also stress the need to prevent the creation of false markets on a takeover.

The Markets in Financial Instruments Directive (2004/39) came into force in 2007, having been implemented in the UK via a number of statutory instruments.[181] This Directive[182] replaces the Investment Services Directive

---

106(2) of their Companies Act 2006. In Europe, Professor Noack has been a leading exponent of better use of information technology in this context – see (1998) 9 EBLR 100.

[175]   See T. Naruisch and F. Liepe [2007] JBL 225 at 235–7.

[176]   Note in particular Art 8 (right to participate in general meeting by electronic means). See the comment in (2007) 28 Co Law 337.

[177]   On the 'Big Bang', see J.L. Jones (1986) 7 Co Law 99.

[178]   For the Lamfalussy process (2001), which was designed to speed up the adoption of measures in the financial services arena, see A. Schaub [2005] 13 Jo of Fin Reg and Comp 110.

[179]   The UK banned insider trading in 1980. Singapore had already taken this step in 1970 – see W.Y. Wan (2007) 28 Co Law 1200. The US proscription in effect dates back to 1961 when a general anti-fraud provision (rule 10b5) was first applied to it.

[180]   See *Alpine Investments* (C384/93) [1995] 2 BCLC 214.

[181]   See SI 2007/126, SI 2007/763, SI 2007/2160 and SI 2007/2932.

[182]   For illuminating accounts of MIFID, see N. Moloney (2006) 55 ICLQ 982, J.D. Haines (2007) 28 Co Law 344.

(1993/22) and seeks to ensure competition in stock markets across the EU is not distorted by local restrictive practices. Investment firms, by securing a passport from their home state, can now operate freely in any EU stock market.

5   COMMON PROBLEMS/ FAMILIAR RESPONSES

The aforementioned survey reflects the truism that in the modern world the regulation of companies raises common concerns, demanding comparable (but not necessarily the same) responses.

3. Commonality of fundamental principles

1 INTRODUCTION

We saw in Chapter 2 that all corporate law regimes seek to achieve certain basic policy goals. It is hardly surprising, therefore, to find that all systems of corporate law have a common core of substantive rules directed towards the attainment of those same broad objectives. In the first chapter in their edited work *The Anatomy of Corporate Law*, Henry Hansmann and Reinier Kraakman observe that, notwithstanding inevitable cultural differences in corporate law, 'the underlying uniformity of the corporate form is at least as impressive'.[1] They continue on the same tack, thus: 'Business corporations have a fundamentally similar set of legal characteristics – and face a fundamentally similar set of legal problems – in all jurisdictions.'[2]

They identify *five* common features of any corporate system in another paper.[3] The effect of this homogeneity from the perspective of English law is that there is now limited scope for cross-fertilisation of radically new ideas from other corporate systems. A law of diminishing returns is in operation. But possibilities do exist for subtle modifications in the common core.

Before examining the potential for change we must ask ourselves the question: 'What are these common core principles?'

2 THE COMPANY AS A SEPARATE ENTITY

If ever there was a universal principle of corporate law, it is the concept that a company is to be regarded as a separate entity with its own distinct rights and obligations. This is a sine qua non of any corporate law model. This principle,

---

[1] (2004) (OUP) at 1.
[2] Ibid at 1.
[3] These are: 1. legal personality; 2. limited liability; 3. shared ownership of capital by investors; 4. delegated management to directors; 5 transferable shares – see H. Hansmann and R. Kraakman in J.N. Gordon and M.J. Roe (eds), *Convergence in Corporate Governance* (2004) (CUP) at 34.

which had been part of the subconscious of corporate law jurisprudence from the earliest days, was finally determined in English law by the House of Lords at the end of the 19th century in *Salomon v Salomon & Co Ltd*,[4] an iconic decision that has attained the status of a world precedent in the common law family. Any perusal of company law texts from a range of jurisdictions will confirm the universal pre-eminence of this ruling. It has its own counterparts in all company systems based originally upon English law.[5] The idea is also adopted in civil law jurisdictions. Its celebrated position in English law has been cemented by the approval it received from the House of Lords in *Williams v Natural Life Health Foods*,[6] a clear policy decision in favour of preserving the benefits of incorporation. The application of the separate personality rule in the context of the globalised business environment was underscored in *DTI v Rayner*,[7] where the House of Lords ruled that the Member States who made up the International Tin Council were not responsible for its debts to brokers when the world commodity market for tin collapsed.

This principle has even been supported by the International Court of Justice in the celebrated *Barcelona Traction* case.[8] Here we were concerned, somewhat belatedly, with the legal consequences of the expropriation in 1938 in the context of the Spanish Civil War of the assets of the Barcelona Traction Company. This company had been incorporated in Canada in 1911, with a view to constructing a transport system in Spain. To add to the legal complications, the majority of shareholders (some 88 per cent) were based in Belgium. Many years after the event, the Belgian shareholders, acting through the Belgian government, sought compensation from Spain. The International Court of Justice ruled the claim inadmissible because the proper claimant should have been the state of Canada, as technically it was a Canadian citizen (that is, the company itself) which had been deprived of its property. Canada had made no such claim. The separate corporate personality principle has thus been established as a global legal standard, a point that is reflected in the jurisprudence of other supranational courts.[9]

---

4   [1897] AC 22. See Lord Cooke in his Hamlyn Lecture, *Turning Points of the Common Law* (1997) (Sweet & Maxwell) at chapter 1. For a superb review of the status of this principle a century later, see R. Grantham and C. Rickett (eds), *Corporate Personality in the 20th Century* (1998) (Hart).

5   See, for example, *Gumede v Bandha Vukani Bakithi Ltd* 1950 (4) SA 560. In India, there are many state-owned corporations – see I. Carr [1991] 10 ICCLR 339.

6   [1998] 1 WLR 880.

7   [1990] 2 AC 418. For discussion, see C. Greenwood [1990] CLJ 8.

8   [1970] ICJ Rep 3. See H. Briggs (1971) 65 Am Jo of Int Law 327.

9   The ECHR at Strasbourg made use of the concept in *Agrotexim v Greece* (1996) 21 EHRR 250.

One pervasive consequence of the principle is that where there is a group of companies, all companies within the group are viewed as distinct entities,[10] each with their own rights and liabilities. In reality, this means that parent companies can avoid many liabilities of their subsidiaries, unless they have explicitly guaranteed their obligations. This logical application of the *Salomon* rule at a secondary level is valued highly by international commercial interests and is the bedrock on which the multinational corporation exists. This has been underlined on a number of occasions in English law through rulings such as *Lonrho v Shell Petroleum*[11] and *Adams v Cape Industries*.[12] In this latter instance, the Court of Appeal confirmed that there is nothing improper in an international group of companies structuring their business affairs in such a way as to reduce the exposure of the parent company to risk by insulating it from the potential liabilities of subsidiaries operating in another state. Multinationals are thus able to use subsidiaries to generate profits (which will be remitted to the holding company as dividends) in high risk jurisdictions, without worrying about the attendant liabilities. As Slade LJ said:[13]

> . . . we do not accept as a matter of law that the court is entitled to lift the corporate veil as against the defendant company which is a member of a corporate group merely because the corporate structure has been used so as to ensure that the legal liability (if any) in respect of particular future activities of the group (and correspondingly the risk of enforcement of that liability) will fall on another member of the group rather than the defendant company.

He continued by concluding: 'Whether or not this is desirable, the right to use a corporate structure in this manner is inherent in our corporate law.'[14]

The principle was also applied in *Colt Group v Couchman*,[15] so that a small distinct company operating within the parameters of a multinational car manufacturing group could take advantage of the 'small employer' concession granted under English law from the obligations imposed with regard to measures dealing with disability discrimination. An odd conclusion, but perfectly logical.

An interesting Irish case again reflects the basic tenet that group members are separate entities. In *O'Ferral v Coughlan*[16] directors of an Irish subsidiary

---

10   But note Blumberg coined the distinction between the formal 'entity' approach and the more realistic 'enterprise' approach – see P.I. Blumberg, *The Multinational Challenge to Corporate Law* (1993) (OUP).

11   [1980] 1 WLR 627.

12   [1990] BCLC 479.

13   Ibid at 520.

14   Ibid.

15   [2000] ICR 327.

16   [2004] 4 IR 266.

of a global multinational faced sanctions for failing to fulfil their responsibilities as directors. In response, they argued that their role was limited because the group was effectively controlled from abroad. That contention did not go down well in the Irish courts. Directors were responsible for the way in which their company operated and they could not evade that responsibility by pointing to some invisible overseas controlling hand.

The orthodox approach towards this analysis of group relationships has not always been universally favoured in the English courts. In *DHN v Tower Hamlets LBC*,[17] Lord Denning found a way to circumvent it by arguing that a group of companies could in appropriate circumstances be viewed as a 'single economic entity'. This suggestion, which alarmed both the business community and the majority of corporate lawyers, for the most part was rebuffed in the UK[18] and across the globe.[19] After *Lubbe v Cape Industries (No. 2)*,[20] however, one suspects that application of the separate personality principle in the group context is not entirely bullet proof. One interpretation of this high profile case was that the English courts permitted the injured South African miners and their dependants to bring their action in English law because they had a fair prospect of establishing parental liability for the actions of the employing South African subsidiary. These stirrings suggesting a departure from orthodoxy have been reinforced by *Gross v Rackind*,[21] where the Court of Appeal held that when considering whether a member of a company had had his interests unfairly prejudiced by the conduct of the company's 'affairs', it might be appropriate to examine the conduct of the affairs of other group members. The most recently reported Court of Appeal cases in this area suggest that there is still life in the single economic entity perspective,[22] but the position as ever remains confused and unpredictable.[23] One cannot help harbouring the suspicion that cases in this context are decided on their merits, with retrospective rationalisation being then employed to produce the desired conclusion.

One can see why there is a problem here. In many instances, applying the concept of separate personality in the group scenario offends against basic

---

[17] [1976] 1 WLR 852.
[18] See, for example, *Woolfson v Strathclyde Council* (1979) 38 P & CR 521 and *Adams v Cape Industries* [1990] 2 WLR 657.
[19] *Industrial Equity v Blackburn* (1977) 137 CLR 567, *Re Securitibank (No. 2)* [1978] 2 NZLR 136, *State v Dublin CC* [1985] ILRM 513, *Allied Irish Coal v Powell Duffryn* [1997] 1 ILRM 306, *AG v Equiticorp* [1996] 1 NZLR 528.
[20] [2000] 1 WLR 1545. See P. Muchlinski (2001) 50 ICLQ 1.
[21] [2004] EWCA Civ 815, [2005] BCC 11.
[22] *Beckett Investment Management Group v Hall*, The Times, 11 July 2007 for a pro- *DHN* approach
[23] *Millam v The Print Factory* [2007] EWCA Civ 322 for a more orthodox view.

justice and commonsense. Persons dealing with a company within a group may not always appreciate the subtleties of the situation. These are powerful forces of intuition for any corporate law system to reckon with. More compelling, however, is the fear on the part of national courts that to discard separate personality within groups could lead to damaging economic consequences. The spectre of 'multinational flight' exerts a powerful constraint upon judicial activism in this respect.

Moving away from the high profile issue of groups for a moment, although the principle of separate personality is well established in English law, there is equally abundant (though unpredictable) authority for 'lifting the veil' in a range of situations. The jurisprudence here is voluminous and many academics have sought to rationalise it.[24] This may arise through statute, though the pre-eminence of the separate personality presumption requires explicit displacement. So, for example, a group of companies may be 'associated' for fiscal or employment law purposes.[25]

The courts[26] have also been prepared to lift the veil in a number of instances, where overseas companies have been suspected of being used as a vehicle to cover up fraud. For instance, in *X Bank v G*,[27] the Court of Appeal indicated that interlocutory remedies may be available to stop this activity by restricting the transfer of assets out of the jurisdiction or the disposal of shares in the company even if it involves disregarding the corporate veil. Again, in *Gencor v ACP Ltd*,[28] Rimer J had no hesitation in lifting the veil and treating an offshore company set up by the defendant director, who had diverted company profits to himself through it, as his 'creature' and equivalent merely to his offshore bank account. A third example is offered by *Kensington International v Republic of Congo*,[29] where the veil was lifted by Cooke J with respect to a state-owned company where the circumstances pointed to sham transactions designed to defeat creditors. Foreign-based sham companies therefore cannot in principle be used to stash away ill-gotten gains, though there is no denying the fact that this may be an effective strategy in practice. Chasing misappropriated assets overseas is never an easy task, though with advances in comity between legal systems, the cause is not a completely lost one.

---

[24] For recent attempts see M.T. Moore [2006] JBL 180, where the point is reiterated that the approach of English law is unsustainable.
[25] On association of groups, see, for example, Employment Rights Act 1996, s. 231 and VAT Act 1994, s. 43. See also *Dimbleby v NUJ* [1984] 1 WLR 427.
[26] For an empirical study, see C. Mitchell [1999] 3 CFILR 15.
[27] The Times, 13 April 1985.
[28] [2000] 2 BCLC 734
[29] [2006] 2 BCLC 296. See also *Trustor AB v Smallbone (No. 2)* [2001] 1 WLR 177.

The practice of lifting the corporate veil is found in all corporate law models, and indeed, it is more prevalent beyond our shores.[30] Within the US corporate law system the mere fact that a company has been undercapitalised may trigger such an approach, so as to deny an insider creditor the benefit of equal treatment under the pari passu distributional rule.[31] Such a creditor may, in effect, be subordinated to the rights of outside creditors by the court using its discretion to defer its claim.

Another qualification to note is that not all jurisdictions adopt a common stance on the attributes that flow from having corporate personality. For example, there is some disagreement as to what extent companies can enjoy fundamental rights: for example, the privilege against self-incrimination.[32] Although this idea has been accepted in the UK, it has not attracted much support in the USA, Canada or Australia. In *Santa Clara County v South Pacific Railroad Co,*[33] the US Supreme Court had to decide whether corporations could enjoy the protection of the 14th Amendment (equal protection under the law). The Supreme Court ruled (without permitting argument on the point) that companies did enjoy the protection of the 14th Amendment. In Europe, the European Convention on Human Rights and Fundamental Freedoms has helped to clarify the position on a number of issues relating to fundamental rights in the corporate context.[34] Thus, we know that companies enjoy the protection of property rights. They may also enjoy a right to protect their commercial reputation, according to the House of Lords in *Jameel v Wall Street Journal.*[35]

---

[30]   For a selection of overseas scholarship on this issue, see J.M. Dobson (1986) 35 ICLQ 839 (Argentina), S. Gates (1984) 12 ABLR 162 (Australia), J. Rinze (1993) 14 Co Law 143 (Germany), P. Hood [2001] JBL 58 (Scotland), A. Daehnert (2007) 18 ICCLR 393 (Germany). The Canadian courts, like their US counterparts, seem more inclined towards lifting the veil – see A. Hargovan and J. Harris (2007) 28 Co Law 58.

[31]   For an early account of this US approach, see H. Ballantine (1925) 14 Calif L Rev 12. The leading US cases now are *Taylor v Standard Gas* (1939) 306 US 307, *Pepper v Linton* (1939) 308 US 295 – these cases establish the so-called 'Deep Rock' doctrine. See C.L. Israels (1942) 42 Col L Rev 376, M. Whincup (1981) 2 Co Law 158, R. Schulte (1997) 18 Co Law 2.

[32]   See G. McCormack, chapter 20 in D. Feldman and F. Meisel (eds), *Corporate and Commercial Law: Recent Developments* (1996) (Lloyd's of London Press), D. Milman [2000] (3) SMCLN 1.

[33]   (1886) 118 US 394.

[34]   See A.J. Dignam and D. Allen, *Company Law and the Human Rights Act 1998* (2001) (Butterworths), A. Aldred (2002) 23 Co Law 241. See *Pine Valley Developments Ltd v Ireland* (1992) 14 EHRR 319 and (1993) 16 EHRR 379, *Tinnelly & Sons Ltd v UK* (1999) 27 EHRR 249.

[35]   [2006] UKHL 44. Thus there is no need to prove special damage before suing in libel.

3   LIMITED LIABILITY

The notion of limited liability flows directly (but not inexorably) from the concept of separate corporate personality. Those who subscribe for shares in limited companies have their exposure to risk capped at the level of their investment. Therefore, once shares are fully paid up, there is no residual liability for shareholders. This is a universal concept, first adopted in the US in the early 19th century,[36] then in English law in 1855 via the Limited Liability Act.[37] France introduced it into its system of company law in 1867.[38]

The commercial significance of limited liability cannot be overstated. In *Re London and Globe Finance Corporation Ltd*, Buckley J declared:[39]

> The statutes relating to limited liability have probably done more than any legislation in the last fifty years to further the commercial prosperity of the country. They have, to the advantage as well of the investor as of the public, allowed and encouraged the aggregation of small or comparatively small sums into large capitals which have been employed in undertakings of great public utility, largely increasing the wealth of this country.

Again this is a corporate law standard, but there are subtle variations in the way in which it is applied in the group context. In particular, New Zealand has pioneered the mechanism of 'contribution orders', under which a controlling company which has interfered in the management of an insolvent subsidiary can be required to contribute to the assets of that subsidiary on liquidation. The current mechanism, which dates back to 1980, is found in ss. 271–2 of the Companies Act 1993 and is extended by the Companies Amendment Act 2006 to voluntary administrations. Pooling orders which ignore the separate assets/ liabilities of group members and facilitate a more efficient winding up/ administration of a group are also a possibility. These ideas have travelled. The model of contribution orders was adopted by the Irish in s. 140 of their Companies Act 1990. Pooling orders under Irish law are based on s. 141 of the said Act. Having noted that, in both New Zealand and Ireland this mechanism does not appear to have been extensively used, which might indicate a lack of

---

[36]   New York introduced it in 1811 and it had spread to the east coast states by 1830. For the arrival of limited liability into the USA, see A. Santuari (1996) 17 Co Law 281.
[37]   See L. de Koker (2005) 26 Co Law 130. For the spread of the idea of the limited liability company with separate personality throughout the colonies, see R. McQueen (2008) 17 Griff L Rev 383.
[38]   Though limited liability partnerships pre-dated such companies. See generally, M. Lobban [1996] 25 Anglo-Am L Rev 397 at 411. Note also A. Santuari (1996) 17 Co Law 281.
[39]   [1903] 1 Ch 728 at 731. For general discussion, see B. Pettet [1995] CLP 124.

practical utility.[40] Other jurisdictions seek to attain the same result, but by more circuitous methods. Thus, in Europe, an interfering parent company can often be made liable for its subsidiaries' debts.[41]

The importance of limited liability is reflected by the pressure placed on the government by professional firms to introduce the LLP, pressure that produced dividends in the form of the Limited Liability Partnerships Act 2000.

Although we have all come to accept limited liability as a permanent feature of the corporate law landscape, that is not to say that it has escaped criticism from those who question its role in a modern economy.[42] Certainly, some critics would argue that, for a developed economy where access to investment funding is not difficult, the idea of limited liability should now be questioned as part of a balanced debate.

4 LEGAL RECOGNITION FOR SHARES: PROTECTION FOR SHAREHOLDERS

Modern capitalism has at its heart the instrument of the share. Indeed, the shareholder-oriented model is the Western liberal capitalist paradigm.

It used to be the case that all shares had to possess a par value – that is, a nominal monetary figure that appeared on the face of each share. That attribute was seen as essential for the operation of the share capital maintenance doctrine whose historic role has been noted above. For example, the rule prohibiting the issue of shares at a discount (see now CA 2006, s. 580) could not operate without the par value concept. However, the idea that shares must have a nominal value has become tarnished, one of the problems being the lack of correlation with market value. It has been displaced in many jurisdictions which either permit or oblige companies to issue no par value shares.[43] In the 1950s, the Gedge Committee[44] recommended the mandatory par value requirement to be abolished for English law, but nothing was done to implement that proposal. The Company Law Review adopted the position that the concept should be scrapped for private companies.[45] However, this would

---

[40] For the position in New Zealand, see R.P. Austin, chapter 4 in R. Grantham and C. Rickett (eds), *Corporate Personality in the 20th Century* (1998) (Hart).

[41] See generally E.J. Cohn and C. Simitis (1963) 12 ICLQ 189.

[42] See S. Griffin (2004) 25 Co Law 99, T. Morgan (2003) 24 Co Law 194.

[43] For Canada, see CBCA, s. 24 (mandatory). No par value shares were introduced into South Africa in 1973, whereas Singapore did not take this step until 2005. They were recognised in the Isle of Man by s. 29 of the Companies Act 2006.

[44] (1954, Cmnd 9112) paras 11 and 27. The Jenkins Committee in 1962 took a similar view (see Cmnd 1749, para 34).

[45] *Final Report* (URN 01/942).

have created an anomaly with public companies (where the concept had to be retained in order to ensure compliance with the EC Second Company Law Harmonisation Directive) and so the status quo prevailed. Accordingly, in the Companies Act 2006, the par value concept is retained; indeed, it is specifically reinforced by explicit statutory provision (s. 542).

Shareholder membership is the relationship at the heart of the modern company. The idea of one share one vote is an ideal espoused by many (but not all) company law systems. Companies that do not adhere to this principle may be denied access to the capital-raising facility of public stock exchanges. But it is not universally adhered to even in English law. Private companies may use a system of weighted votes on shares.[46] In Scandinavian corporate law systems, weighted votes are not uncommon. This tradition caused some difficulty in the protracted debate surrounding the introduction of the EC Takeovers Directive (2004/25/EC). Eventually concessions had to be made in order to secure adoption of the Directive.[47] Another variant is cumulative voting rights, for example, on the election of directors. This clever vote accumulation device which empowers small shareholders by allowing them to target their overall voting power tactically is used in some US-inspired corporate law jurisdictions.[48]

If shares exist, there must be cost-effective procedures designed to facilitate share transfers. The English courts have talked about a presumption of transferability.[49] However, the preference has always been for a registration procedure linked to transfer. In private companies, this has produced a situation where directors usually enjoy discretion not to register certain transferees (see Table A, Art 24, which will be replicated in the new Table A, Art 26(5) with effect from 1 October 2009). The justification for this right to block a share transfer lies in the fact that private companies may still be viewed in some quarters as exclusive clubs. The Companies Act 2006 modifies the position here by requiring directors within two months to give reasons for a refusal to register a transfer (see s. 771).[50] English law has been more hostile than its European counterparts to bearer shares or share warrants which can be trans-

---

46   *Bushell v Faith* [1970] AC 1099.

47   For the story behind the painful birth of this Directive, see B. Clarke, *Takeovers and Mergers Law in Ireland* (1999) (Round Hall Press) chapter 4.

48   See, for example, MBCA, s. 33 (USA), CBCA, s. 102 (Canada), India Companies Act 1956, s. 265. Both South Korea and China have adopted this mechanism.

49   *Weston's case* (1868) LR 4 Ch App 20 at 27–8 per Page-Wood LJ.

50   This issue of blocking share transfers in private companies was discussed by the Company Law Review, which in its Final Report recommended change by requiring refusals to be reasoned (see URN 01/942, paras 7.42–7.45).

ferred as negotiable instruments without registration.[51] Grudging acceptance has been the standard response in this country, but share warrants have now received the legislative seal of approval in the Companies Act 2006 (see s. 122 which permits the issue of share warrants de novo). Share warrants are also accepted by Art 51 of the new Model Articles for Public Companies. Equally, any transfer facility must respect the terms of the arrangement under which those shares were originally acquired; transfer restrictions, for example in private companies, may be justified.[52] Electronic modes of transfer should be considered – witness the CREST system,[53] which replaced the ill-fated TAURUS model in 1996.

Shares will not be popular investments if mechanisms are not put in place to ensure that the investment is protected from expropriation at the hands of managers, other shareholders or outside forces. Shareholder protective mechanisms may range from the provision of substantive rights, through the maintenance of grievance procedures or by other institutional mechanisms. The compulsory purchase procedure only operates in the context of a genuine takeover bid.[54] Shareholder rights may in some cases be inalienable.[55] Shares are items of property and are guaranteed protection as such by Art 1 of the First Protocol European Convention on Human Rights and Fundamental Freedoms. This point has been confirmed in *Lithgow v UK*[56] and *Pafitis v Greece*,[57] though, as always, the point needs to be reiterated that ECHR rights are not absolute.[58]

Shareholder protection encompasses the economic expectation of shareholders in a target company to receive a premium for their shares in the event

---

[51] See, for example, *Colonial Bank v Cady & Williams* (1890) 15 App Cas 267 – refusal by court to treat registered shares as negotiable instruments in spite of evidence that they were being dealt with as such in the market.

[52] For typical private company share transfer curbs, see CA 1985, Table A, Art 24 and the philosophy reflected by cases such as *Charles Forte Investments v Amanda* [1964] Ch 240. See now Art 26 of the new Model Articles for Private Companies Limited by Shares (SI 2008/3229).

[53] See CA 1989, s. 207 and the Uncertificated Securities Regulations 1995 (SI 1995/3272).

[54] *Re Bugle Press Ltd* [1961] Ch 270.

[55] *Re Peveril Gold Mines* [1898] 1 Ch 122, *Exeter City AFC v Football Conference* [2004] BCC 498. But compare *Re Vocam (Europe) Ltd* [1998] BCC 396.

[56] (1986) 8 EHRR 329.

[57] (1999) 27 EHRR 566.

[58] *Bramelid and Malstrom v Sweden* (1982) 5 EHRR 249. See also *Re Waste Recycling Group Ltd* [2004] 1 BCLC 352.

of a takeover bid. This expectation is jealously guarded in English[59] and American law, but it is a novel idea for much of continental Europe.[60]

5   REGULATING DIRECTORS AS MANAGERS

Even in the smallest of companies the idea that shareholders are the best persons to manage the enterprise is not without its critics. The solution of shareholder management in larger undertakings becomes a practical impossibility. Management delegated to an expert body of agents is therefore necessary. The concept of management by directors is enshrined in Art 70 of Table A (soon to be replaced under New Model Articles set forth in SI 2008/3229 by Arts 3 and 4), but strangely not in the Companies Act itself. It is apt therefore to talk about the managerial prerogative. But what should this encompass? First and foremost, it should permit directors maximum flexibility in managing the business. That does not mean complete freedom. We have encountered the ultra vires rule as an obsolete example of managerial constraint. Permitting directors to fetter their powers may be appropriate in limited circumstances.[61] In modern times, this prerogative has been impinged upon in various ways – for example, by environmental law, consumer law and competition law. It is also the traditional approach in English law to prohibit arrangements under which directors are exempted from liability for breach of duty (witness CA 1985, s. 310[62]), but this approach has begun to fray at the edges in recent decades with the introduction of indemnity insurance arrangements[63] and costs indemnities.[64] The Companies Act 2006 introduces a new provision which seeks to clarify the position. Looking at the issue of stakeholders and enlighted shareholder value, s. 172 of the Companies Act 2006 states that although directors have a duty to promote the success of the company (in the sense of acting for the benefit of members), they must also take into account long-term issues and the interests of stakeholders such as employees, the local community, suppliers and the environment. They should also have regard to the need to act fairly in business. What we have here is a move away from

---

59   Hence cases such as *Howard Smith v Ampol Petroleum* [1974] AC 821 and the resistance to poison pills.
60   This was one reason why the issue of defensive measures poisoned the debate over the adoption of the Takeovers Directive.
61   See *Thorby v Goldberg* (1964) 112 CLR 597 and *Fulham FC v Cabra* [1992] BCLC 863.
62   See now CA 2006, s. 232.
63   See CA 1989, s. 137 (CA 1985, s. 310(3); CA 2006, s. 233).
64   See The Companies (Audit, Investigations and Community Enterprise) Act 2004, ss. 19 and 20, superseded by CA 2006, ss. 234–8.

shareholder wealth-maximisation rhetoric to a perspective focusing upon the idea of stakeholders and the socially responsible company. But critically, the broader 'responsibilities' mentioned appear to be unenforceable by this wider cohort of stakeholders under established mechanisms in UK company law.[65]

This has been heralded in some quarters as representing a fundamental change in priorities. That is not so – drawing on the experience with s. 309 of the Companies Act 1985 (a provision that was superseded by s. 172, CA 2006), which has often worked to the benefit of the managerial interest – all that it will achieve is the accumulation of paperwork to show that directors have considered (and usually then dismissed) a range of stakeholder concerns in favour of maximising shareholder wealth.[66] At the end of the day, a director's tenure in office is in the hands of shareholders. That said, with the arrival of the state as a shareholder in a number of large private-sector public companies in the wake of the world financial crisis, it may be that the state will use its power as a shareholder to move towards enforcing these wider management goals.

A corpus of substantive law dealing with directors should cover issues such as appointment, removal, powers and duties. Precise principles may vary from jurisdiction to jurisdiction, but all of these functional matters must be addressed in some way or another. Transparency and accountability are essential requirements.

6 PROVIDING FOR EQUALITY OF CREDITORS

Where a company becomes insolvent, the starting proposition is that all unsecured creditors rank equally, irrespective of the amount of their debt or the date when it was incurred. In practice, where there is an insufficiency of assets, such creditors will be repaid rateably, with a proportion of the amount due to them. This is known as the pari passu principle and again, it forms the bedrock of many corporate law systems.[67] There are numerous exceptions (both at

---

[65] For an in-depth study, see A. Keay (2007) 28 Co Law 106.

[66] This cynicism is borne out of the experience with s. 309 CA 1985 which, far from limiting the managerial prerogative, has made it more flexible by allowing directors greater room for manoeuvre if they wish, when reaching managerial decisions.

[67] On this rule in English law, see Insolvency Act 1986, s. 107 and *British Eagle International Airlines v Cie Nationale Air France* [1975] 1 WLR 758. By coincidence, this issue has been revisited by the High Court of Australia in *IATA v Ansett* [2008] HCA 3, where revised IATA regulations have been upheld as not being contrary to the pari passu policy – for perceptive comment, see M. Bridge (2008) 124 LQR 379. The English Court of Appeal was heavily influenced by the pari passu idea in *Re Buckingham International plc (No. 2)* [1998] BCC 943. The principle was also

common law and through legislation) to this rule and as a result, there is considerable academic debate as to the current status of this rule. Respected scholars such as Rizwaan Mokal[68] and Look Chan Ho[69] would argue that the pari passu rule as commonly understood is a myth. In spite of these well-argued reservations, it remains the case (rightly or wrongly) that the principle of pari passu distribution is still applied as a basic philosophy underpinning many winding-up models across the globe.[70] It is sometimes difficult to disentangle myth from reality.

Although we have asserted that the pari passu rule may be viewed as the starting point, there are exceptions.[71] One of these relates to preferential creditor status.[72] It is not uncommon to find that certain creditors, typically government agencies and employees, are given favourable treatment. As far as the state protecting itself is concerned, this has long been regarded as unfair and a blot on the landscape of the system. The Cork Committee[73] was severely critical of its continued existence. Preferential status for state debts has been discarded in many jurisdictions,[74] including Australia,[75] though surprisingly it

---

endorsed by the Privy Council in a conflicts of law scenario in *Wight v Eckhardt Marine* [2003] BCC 702. It is standard fare in all legal systems derived from English law – see, for example, India Companies Act 1956, s. 528, Corporations Law, s. 555 (Australia), Companies Act 1993, s. 313 (New Zealand), Companies Act 1963, s. 275 (Ireland). See D. Milman, in A. Clarke, *Current Issues in Insolvency Law* (1991) (Stevens) at 57–85, also V. Finch [2000] Ins Law 194. The pari passu debate took an interesting turn in *Sons of Gwalia v Margaretic* [2007] HCA 1, where the High Court of Australia ruled that shareholders who had been misled into investing in the company could be treated as creditors. This surprising decision has provoked a government review.

[68]   *Corporate Insolvency Law* (2005) (OUP) especially Chapter 4. See also his perceptive essay in [2001] CLJ 581.

[69]   For the views of Look Chan Ho on this controversy, see (2003) 19 IL & P 155, and [2004] JIBLR 54.

[70]   Blackburne J used it to justify his ruling in the test case of *Re Courts plc* [2008] EWHC 2339 (Ch), [2008] BCC 917 (no selective disapplication of the prescribed part). It was an important element in the advice tendered by the Privy Council in the British Virgin Islands case of *Hague v Nam Tai Electronics Inc* [2006] UKPC 52, [2007] 2 BCLC 194.

[71]   In Australia under s. 562A of the Companies Act 2001, policyholders of an insolvent insurance company enjoyed protected status – see *Re HIH Casualty and General Insurance Co* [2006] EWCA Civ 732 (reversed appeal to the HL sub nomine *McGrath v Riddell* [2008] UKHL 21, [2008] BCC 349).

[72]   First introduced into English law in 1888. See A. Keay and P. Walton [1999] CFILR 84 and [1999] Ins Law 112.

[73]   Cmnd 8558 (1982).

[74]   Thus state preferential claims have been dropped in Germany and Austria. For an instructive comparative survey see A. Keay, A. Boraine and D. Burdette (2001) 10 Int Insolv Rev 167.

[75]   Australian Crown preferential claims in respect of unpaid tax were abandoned in 1993.

has been retained in New Zealand.[76] In the UK, Crown preferential debt status was finally surrendered by the Enterprise Act 2002.[77] Preferential status has not disappeared completely in English law – it survives for certain employee claims and other specialised debts – but its long-term future is under threat. The problem here is that it is inconsistent on the one hand to view employees as stakeholders and then to featherbed them in the event of enterprise failure.[78]

7   PROVIDING FOR DIFFERENTIAL TREATMENT FOR PUBLIC/PRIVATE COMPANIES

This is a characteristic distinction found in corporate law models across the globe – for example, in Australia,[79] in South Africa[80] and on the Continent of Europe.[81] Clearly, different issues arise when one is considering an appropriate corporate regime for a large company with a multiplicity of dispersed shareholdings as compared with a small private 'close' company. One of the problems endemic in English law has been the tendency to use the former model as the default position, with token gestures to the latter. The elective regime for private companies introduced by CA 1989, s. 116 (inserting s. 379A into CA 1985) is perhaps the clearest example of a more focused approach towards private companies. Explicit provision on written resolutions for private companies is to be found in ss. 288 et seq. of the Companies Act 2006. The European Union initiatives have in the past also fallen into that trap of over-obsession with public companies. As far as the UK is concerned, that strategy is dead and buried with the Company Law Review. The governing

---

[76]   See s. 312 of New Zealand Companies Act 1993. The Insolvency Act 2006 surprisingly did not change the position in New Zealand – see D. Brown and T.G.W. Telfer, *Personal and Corporate Insolvency Legislation* (2007) (LexisNexis NZ) at 86 et seq.

[77]   Section 251, with effect from 15 September 2003.

[78]   See D. Milman in A. Clarke, *Current Issues in Insolvency Law* (1991) (Stevens) at 57 and C.L. Symes, *Statutory Priorities in Corporate Insolvency Law: An Analysis of Preferred Creditors* (2008) (Ashgate).

[79]   In Australia there are distinctive rules for the proprietary company (designated Pty).

[80]   Close Business Corporations Act 1984 – discussed by J.J. Henning in (2007) 28 Co Law 253.

[81]   For example, in Germany there are separate regimes for public companies 'aktiengesellschaft' (AG) in the form of the 1965 Act and for private companies 'Gesellschaft mit beschranker Haftung' (GmbH). On the latter, see K. Muller, *The GmbH – A Guide to the German Limited Liability Company* (3rd edition, 2006) (Kluwer).

philosophy now is 'Think Small First'.[82] Thus, the Companies Act 2006 focuses upon small companies first and then considers whether variants are appropriate for larger counterparts. A similar strategy has been commended in Ireland by the First Report of the Company Law Review Group[83] and indeed the proposed new Irish Companies Bill seems to reflect that wisdom. As far as Europe is concerned, the *Centros*[84] bombshell has led to a major reappraisal of the traditional harmonisation obsession with public companies. There is now a real push towards introducing a standardised format for a European Private Company.[85] So, for example, in July 2007 the European Commission published a consultative document dealing with the proposed European Private Company Statute.[86] Events on the ground might suggest that that is already occurring, with minimum share capital requirements for private companies gradually being watered down.

8   ESTABLISHING EFFECTIVE PROCEDURES FOR THE INCORPORATION/DISSOLUTION OF COMPANIES

This is a pragmatic matter, but an absolute prerequisite for any effective system of corporate law. Most corporate law models have provision for the winding up and eventual dissolution of companies. There is a constant search for cost-effective variations. So, for example, in English law, a procedural device for the quick dissolution of hopelessly insolvent companies with no assets was introduced in 1985 on the back of proposals from the Cork Committee[87] (see now Insolvency Act 1986, s. 202). This idea was extended to administration of companies by the Enterprise Act 2002 by the provision of a dedicated exit option for hopelessly insolvent concerns (see Schedule B1 of the Insolvency Act 1986, para 84). This latter facility has proved its worth.[88]

---

82   URN 01/942, para 1.53
83   (2001) Chapter 3.
84   (Case C212/97) [2000] Ch 446 – see T. Tridimas (1999) 48 ICLQ 708.
85   See [2008] SMCLN 1 for the latest developments. See also J. Schmidt (2006) 27 Co Law 99 at 108.
86   This consultation took the form of a questionnaire sent to interested parties.
87   Cmnd 8558, paras 649–51.
88   Para 84 of Sched B1 has been interpreted in a user-friendly way – see *Re GHE Realisations Ltd* [2006] BCC 139.

9 ENSURING THAT COMPANIES REMAIN SUBJECT TO STATE CONTROL

This is a more controversial heading. Adherents to the Chicago school of thinking would raise objections in principle. On the other hand, as corporations are now recognised as citizens of a state and subject to the protection of fundamental rights in many jurisdictions, there is no reason why they should be immune from state control. Most commentators agree that there is a need for public control via the disclosure philosophy. In English law, one could cite DTI investigations[89] and the possibility of winding up in the public interest[90] as further manifestations of the desire to maintain some state control. Winding up in the public interest extends to foreign companies, provided a sufficient jurisdictional link with English law can be established.[91] Companies can be required to change their names (see CA 1985, s. 32; CA 2006, s. 76). The fact that where companies are dissolved and surplus unclaimed assets devolve upon the state via the concept of *bona vacantia*[92] might also indicate the underlying nature of the relationship between companies and their ultimate progenitor, the state. The fact that the state can nationalise companies[93] or bail out stakeholders in the event of market failure[94] shows where the real power

---

[89]   CA 1985, s. 432. See the discussion in *Norwest Holst Ltd v Secretary of State for Trade and Industry* [1978] Ch 201.

[90]   Insolvency Act 1986, s. 124A. Strangely, this facility is not available in Ireland – see First Report of Company Law Review Group (2001) para 15.2.3.

[91]   *Re Titan International Inc* [1998] 1 BCLC 102 at 108–9 per Peter Gibson LJ.

[92]   CA 1985, s. 656, restated in CA 2006, s. 1012.

[93]   For nationalisation of UK companies, a dominant feature of the late 1940s, see the Coal Industry Nationalisation Act 1946. In the 1970s, nationalisation again became a prominent issue – see Aircraft and Shipbuilding Act 1977. When Railtrack got into financial difficulties at the turn of the decade, it was effectively nationalised via being put into a special administration regime in 2001. For this administration and its outcome, see S. Plant (2002) 18 IL & P 18 and S. Elboz (2002) 18 IL & P 187. An attempt by shareholders to challenge this governmental intervention via a class action failed in 2005. In Malaysia, the so-called Danaharta Act 1998 was used to exert state control over companies distressed in the wake of the 1997 financial crisis – see M. Likosky, *The Silicon Empire* (2005) (Ashgate). A somewhat similar regime called special administration was applied in the Italian Parmalat insolvency. For a flavour of the global impact of the Parmalat collapse, see *Parmalat Capital Finance Ltd v Food Holdings Ltd* [2008] UKPC 23.

[94]   As evidenced by the billions of pounds pumped into Northern Rock in 2007–8, finally resulting in the nationalisation of that company. See Banking (Special Provisions) Act 2008. For comment on Northern Rock, see R. Tomasic (2008) 29 Co Law 297 and (2008) 29 Co Law 330. For the EU implications of this state support, see C. Bamford (2008) 29 Co Law 65. A similar, but in this case a public/private, bailout was extended to Bear Stearns by the US Federal Reserve in March 2008, leading to the

lies. The real question is how far this characteristic should intrude into the mainstream of companies regulation. That very question will exercise the minds of policymakers and regulators in the months to come.

When considering state control, we need to distinguish between state control in the general public interest and the notion of state control designed to protect the direct economic interests of the state. The debate over the use of golden shares, discussed below in Chapter 4, is apposite here. In post-privatisation economies, this is a common issue that raises concerns best dealt with later in this study.

10 MAINTAINING CONFIDENCE IN CAPITAL MARKETS

If we persist with our expansive view of the parameters of corporate law, this item must be covered. The links between capital market regulation and the operations of companies are too close to ignore. The regulation of insider trading/market abuse springs to mind. English common law has had at its disposal principles which might be useful to discourage improper conduct in the market[95] but in *Percival v Wright*,[96] it appeared to send out a message that it was not improper for directors to exploit their position in share transactions with members through insider dealing. Such behaviour could not be challenged by individual shareholders. The courts of the Commonwealth[97] were

---

sale of that investment bank to a competitor at a greatly reduced price, reflecting its current perceived share market valuation. More evidence of Federal intervention came in the wake of the rescue operation for the leading private financial institutions Fanny Mae and Freddie Mac in 2008. After refusing to save Lehman from collapse in September 2008, the Federal government then produced a plan to spend trillions of dollars in buying up 'toxic' debts. Meanwhile, back in the UK at the same time, the British government waived domestic competition laws to allow Lloyds Bank to take over Halifax plc as part of a rescue operation. There is evidence that within the EU, the European Commission is taking a relaxed view of state aids in the wake of the global financial crisis.

   [95]   *R v De Berenger* (1814) 3 M & S 67. For a fascinating account of the real story behind this case featuring Admiral Lord Cochrane as one of the defendants, see R. Dale, *Napoleon is Dead: Lord Cochrane and the Great Stock Exchange Scandal* (2007) (Sutton Publishing). Cochrane was eventually vindicated in 1832, but doubts still remain as to his culpability. See also D. Cordingly, *Cochrane the Dauntless* (2007) (Bloomsbury Publishers) chapter 15. Full details of the trial can be sourced from the contemporary work of B. Gurney, which is electronically available through Project Gutenberg.

   [96]   [1902] 2 Ch 421.

   [97]   *Coleman v Myers* [1977] 2 NZLR 225, *Bruninghausen v Glavanics* [1999] NSWCA 199.

less reluctant to castigate such opportunistic behaviour. Insider dealing was made a criminal offence in English law in 1980[98] and it is still a crime under the Criminal Justice Act 1993.[99] With the advent of the Financial Services Authority[100] and EC Market Abuse Directive,[101] the regulatory matrix has been firmed up by the addition of new 'smart' sanctions. These include administrative penalties. Under Part VIII of the Financial Services and Markets Act 2000, the FSA can impose such penalties for breaches of the Code of Practice on Market Abuse (see s. 123 FSMA 2000 for the particular provision here).

11 ENABLING COMPANIES TO GROW AND RESTRUCTURE

There are several points that could be included under this umbrella principle. Any effective system of corporate law must develop procedures for the acquisition of companies through takeover, whether that be private acquisition via a contractual process, a friendly merger or hostile takeover. Equally, mergers should be addressed, as should situations of financial distress requiring restructuring. This latter characteristic has become a dominant feature in global corporate law reform in the past 25 years. If one wished to find support for the existence of such a general principle at common law outside the parameters of explicit statutory provision, the Court of Appeal judgment in *Ord v Belhaven Pubs*[102] would offer such support, in that the Court of Appeal there affirmed the right of a company to restructure, notwithstanding the damaging effect of such a restructuring upon a third party.

---

[98] Companies Act 1980 s. 72 – see now Criminal Justice Act 1993, s. 52. Ireland has favoured civil sanctions but there can be enforcement problems there – see B. Clarke [2009] JBL 68 for discussion of recent litigation in the Irish courts.

[99] On Part V of the Criminal Justice Act 1993, see K. Wotherspoon (1994) 57 MLR 419.

[100] The FSA replaced the Securities and Investments Board in 1997.

[101] EEC/2003/6. On market abuse, see A. Haynes (2007) 28 Co Law 323.

[102] [1998] 2 BCLC 447.

4. Foreign shareholders and non-resident controllers

1 EXPLOITATION OF UK COMPANY LAW BY FOREIGN ENTRANTS

In this chapter, we propose to consider the relationship between UK Company Law and a range of overseas players, namely foreign shareholders and non-national directors. Issues connected with the non-residence of an actor (as opposed to foreign nationality) will also be addressed in the course of the discussion.

This is a topical question at the start of the 21st century. There is much media attention being paid at the moment to the fact that UK firms are being bought up by foreign investors at a record rate.[1] The number of English Premier League football clubs falling under overseas control has merely served as a microcosm highlighting this more pervasive issue for the average man and woman in the street.

2 THE OVERSEAS SHAREHOLDER

2.1 Statistical Significance

Since the dawn of modern company law, overseas shareholders have always been present on the UK corporate scene, because the City of London has always been seen as a magnet for foreign capital.[2] For example, in the 18th century foreign investors are believed to have held some 15 per cent of government bonds. One reason for this was the availability of a capital market operating within a stable political economy. Moving forward to the 20th

---

[1]   See *The Times*, 8 November 2006, p. 54.

[2]   For a history of the City of London and the drive to attract foreign capital, see R.C. Michie, *The London Stock Exchange: A History* (1999) (OUP). More generally, see G. Gilligan, chapter 1 in B.A.K. Rider and M. Andenas (eds), *Developments in European Company Law, Volume 1/96* (1997) (Kluwer) for a historical review of the City and its ability to maintain self-regulatory regimes.

century, as far as public companies are concerned it has been possible for many years to track the participation rate of the overseas investor. An examination of the data produced by what is now the Office of National Statistics[3] reveals a clear pattern of increasing foreign 'penetration' of the UK equities scene. Focusing on the position for listed companies for various dates over the past 30 years, the statistics are revealing:

- 1981 – 4 per cent of equities owned by foreign shareholders;
- 1994 – 16.3 per cent of equities owned by foreign shareholders;
- 1997 – 24 per cent of equities owned by foreign shareholders;
- 2004 – 33 per cent of equities owned by foreign shareholders;
- 2006 – 40 per cent of equities owned by foreign shareholders.

It is also possible from analysing these percentages to gain an understanding of which national groups are buying into 'UK plc'. Looking at the 1997 figures, the key foreign groups today appear to hail from the EU (20.3 per cent), the USA (51.2 per cent) and Japan (2.8 per cent). The proportion of Chinese shareholdings is growing. Foreign investors these days are increasingly not private individuals, nor indeed foreign private businesses, but rather 'sovereign investment (or wealth) funds', with huge quantities of petro-dollars to invest. This rapidly evolving phenomenon has caused disquiet in some quarters.[4] The irony here, of course, is that the concerns are being raised in those very economies which for generations have pioneered free capital markets and have decried protectionism. This reversal of fortunes has been lost on those countries calling for an international code of conduct governing investment by sovereign wealth funds, demands that were vociferous at the Davos World Economic Summit in 2008.[5] The European Commission has also raised concerns on this matter[6] and the International Monetary Fund is examining the phenomenon.[7] In fairness to those putting forward these views, it should be noted that some of the concerns currently being aired relate more to the lack of transparency on the part of the ultimate acquirer and less to the identity of the new shareholder. In a final twist of irony, those concerns were suddenly silenced in the final months of 2008, as leading financial institutions

---

[3]   Formerly Central Statistical Office.
[4]   See the *Sunday Times Business Supplement*, 9 September 2007 at p. 13, the *Times*, 15 October 2007 at p. 42, also *The Times*, 22 December 2007 at pp. 56–7. For Japanese concerns, see *The Times*, 8 February 2008.
[5]   See the *Independent*, 25 January 2008.
[6]   For the Commission's views here, see its Communication of 27 February 2008 – the Commission favours transparency but also a balanced response to the issue.
[7]   See the IMF website March 2008 – www.imf.

in the West sought fresh capital injections from *any* available source in the wake of the worldwide credit crunch.

2.2   Judicial Support for Foreign Shareholders

English law has generally adopted a welcoming approach to foreign share-holders. As an imperialist nation, wedded to notions of free trade since the demise of the Navigation Acts[8] and the abolition of the Corn Laws,[9] it could hardly take a different stance. So, for example, it has always been the case that foreign individuals could become subscribers to the memorandum.[10] The fact that a foreign state became a shareholder in a UK company as a result of a local nationalisation process is immaterial.[11] Bearer shares have been available in English law for over 100 years[12] – such securities are highly attractive to foreign investors. Annual General Meetings of UK companies apparently could be held abroad, provided the articles of association did not prohibit this.[13] The Companies Acts have, for many years, contained provisions permitting the setting up of local branch registers of foreign non-resident shareholders. These provisions, which in future will be located within CA 2006, ss. 129–35[14] only operate where the company is trading in that foreign

---

[8]   The Navigation Acts 1650–63 were designed to protect the English merchant fleet, particularly from Dutch competition. They were repealed in 1849. Sir David Hughes Parry regarded them as a legislative expression of the economic theory of mercantilism – see (1931) 47 LQR 183 at 198.

[9]   The Corn Laws restricted the import of foreign corn and were another protectionist measure designed to protect British farmers (at the expense of consumers). They were repealed in 1846.

[10]   *Princess of Reuss v Bos* (1871) LR 5 HL 176.

[11]   *Williams and Humbert Ltd v W & H Trade Marks (Jersey) Ltd* [1985] 1 All ER 619.

[12]   *Bechuanaland Exploration Co v London Trading Bank Ltd* [1898] 2 QB 658. See also *Edelstein v Schuler* [1902] 2 KB 144 (negotiability of bearer debentures). Some jurisdictions exemplify a hostility to bearer securities – see the Isle of Man Companies Act 2006, s. 30.

[13]   There is a lack of clarity here. The only restriction imposed by English law on holding shareholder meetings abroad seems to be the unfair prejudice jurisdiction which has been invoked in this context – see *McGuinness v Bremner plc* [1988] BCLC 673, where an attempt to delay and then to hold an EGM outside the jurisdiction was overturned by the Scottish courts. A shareholder has a right at common law to attend and vote at meetings. This issue of the venue for meetings was commented upon in the First Report of the Irish Company Law Review Group – see para 6.5.7, where it was noted that there is no right to hold an AGM abroad unless this is permitted by the articles or unless the shareholders agree. The possibility of holding company meetings outside the jurisdiction is envisaged by the Isle of Man Companies Act 2006, s. 67(3).

[14]   Formerly s. 362 of and Sched 14 to CA 1985.

jurisdiction where shareholder residence is located. The jurisdictions where a local branch register may be kept are listed in s. 129(2) – these are basically former British colonies. A local branch register must be open to inspection in the UK (s. 132). Local courts may be given the power to rectify a branch register (s. 134). The 2006 Act here makes no significant changes in the substance of the pre-existing law.

The desire to encourage foreign share ownership was one of the factors that influenced the decision of Harman J in *Re Scandinavian Bank plc*.[15] Here we had a public company incorporated under English law wishing to rearrange its capital structure in order to create a class of shares denominated in a range of foreign currencies (in particular, US dollars). This possibility was not specifically addressed by the Companies Act 1985. The indications in the common law were that this option would not be permitted, as there was a presumption (based upon some influential obiter dicta[16] of Lord Wright in the 1930s) that shares in UK companies had to be denominated in sterling. Nevertheless, after taking evidence and hearing the views of an amicus curiae, Harman J ruled that denomination of shares in foreign currencies should indeed be permitted. Cocktails of foreign currencies could also be used, provided no company had a single share denominated in multiple currencies. Various factors informed the judgment. Firstly, there had been a change of approach by the English judiciary with regard to the pre-eminence of sterling in matters of court judgment. The English courts could now award compensation denominated in a foreign currency if that was appropriate.[17] Secondly, the evidence indicated that the Registrar of Companies had already registered a number of companies having non-sterling shares; the cat had therefore been let out of the bag. To deny this progressive possibility now would seriously embarrass the bureaucrats by revealing a flaw in the system. The decision was therefore permissive. Harman J did, however, indicate *two* restrictions on non-sterling shares:

(i) No single share could be denominated in multiple currencies; 'schizophrenic' shares were not to be allowed.

---

[15]   [1988] 1 Ch 87.

[16]   *Adelaide Electric Supply Co Ltd v Prudential Assurance Co Ltd* [1934] AC 122.

[17]   See *Miliangos v Geo Frank Textiles Ltd* [1976] AC 443 – discussed in R. Bowles and J. Phillips (1976) 39 MLR 196 and F.A. Mann (1976) 92 LQR 165. Having said that, it is a rule of liquidation law that for matters of administrative convenience, proof of debts must be converted into equivalent sterling amounts at the date of liquidation – *Re Lines Brothers Ltd* [1983] Ch 1. For currency conversion processes in the context of a scheme of arrangement, see *Re Telewest Communications (No. 2)* [2005] 1 BCLC 772.

(ii) In the case of a plc, there must be at least £50,000 worth of shares denominated in sterling in order to comply with the terms of s. 118 of the Companies Act 1985 (see now CA 2006, s. 763).

This conclusion was welcome. It made UK company shares more attractive to foreign investors and will also facilitate the usage of the euro. It has received the statutory imprimatur, in that the Companies Act 2006, s. 542[18] specifically permits the issue of foreign denomination shares. Indeed, it has gone so far as to introduce a new tranche of provisions (ss. 622–8) which enable companies to redenominate shares into foreign currencies, provided specified procedures are adhered to. As these provisions do not come into effect until 1 October 2009, we shall have to wait and see if they are widely utilised.

If we discount the now defunct exchange control regime,[19] one exception to this welcoming approach is reflected in the House of Lords judgments in *Daimler v Continental Tyre*.[20] This case involves the quaint procedural rule, founded in public policy, that the English courts would not aid an alien enemy in time of war. Here we had a company suing in the English courts during the First World War.[21] The company had been incorporated in England, but was controlled by foreign shareholders with strong connections in Germany. The House of Lords, ignoring the concept of the separate personality of the company, held that the company was an alien enemy. Lord Parker explained[22] this ruling on the grounds that the problem did not lie in the existence of foreign shareholders, but rather in foreign control. With due respect, this analysis seems to involve splitting hairs. The case owes much to wartime emergency conditions; a scenario that has generated some hostile legislation[23] as far as shareholders are concerned. But the precedent may be more wide-reaching, in that a similar approach has been applied[24] in peacetime, where foreign shareholders (admittedly from a friendly country) were using an English company to circumvent protectionist regulatory legislation in the film industry.

---

[18] See CA 2006, s. 542.
[19] Exchange Control Act 1947, ss. 8–10. Exchange control was abolished in 1987.
[20] [1916] 2 AC 307.
[21] One could also note that wartime pressures led to the enactment of the Registration of Business Names Act 1916.
[22] [1916] 2 AC 307 at 345.
[23] See, for example, the Companies (Foreign Interests) Act 1917, which prohibited alteration of articles without governmental consent where the original article capped share ownership by aliens, and the Trading with the Enemy Act 1939, s. 7.
[24] *Re FG Films Ltd* [1953] 1 All ER 615.

2.3 Problems in EU Law

In view of the traditionally welcoming attitude of English law in peacetime conditions towards foreign shareholders, the facts of *Factortame*[25] may seem curious. The problem arose here because of concerns centring on 'quota hopping' and the operation of the EU Common Fisheries Policy. Each Member State had allocated to it a quota, but that quota could be exploited by foreign fishermen buying up UK fishing boats by acquiring the companies that operated such boats. This provoked national disquiet, largely fuelled by underlying hostility towards the concept of the EU in general. Accordingly, the UK government secured the enactment of the Merchant Shipping Act 1988. This legislation placed restrictions on the right of foreigners to acquire control of UK fishing companies by imposing nationality/residence requirements. This legislation was challenged by the Spanish fishermen in the English courts and references to the European Court of Justice were required on a number of occasions to clarify the position.[26] On the central substantive issue, the European Court of Justice ruled[27] that it was contrary to the principles of freedom of establishment and free movement of capital for the 1988 Act to restrict Spanish shareholders taking control of English fishing companies. As a result of this finding, the proceedings were rejoined in the English courts and the UK government was compelled to pay a substantial sum by way of compensation to the Spanish fishermen under the emerging principle of EC law of 'state liability'.[28]

The importance of freedom to participate in the share capital of EC companies is also reflected by *Proceedings brought by Manninen (C319/02)*.[29] The point at issue here was whether a Finnish tax credit system could operate in such a way as to disadvantage Finnish taxpayers who received dividends from Swedish (as opposed to Finnish companies). The European Court of Justice held that this was not consistent with Art 56 of the Treaty, because it effectively discouraged Finnish investors from investing in the share capital of companies incorporated in other Member States.

---

[25] [1990] ECR 2466.

[26] See *Factortame (C221/89)* [1991] ECR I-3905 (main substantive ruling on freedom of establishment and freedom of capital). Note also *Factortame (C213/89)* [1990] ECR I-2466 (interim relief) and *Factortame (C48/93)* [1996] ECR I-1029 (state liability).

[27] [1990] ECR I-2466.

[28] *Factortame (C48/93)* [1996] ECR I-1029, applying *Francovich v Italy (C6 and 9/90)* [1991] ECR I-5537.

[29] [2005] 2 WLR 690.

This policy of encouraging cross-border ownership of shares will receive a further boost when a new EC Directive (36/2007)[30] is implemented. At the moment, it is estimated that one-third of shares in EU companies is owned by non-resident shareholders, yet the fact of non-residence can place barriers in the way of shareholder empowerment. Under the new Directive, many of these barriers will be swept away. For instance, notice periods for shareholder meetings will be standardised at 21 days. Shorter periods will only be allowed where electronic voting is in operation. Websites are to be encouraged as a tool for communicating with shareholders. These reforms are welcome and will, of course, promote further convergence in corporate law.

2.4 Equal Treatment; Not Better Treatment

Although foreign shareholders are welcome, they are only received on the understanding that they become subject to the same obligations as native shareholders. This fundamental point was exemplified by *Re FH Lloyd Holdings plc*.[31] Here we were concerned with the rules contained in what became Companies Act 1985, Part VI (now Part 22 of the Companies Act 2006), requiring those investors acquiring beneficial interests in UK public companies to disclose the nature of that interest. In order to circumvent that obligation, it has become the practice for reclusive acquirers to hide behind foreign nominees. Typically, such investors would build up a strategic stake in a UK company in a clandestine fashion and then would pounce in the market through what became known as a 'dawn raid',[32] denying the directors of the company any opportunity to react. To counteract this stratagem, the law enables the company to apply to the court for a freezing order on the shares registered against the name of the nominee, if the nominee refuses to identify the real beneficial owner.[33] This was similar to the scenario that presented itself to the court in this case. Here the foreign nominee (for whose intermediate benefit shares were held by an English nominee) faced with the possibility of being subjected to a share-freezing order was an institution based in Luxembourg and it refused to disclose the identity of its client (the beneficial share owner), possibly because to do so would result in an infringement of Luxembourg law. Nourse J ruled that those foreign shareholders who acquire

[30]   For background, see (2006) 27 Co Law 119.
[31]   [1985] BCLC 293 – noted by D. Milman in (1985) 6 Co Law 184. Compare the approach of the Federal Court of Australia in *ASC v Bank Leumi Le Israel* (1996) 21 ACSR 474.
[32]   For discussion, see M.T. Lazarides (1983) 4 Co Law 66.
[33]   See CA 1985, s. 212 and soon CA 2006, ss. 793 et seq. See generally D. Milman and D. Singh (1992) 13 Co Law 51.

shares in UK public companies become subject to the same obligations as local shareholders and those obligations cannot be relieved by commitments under local law. The articles of association form the proper law of contract with members and that proper law was English law. The lex situs of the shares was also English law. The position was made no different by the reluctant party being only an intermediate beneficial holder – the trust property of the shares was located in England and therefore jurisdiction was engaged. Nourse J put it succinctly when posing the rhetorical question: 'Why should a true foreigner, while able to enjoy all the benefits of holding shares in an English company, be intended to escape the burdens?'[34] Having made that point, it is clear that English law does not completely disregard the predicament that a foreign shareholder might find himself in.[35]

A similar refusal to accept special pleading on behalf of foreign share-holders was exemplified in *Winpar Holdings v Joseph Holt plc*.[36] Here the Court of Appeal held that it was not fatal to the operation of the compulsory share purchase procedure found in CA 1985, s. 428 (restated in Chapter 3 of Part 28 of the Companies Act 2006) that each and every foreign share-holder had to be supplied with documentation relating to the bid in their home jurisdiction. That was not feasible in every case. It was common prac-tice in such offers to identify forbidden territories in which offers would not be directly communicated; shareholders from such territories would have to rely on methods of communication used in the UK, such as a notice in the *Financial Times*. However, city practices with regard to communications with overseas shareholders left something to be desired, as Peter Gibson LJ indicated:[37]

> However, I would add this caveat. I have some unease as to the practice, which appears to become standard in the City, of not directly communicating a takeover

---

[34]   Ibid at 299.

[35]   Notwithstanding the apparently uncompromising approach reflected in the above quotation, the English courts have acknowledged that a foreign shareholder may be given a short period of grace to enable advice to be taken on the position under English law – *Re Lonrho plc (No. 2)* [1989] BCLC 309. Here the court had to weigh speed of communication against the need to respect local religious practices and days of observance.

[36]   [2002] BCC 174. Similar reasoning may be said to explain the decision in *Mutual Life Insurance Co of New York v The Rank Organisation* [1985] BCLC 11. See also *Parkstone Ltd v Gulf Guarantee Bank plc* [1990] BCC 534, which offers another illustration of the practical difficulties that can arise when communicating with foreign shareholders. Here Warner J adopted a flexible interpretation of the articles to facilitate the sending of postal notices to shareholders based in Gibraltar.

[37]   Ibid at 196.

offer to persons in the forbidden territories, understandable though that practice is in view of the difficulty and cost of complying with local securities regulations This judgment should not be taken as blessing that practice whatever the circumstances.

It remains to be seen whether this advice is taken to heart.

3   CONTROLLING FOREIGN PARTICIPATION IN STRATEGIC COMPANIES

Notwithstanding what has been said above, it has long been the case that the UK corporate law model has been prepared to accept the idea that certain companies operating in strategic areas of the economy (for example, transport, energy and the defence sector) should be permitted to place restrictions on foreign shareholder participation. This may be achieved through a special regulatory structure based upon legislation or by a domestic provision in the articles of association of the relevant company. Such a strategy is often carried out through the mechanism of what is colloquially described as a 'golden share'.[38] A 'golden share' may enable the holder (usually a ministerial representative of the government) rights to veto the transfer of the business or the acquisition of control by a foreign shareholder. Typically, a 'golden share' arrangement is put in place in the wake of the privatisation[39] of a sector of the economy that was formerly under public ownership, so the state is able to gain the immediate financial rewards of privatisation from the proceeds of share sales, whilst retaining a degree of control over the sector. Truly a case of having one's cake and eating it!

This policy is now suspect, in that it potentially infringes EC law rules against discrimination with regard to participation in capital, in particular Art 56 of the EEC Treaty. During the 1990s, the European Commission had indicated to the UK government its concerns about the use of 'golden shares'. There is evidence that such devices were being quietly dropped in the UK,[40]

---

[38]   For an account of the legal issues associated with privatisation, see C. Graham and T. Prosser (1987) 50 MLR 16, C. Graham (1988) 9 Co Law 23 and A.P. Rutabanzibwa (1996) 17 Co Law 40.

[39]   See M. Likosky, *The Silicon Empire: Law, Culture and Commerce: Global Perspectives* (2005) (Ashgate) at 44–51. Privatisation, the brainchild of the Thatcher government in the 1990s, has spread as a commercial culture across Europe and to many jurisdictions whose economies were formerly dominated by a state-controlled sector. Complicated transitional issues can arise where an enterprise is switched between public and private owners and vice versa – see *R (on the application of National Grid Gas plc [formerly Transco plc] v Environmental Agency* [2007] UKHL 30.

[40]   See (2004) 25 Co Law 244.

but were still being maintained (and, in some cases, introduced) in other EU states. The principles governing this usage of 'golden shares' were explained in June 2002 by the European Court of Justice in *Portugal et al v Commission (Cases C367/98 and C483/99).*[41] In this instance, the Court of Justice was invited to give its views on three 'golden share' arrangements adopted respectively by the Portuguese, French and Belgian governments. The Portuguese arrangement related to privatisation issues in general, and capped foreign shareholders. The European Court of Justice ruled that this arrangement could not be objectively justified. In the case of the French 'golden share', in an oil company, the restriction was rejected. Again, the approach of the Court was to rule this arrangement to be contrary to EU law and unjustified. In the third case, that involving the Belgian veto designed to protect its energy supplies, the Court of Justice here found in favour of the Belgian government. Transparency and proportionality linked to a real public need seem to be the essential requirements for a golden share or equivalent regime to survive scrutiny by the ECJ. The reluctance of national governments to accept this loss of state control was apparent by virtue of the fact that some twelve months after this ECJ ruling, Portugal had to be reminded of the need to comply. A similar approach was taken by the European Court of Justice in *Commission v Italy (C58/99),*[42] where Italian privatisation laws that retained special powers for the state in the privatised companies were found to be incompatible with freedom of establishment and free movement of capital.

Subsequent to these cases, other proceedings have arrived at the door of the Court of Justice. In *Commission v Spain (C463/00)*[43] and the *Commission v UK (C98/01),*[44] it was necessary to give judgment on the legality of a general Spanish privatisation law and on the 'golden share' in British Airport Authorities (BAA), which capped foreign share ownership in the company. In both instances, a finding of incompatibility was made, with the restrictions being unjustified. In the case of BAA, it was seen as an unwarranted restriction on free movement of capital. Other cases of similar ilk and portent are *Commission v Italy (C174/04)*[45] and *Commission v Netherlands (C282 and 283/04).*[46]

'Golden shares' are not the only devices which can be used to restrict foreign acquisitions. Witness the so-called 'Volkswagen law', which restricted voting rights in Volkswagen to prevent any shareholder having more votes

---

41 [2003] 2 WLR 1.
42 [Unreported]. See also *Commission v Belgium (C503/99)* [2002] ECR I-4809.
43 [2003] ECR I-4581.
44 [2003] ECR I-4641.
45 [2005] ECR I-4933.
46 [2006] ECR I-9141.

than the state of Saxony, thereby effectively blocking a foreign takeover. This arrangement was struck down by the European Court of Justice in *Commission v Germany (C112/05)* in 2007.[47]

The conclusion must therefore be that each case turns on its own facts, though with a strong presumption that 'golden shares' (and comparable arrangements) do indeed infringe EU law. Had these rulings been handed down 20 years ago, they would have had serious implications for UK privatisation policy. As it happens, the British government has quietly abandoned most of its 'golden share' arrangements.[48] A blemish on the face of our open-door policy has fortunately been swept away.

4   FOREIGN (OR NON-RESIDENT) DIRECTORS

Although English Law does require the nationality of company directors to be disclosed on business letters,[49] there is no significant nationality barrier placed in the way of those individuals who wish to become directors of companies incorporated in this country.[50] Some have argued that this latitude may be abused by foreign undesirables becoming directors of British companies,[51] but this relaxed approach is fortunate because such an explicit nationality requirement would almost certainly be contrary to EC law, on the grounds that it infringes either the Art 43 guarantee of freedom of establishment or more likely the Art 49 freedom to provide services (that is, directorial services).[52] Equally, the more subtle ploy of requiring directors to be resident in the UK would again infringe those same principles as this would be seen by the ECJ as in substance an indirect contravention of the basic principle of non-

---

[47]   [2008] 1 CMLR 643. For background on this Volkswagen affair, see F. Sanders (2008) 14 Col Jo of Euro Law 359.

[48]   Though it appears to have retained a special share in the sell-off of its remaining interests in the Aldermaston atomic weapons research establishment – see the *Independent*, 20 December 2008.

[49]   See CA 1985, s. 289(1)(a)(iv).

[50]   Other countries have had fewer qualms – see, for instance, Canadian Business Corporations Act, s. 100(3). In Switzerland, there is a requirement that the majority of the board should be Swiss resident – see O.C. Meier-Boeschenstein [1994] JBL 212. There have been questions raised as to whether English law is too lax in vetting those individuals who may become a director – there have been instances where wanted criminals and suspected war criminals have been recorded as directors of British companies – see the *Times* 21 February 2008, p. 28.

[51]   For example, it has been alleged that war criminals are using British companies to mask their commercial activities – see the *Times*, 21 February 2008, p. 28.

[52]   It would also breach Art 12 EC (discrimination on grounds of nationality).

discrimination.[53] Here we have clear authority in *Commission v Spain (C114/97)*,[54] where the European Court of Justice ruled that a Spanish law requiring directors of private security companies to be Spanish nationals was discriminatory. Again, in the EFTA case of *Rainford-Towning (E-3/98)*,[55] it was held that a comparable Liechtenstein law offended the same principle.

Indeed, the empirical evidence would suggest that a growing number of UK companies have directors who are either non-nationals or at least resident outside the jurisdiction. So in 1996 it was estimated that some 300,000 directors of UK companies were non-resident. That figure (which now may be as high as 20 per cent) is likely to grow as the numbers of foreign shareholders expand.

In the same way that nationality is an irrelevance when determining the obligations of shareholders, so directors do not escape their responsibilities under English law by virtue of foreign nationality or residence abroad. In *Re Seagull Manufacturing Co Ltd*,[56] the English courts were required to determine whether a non-resident director could be subject to the investigatory procedures specified in the Insolvency Act 1986. In answering this question in the affirmative, the court stressed that it was important for the integrity of UK Company Law to extend the purview of these provisions to this scenario. Peter Gibson J explained:

> I can see no reasons of comity which would prevent those who voluntarily were officers or otherwise participated in the formation or running of an English company being capable of being summoned by the English court for the purposes of public examination.[57]

The observation was made by Hirst LJ that, with advances in communications technology, managing a UK company from overseas was an increasingly attractive possibility. English law had to rise to that challenge:

> The efficient and thorough conduct of such investigation by the official receiver is of great public importance, as several recent notorious cases have demonstrated.

---

[53] See *Mund and Fester v Firma Hatrex International Transport (C398/92)* [1994] ECR I-467. The Danes had a residence requirement for directors until 2004.

[54] *Commission v Spain (C114/97)* [1999] 2 CMLR 701. See also *Commission v Belgium (Case C355/98)* [2000] 2 CMLR 357. These cases all involved directors of private security firms – public interest could therefore not be used to justify the differential treatment.

[55] *Rainford-Towning* [1999] 1 CMLR 871. See also *Re Pucher* [2002] 2 CMLR 3 (EFTA case in which Liechtenstein residence requirement for company directors ruled unlawful).

[56] [1993] BCC 241.

[57] Ibid at 246.

This process would be frustrated if, for example, a director, who had with the aid of modern methods of communication run the company entirely from abroad, was immune from public examination . . . The same applies to a director who has defrauded the company in England and then absconded abroad shortly before the liquidation.[58]

In *Re Seagull Manufacturing Co Ltd (No 2),*[59] much the same point was made by the judge, Mary Arden QC, in the context of the operation of the director disqualification regime against non-resident directors. Here the judge dismissed an application to restrain the commencement of director disqualification proceedings against a director who was not present in the jurisdiction in circumstances where the alleged misdeeds may have occurred outside the jurisdiction. Mary Arden QC ruled that s. 6 of the Company Directors Disqualification Act 1986 was meant to have extraterritorial effect:

Accordingly, in my judgment, Parliament must be presumed to have been legislating not simply for British subjects and foreigners who happened to be here at the relevant time, but also for other foreigners who were out of the jurisdiction at the critical time. Likewise, in relation to conduct, section 6(1) contains no territorial restriction. Accordingly, the court must ask what is the conduct in respect of which Parliament must have been presumed to have been legislating?[60]

This conclusion was explained thus:

There are two factors which, in my judgment, indicate that the conduct in question in section 6(1) need not be conduct which occurred within the jurisdiction. The first such factor is the definition of 'company' to which I have already referred. This includes foreign companies and the acts of the directors of those companies are likely to have taken place abroad, and Parliament must have been presumed to have been legislating with that in mind.[61]

She continued:

Secondly, in these days of modern communications, a person may conduct himself as a director in such a way as to affect persons within the jurisdiction without himself ever entering the jurisdiction. Again, in my judgment, Parliament must be presumed to have been legislating with this in mind, and, accordingly, by plain implication, to be taken to have been referring to conduct wherever committed.[62]

---

58   Ibid at 250.
59   [1993] BCC 833. A director can be disqualified even if his COMI is located abroad – *Official Receiver v Stojevic* [2007] EWHC 1186 (Ch), [2008] Bus L R 641. In Ireland similarly, it has been held that a restriction order can be granted against a nonresident director – *Fennel v Frost* [2003] 1 IR 80 and *O'Ferral v Coughlan* [2004] 4 IR 266.
60   [1993] BCC 833 at 841.
61   Ibid at 841.
62   Ibid at 841.

Non-residence arguably was one of the reasons for the imposition of a 12-year disqualification in respect of an individual in *Official Receiver v Vass*[63] who had based himself offshore in Sark and had taken on no fewer than 1313 directorships of UK companies with complete disregard for the attendant responsibilities!

This judicial policy was taken a step further in *Re Howard Holdings Inc*[64] where the English courts indicated that foreign non-resident directors of a foreign company, which was being wound up under English law, could in theory become subject to wrongful trading liabilities pursuant to s. 214 of the Insolvency Act 1986.

In *Re Mid East Trading Ltd*,[65] the investigative procedures in s. 236 of the Insolvency Act 1986 were made available to the liquidators of a foreign company being wound up within the jurisdiction to permit the production of documents located overseas. Although the case does not focus upon action taken against foreign-based officers, the points made in the judgment by the Court of Appeal on the need to balance carefully competing interests are apposite. Any extension of sovereignty must be justified.

Although legal systems can deal with the non-residence issue by stretching the meaning of substantive problems, there is no denying the practical difficulties involved in imposing corporate law standards against directors who are outwith the jurisdiction. This point was noted in Ireland in the First Report of the Company Law Review Group with regard to the difficulties often encountered in prosecuting such individuals.[66]

5   THE CORPORATE DIRECTOR PHENOMENON

Although there is no objection to foreign or non-resident directors, there is scope for abuse where a company is allowed to become a director of a UK-registered company. Unusually, English law has for many years permitted companies to become directors of other companies (see CA 1985 s. 289(1)(b)). This point was settled many years ago by Warrington J in *Re Bulawayo Market and Offices Co Ltd*.[67] Furthermore, the nationality of the corporate director is

---

63   [1999] BCC 516. See the news item in (1999) 20 Co Law 117 and L. Hitchens [2000] CFILR 359.

64   [1998] BCC 549 – noted by K. Dawson in [1999] Ins Law 67.

65   [1998] BCC 726.

66   See para 8.3.15, where it was suggested that changes should be made in the rules on service of prosecution papers to address this difficulty.

67   [1907] 2 Ch 458.

immaterial. The potential for abuse here was exemplified by *Official Receiver v Brady*,[68] where Jersey-based companies were used as part of a scheme designed to disguise the participation of certain individuals in UK companies. Most jurisdictions do not take such a liberal approach. Even the offshore jurisdiction of the Isle of Man banned corporate directors until the enactment of reforms in 2006 (see Chapter 1 above). Ireland maintained its position of opposition in the First Report of the Company Law Review Group.[69] The position in English law has been reviewed recently. At one stage, it seemed likely that a prohibition would be introduced on corporate directors.[70] The government[71] has backed away from this draconian option (possibly because of the fact that there are many thousands of corporate directors recorded at present and to replace all of these would be a massive task). Instead, the new rule, which is now applied under s.155 of the Companies Act 2006 with effect from 1 October 2008, is that every company must have at least one natural person acting as a director. If that requirement is met, corporate directors are still viewed as acceptable. It remains to be seen if this classic British compromise achieves the desired goal of eliminating the perceived abuse.

---

[68]   [1999] BCC 259. See also the case mentioned by R. Goddard in (2007) 28 Co Law 281 – based on *Re Citylink Ltd* [2005] EWHC 2875 (Ch).

[69]   (2001) para 11.8.10.

[70]   See Company Law Review, *Final Report* (URN 01/942).

[71]   See White Paper (Cm 6456) (2005).

5. Reception of overseas companies by the English legal system[1]

1 THE INCLUSIVE TRADITION

English law has a long history of affording recognition to foreign entities which have not incorporated as such under the processes provided by English law. Witness the ancient House of Lords precedent of *Henriques v Dutch West India Co*, where the English court gave recognition to a company which had been incorporated in Holland.[2] Even where overt discrimination existed within the English legal system – see, for example, the bar on foreign companies owning land in the UK – such negative treatment has long been ended.[3]

In more recent times, we find a useful illustration of this embracing tradition at work in the case of *Arab Monetary Fund v Hashim (No. 3)*.[4] Here the AMF was allowed to bring proceedings in English law even though it had not been incorporated under English law. The AMF was set up by treaty and had been afforded status as a legal entity by a number of friendly Arab states, with the result that the facilities of English law were made available to it. This House of Lords majority ruling seemed to extend the parameters of the common law. This decision was taken further by the Foreign Corporations Act 1991, which made provision for the recognition of entities incorporated in territories not recognised as states by English law.[5]

---

[1] For scholarly treatment of this subject, see F. Tansinda, chapter 12 in D. Milman (ed.), *Regulating Enterprise* (1999) (Hart). See also his article in (1997) 18 Co Law 98. *Gower and Davies: The Principles of Company Law* (P. Davies, ed.) (7th edition, 2003) (Sweet & Maxwell) chapter 6 also provides some coverage.

[2] (1728) 2 Ld Raym 1532. See also *Lazard Bros & Co v Midland Bank* [1933] AC 289 at 297 per Lord Wright. A more recent overview of the position is provided by Brooke LJ in *Sarrio SA v Kuwait Investment Authority* [1997] CLC 280 at 296.

[3] This change occurred in 1908.

[4] [1991] AC 114 – noted by G. Marston [1991] CLJ 218 and I. Cheyne (1991) 40 ICLQ 981. A similar approach was taken in *Buckmaster & Moore (a firm) v Fado Investments* 1986 PCC 95. For an historical overview of the attitude of the English courts towards foreign state entities, see G. Marston [1997] CLJ 374 and F.A. Mann (1991) 107 LQR 357.

[5] See A. Mayss (1990) 7 Co Law 140 and I. Cheyne (1991) 40 ICLQ 983.

Recognition of foreign companies is without regard to the question of who owns such companies. There is no discrimination against overseas companies owned by foreign governments.[6] Indeed, there may even be a possibility of such companies exploiting the concept of sovereign immunity, though such immunity is limited where commercial activities are involved and in other prescribed circumstances.[7] Having said that, the device of lifting the veil of corporate personality may be engaged in such circumstances, as the court in *Kensington International Ltd v Republic of the Congo*[8] indicated. In other cases, the sensitive diplomatic considerations triggered by state-owned companies may have influenced the ultimate court decision.[9]

Another expression of this non-discriminatory approach can be found in the judgment of Lord Phillips MR in *Jameel v Wall Street Journal*,[10] when it was heard at Court of Appeal level prior to its progression to the House of Lords. In response to a suggestion that the rule of English law that companies did not need to show special damage before suing in libel did not apply to foreign companies, Lord Phillips was most insistent that the same rule should apply.[11]

Why is this welcoming attitude adopted? Undoubtedly, it is a manifestation of comity between courts of friendly jurisdictions. More pragmatically, the consequence of such recognition is that litigation will be allowed to be undertaken in the English law forum. English lawyers will have to be engaged to represent parties and ancillary services used to facilitate such litigation. The invisible earnings of 'UK plc' will thus be increased. This is part of a general strategic approach taken by English law towards 'capturing' foreign-party litigation. It is a strategy that has been given a major boost in recent years with the advent of the EC Regulation on Insolvency Proceedings (1346/2000) (as amended) which allocates primary jurisdiction in cross-border insolvency cases to the jurisdiction where the debtor has its 'centre of main interests' (or 'COMI'). This convenient device (which smacks of the real seat concept) has enabled English law to 'capture' insolvency proceedings related to foreign incorporated companies where their COMI was located here, even though the

---

6   *Williams and Humbert v W & H Trade Marks* [1985] 1 All ER 619.
7   *Mellinger v New Brunswick Development Corp* [1971] 1 WLR 604, *Trendtex Trading Corp v Central Bank of Nigeria* [1977] 2 WLR 356. See also State Immunity Act 1978, s. 3 (waiving immunity for commercial transactions) and s. 8 (waiving immunity with respect to proceedings relating to a corporation in which the state has a membership interest).
8   [2005] EWHC 2684 (Comm), [2006] 2 BCLC 296.
9   See, for example, *Banco Nacional de Cuba v Cosmos Trading* [2000] BCC 910.
10   [2005] 2 WLR 1577 (CA); [2006] UKHL 44.
11   [2005] 2 WLR 1577 at 1611. For discussion, see A. O'Neill (2007) 28 Co Law 75.

place of incorporation is located in another Member State. Although there have been the occasional criticisms[12] of the 'piratical' approach of the English courts, for the most part this Regulation has produced harmony. This particular EC Regulation will be considered in greater depth in Chapter 8.

2   DEFINITION

The law on overseas companies (that is, companies incorporated outside Great Britain) is dealt with by Part 23 of the Companies Act 1985, which will be replaced by Part 34 of the Companies Act 2006 with effect from October 2009.

Where do companies incorporated in other parts of the UK or the British Isles fit into the picture?

Companies incorporated in Scotland are not within the scope of Part 23, but are covered by the Companies Acts and Insolvency Act generally, unless specific excusion is provided for.[13] As far as Scotland is concerned, the position is reflected by *Re Baby Moon Ltd*,[14] where the distinctive nature of the English and Scottish systems was stressed in the context of the English winding-up jurisdiction.

The position is different vis-à-vis Northern Irish companies, which at present fall outside the scope of the Companies Acts and the Insolvency Act.[15] Northern Irish companies at present rank as oversea companies and there are 91 such companies registered under Part 23. The position has changed now that the Companies Act 2006 has come into force, because s. 1284 extends the Companies Acts to Northern Ireland.

Companies incorporated in Channel Islands jurisdictions[16] and in the Isle of Man[17] also deserve special mention. They both fall within the parameters of Part 23. Companies statistics indicate that there are 476 and 515 respectively of these companies operating in the jurisdiction. In *Curragh Investments v Cooke*,[18] the court treated an Isle of Man company as an overseas company.

---

[12]   See *Stojevic v Komercni Banka AS* [2007] BPIR 141.
[13]   See, for example, Companies Act 2006, s. 265. Insolvency Act 1986, s. 440 lists those specific exceptions where the Insolvency Act 1986 does not apply.
[14]   [1985] PCC 103.
[15]   See CA 1985, s. 745 and IA 1986, s. 441 – Insolvency Act 1986 does not apply to Northern Ireland unless provision is specifically identified.
[16]   See Chapter 1 for an explanation of the position here.
[17]   See Chapter 1 again.
[18]   [1974] 1 WLR 1559.

3   NON-RESIDENT COMPANIES: A NOTE

The residency of a company could be relevant for a host of legal reasons – for example, taxation or jurisdictional matters. A company may be incorporated in this country but treated as non-resident for the above purposes. Conversely, a foreign company could be regarded as resident here. The acid test in all cases is to identify where the central control and management is based.[19]

4   FOREIGN ENTERPRISE ACTIVITY IN ENGLAND AND WALES: STRATEGIC OPTIONS

Where a foreign enterprise wishes to undertake business within the English legal jurisdiction, it has a number of options available to it. One choice that is not available is simply to register itself as an English company. Strict corporate law orthodoxy dictates that a company can only be incorporated in one jurisdiction.[20] Other courses of action must, therefore, be evaluated.

4.1   'Going Native'

Firstly, the enterprise could acquire or incorporate a local company. The owners of the foreign enterprise would become the controlling shareholders of the local company. The implications of this strategy have been considered in Chapter 4.

4.2   Formal Admission as an Overseas Company

A second option would be to seek formal recognition for the foreign company under English law. In English law, this is achieved by registration under Part XXIII of the Companies Act 1985 (now Part 34 of the Companies Act 2006). The registration process is painless and there are no risks that registration would be refused.[21] Statistics covering companies registered under Part XXIII are revealing. In the DTI Companies Annual Report for 2005–6,[22] we learn that of 8066 registered overseas companies:

---

[19]   *De Beers Consolidated Mines* [1906] AC 455, *Unit Construction Co Ltd v Bullock* [1960] AC 351.

[20]   *Bulkeley v Shutz* (1871) LR 3 PC 764, *Bateman v Service* (1881) 6 App Cas 386.

[21]   This is not always the case – see New Zealand Overseas Investment Act 1973 (special permission required).

[22]   See DTI Annual Report 05/06, Table E1.

- 2410 were from the USA;
- 1882 were from the EU;
- 1449 were from the Commonwealth;
- 1082 were from other parts of the UK;
- 3653 were from the rest of the world (including 303 from the Virgin Islands and 213 from Japan).

Compare this with the figures for 1993–4 where the total of registered overseas companies was only 4881; we thus have a significant increase over the last decade. In 1987/8, the equivalent figure was 3749; the total has now doubled in two decades. Having said that, the total is still only a small drop in the ocean when compared to the two million plus registered companies in Great Britain.

For many years, the legal rules here were settled. A separate legal regime for overseas companies had been constructed on the recommendation of the Loreburn Committee[23] way back at the start of the 20th century. That regime operated without major problems. So, for instance, the Jenkins Committee[24] in 1962 concluded that it was fundamentally sound and needed only minor surgery. Part XXIII of the Companies Act 1985 was engaged when the foreign company established a place of business within the jurisdiction. Much jurisprudence evolved around the concept of establishing a place of business; the degree of permanence in the link was important.[25] The waters here were muddied[26] by the transposition of the 11th EC Company Law Harmonisation Directive (1989/666) into English law. This Directive used as its critical element the concept of a 'branch', an idea well understood by continental lawyers but new to their English counterparts. In *Etablissement Somafer SA v Saar-Ferngas AG (C33/78)*,[27] a case dealing with jurisdiction under the Brussels Convention, a 'branch' was defined as:

> A place of business which has the appearance of permanency, such as the extension of a parent body, has a management and is materially equipped to negotiate business with third parties so that the latter, although knowing that there will, if necessary, be a legal link with the parent body, the head office of which is abroad, do not have to deal directly with such parent body but may transact business at the place of business constituting the extension.[28]

---

23   Cd 3052 – this led to the enactment of s. 35 of CA 1907.
24   Cmnd 1749, para 525. For suggestions of the need for minor reform see D.G. Rice [1962] JBL 155.
25   *Lord Advocate v Huron and Erie Loan & Savings Co* [1911] SC 612.
26   For a critique of the legislative method using delegated legislation made under s. 2 of the European Communities Act 1972, see J. Rickford in J. de Lacy (ed.), *The Reform of UK Company Law* (2002) (Cavendish) at 6.
27   [1978] ECR 2183.
28   Ibid at 2193.

In the light of this interpretation adopted by the European Court of Justice, in this particular case a French firm with an office in Germany could in principle be sued in the latter jurisdiction.

The position prior to the entry into force of the Companies Act 2006 is extremely complicated and may be summarised thus. Foreign business emanating from non-EU states would only have to register under Part XXIII if they established a place of business within the jurisdiction. Companies incorporated in EU states clearly had to register the establishment of a branch. The real difficulty concerned EU businesses that did not set up a branch, but in some other way were deemed to be establishing a place of business. There were thus *two* separate registration systems for companies which establish branches and places of business, but the relationship between the two regimes was opaque.

The Company Law Review[29] addressed the issue of the two systems for registering overseas companies/branches and came down firmly in favour of a single harmonised model, inevitably based upon the branch idea, which, of course, ensures compliance with our EC obligations. It produced a separate consultative document on this subject in October 1999. Entitled *Reforming the Law Concerning Overseas Companies*,[30] it put forward a solution along the lines that there should be a single system based upon meeting the requirements of the 11th Directive. Simplification and reducing the need for multiple registration were also suggested.

Under Part 34 of the Companies Act 2006, the position will be as follows. A single criterion will be adopted instead of the current dual track system. That will be based upon the concept of an establishment, which will be wide enough to encompass a branch presence and establishing a place of business. Under s. 1044, overseas companies (defined as companies incorporated outside the UK) will have to comply with an obligation to make disclosures (a duty imposed by s. 1046) if they meet certain criteria to be specified by secondary legislation. At the other end of the spectrum, there will be an obligation under s. 1058 to notify the registrar in the event of an overseas company ceasing to have a registrable presence by closing an establishment. We are told by s. 1059 that moving a branch from one jurisdiction in the UK to another is tantamount to closure, which is equated to ceasing to have a registrable presence. It is apparent from the aforementioned summary that much will depend upon the details contained in the as yet unfinalised Draft Overseas Companies Regulations.[31] As things stand at present, these substantial regulations deal with such matters as registration requirements, trading disclosures, accounts and charge registration. Apart from embellishing the Act, they also introduce

---

[29] *Final Report* (URN 01/942) paras 11.21–11.33.
[30] URN 99/1146.
[31] SI 2009/Draft.

some amendments to the Companies Act 2006 itself by modifying s. 1067 (which provides for branches of overseas companies to be given a registered number) to replace the word 'branch' with 'UK establishment'. Once finalised, these will take effect from 1 October 2009.

4.3 Flouting the Law

Thirdly, the foreign entity may seek to disregard both of the previous options. What are the consequences of such behaviour? The legal status of the foreign entity would still be recognised in English law. Moreover, any contracts made by it would remain enforceable. In *Curragh Investments v Cooke*,[32] which was mentioned above, contracts made by an Isle of Man company in this country in circumstances where the company had failed to fulfil its obligations under Part XXIII were held to be enforceable. The court reasoned that, although invalidity may be used as a sanction to support a criminal penalty, there has to be a point of connection between the breach of the technical provision and the use of a civil avoidance sanction. The court could find no such logical connection in this particular instance.[33]

4.4 Redomestication[34]

A route that is not often chosen is to redomesticate the foreign company under English law. As far as English law[35] (and many other legal systems) are concerned, this is not an attractive option, as it would involve dissolution in the home jurisdiction and incorporation in this country.[36] Moreover, it is not possible to simply move a company's registered office from one EU Member State to another.[37] Needless to say, any transition involving dissolution is fraught with legal difficulty, threatens goodwill and therefore is not used widely. A private Act of Parliament, a time-consuming and expensive process, may be required for such a redomestication.[38] It is contrary to company law

---

[32] [1974] 1 WLR 1559. The Jenkins Committee (1962, Cmnd 1749) para 515 would have applauded this ruling.

[33] See the comments of Megarry J, ibid at 1564.

[34] For an excellent review of this subject, see D. Lewis (1995) 16 Co Law 295.

[35] Under the Manx Companies Act 2006, s. 162, foreign companies can simply adopt the 2006 Act, thereby creating a form of redomestication by continuation.

[36] For an insight into some of the issues that can arise, see *Re Datadeck Ltd* [1998] BCC 694 (redomestication of an English company to Delaware).

[37] *Daily Mail (C81/87)* [1988] ECR 5483. For comment, see C. Schmitthoff [1988] JBL 454.

[38] Note The Henry Johnson, Son & Co Ltd Act 1996. See D Lewis (op. cit. note 34) at 297 for comment.

orthodoxy simply to register a company as being incorporated in more than one jurisdiction.[39] A number of other offshore jurisdictions have, however, developed procedures to facilitate this[40] and at one stage it looked as if English law might be moving in that same direction. So, for example, in the Final Report of the Company Law Review[41] (Chapter 14), it was recommended that solvent companies should be allowed to move to scheduled jurisdictions without a break in their corporate identity. Alas, the Companies Act 2006 is silent on this matter. We return to this issue in Chapter 9.

5   APPLICABILITY OF GENERAL PROVISIONS IN THE COMPANIES ACTS

The starting point here is that the Companies Act 1985 (and the Companies Act 2006) do not generally apply to overseas companies.[42] This is the result of section 735 of the 1985 Act, which establishes a *presumption* of non-applicability. A similar presumption is established by s. 1 of the Companies Act 2006, which also in subsection (3) flags up the discrete regime for overseas companies set forth in Part 34. Let us examine a few illustrations of that presumption at work. Unfortunately, in many situations, the legislation is opaque and the courts have been left to resolve the matter.

So, for instance, in *Rover International v Cannon Film Sales*,[43] the question was whether the presumption of a promoter's personal liability in respect of preincorporation contracts (as created by s. 36C of the Companies Act 1985) applied where the company in question was to be incorporated in a foreign jurisdiction. Applying the basic presumption of non-applicability embodied in s. 735, Harman J held that s. 36C (which is now restated by s. 51 of CA 2006) did not encompass this factual situation. Parliament had not intended to legislate for such a scenario. This was an odd conclusion, as the provision was meant to protect the party contracting with the promoter and therefore the national status of the prospective company should be immaterial.

---

[39]   *Bateman v Service* (1881) 6 App Cas 386. See P. Smart [1990] JBL 126.

[40]   See Isle of Man Companies Act 2006, ss. 162 and 167, which allow both foreign companies and local companies to redomesticate provided they are solvent. These provisions appear to date back to 2003 – see (2004) 25 Co Law 114. Note also the Companies (Redomiciliation) Regulations 1996 in Gibraltar.

[41]   URN 01/942 especially at paras 14.3 et seq.

[42]   Under s. 442 of the Insolvency Act 1986, an order in council can extend the Act to companies from the Channel Islands.

[43]   [1987] 3 BCC 369 – decision was reversed by Court of Appeal ([1988] BCLC 710), but on grounds unrelated to the preincorporation point.

The inconvenience of this decision was quickly recognised and the case was neutralised by the Foreign Companies (Execution of Documents) Regulations 1994.[44] These regulations in turn will be superseded by Part 2 of the Draft Overseas Companies (Company Contracts and Registration of Charges) Regulations 2009).

In *Re Dallhold Estates Pty Ltd*, [45] Chadwick J sitting in the High Court was required to decide whether a company incorporated in Western Australia could enter into administration under English law. Possibly relying on comments of Hirst J in the case of *Felixstowe Dock and Rwy Co v US Lines Inc*,[46] the court proceeded on the basis that the provision in s. 8 of the Insolvency Act 1986 did not apply to foreign companies. Having drawn this inference, the court rescued the position by invoking the judicial comity facility embodied in s. 426 of the Insolvency Act 1986 to produce the desired effect (see Chapter 6 below).

A variant on this interpretative conundrum surfaced in *Arab Bank v Mercantile Holdings*.[47] Here Millett J was invited to decide whether the word subsidiary when used in the Companies Act 1985, s. 151 (which prohibits subsidiaries giving financial assistance to the acquisition of shares in their parent) was restricted to domestic subsidiaries or whether it encompassed foreign subsidiary companies. According to Millett J, the former construction was to be preferred, with the consequence that a foreign subsidiary could financially assist the acquisition of shares in the parent.[48] This, of course, assumed that such behaviour was not illegal under the law of the place of incorporation. Furthermore, as Millett J was at pains to stress, the setting up of a foreign subsidiary simply to evade the restrictions imposed by s. 151 would not be tolerated by the English courts. This approach towards the interpretation of the financial assistance bar has recently been followed by Evans-Lombe J in *AMG Global Nominees (Private) Ltd v SMM Holdings Ltd*.[49]

In *Re International Bulk Commodities*,[50] the interpretative question involved s. 29 of the Insolvency Act 1986. Did this permit a foreign company to be placed into administrative receivership under English law? This question was answered in the affirmative.

The availability to a foreign company of the corporate reconstruction procedure mapped out by ss. 425–7 of the Companies Act 1985 (ss. 895–901

---

[44]   SI 1994/950.
[45]   [1992] BCC 394.
[46]   [1989] QB 360. See I. Fletcher [1993] 6 Ins Intell 10.
[47]   [1993] BCC 816.
[48]   This precedent has apparently been confirmed by the Companies Act 2006 – see para 991 in the *Explanatory Notes* to the Act.
[49]   [2008] 1 BCLC 447. Confirmed on appeal sub nomine *AMG Global Nominees (Private) Ltd v Africa Resources Ltd* [2008] EWCA Civ 1262.
[50]   [1992] 3 WLR 238.

of CA 2006) was the issue at stake in *Re Drax Holdings Ltd*.[51] The court
(Lawrence Collins J) found no difficulty in holding that a scheme of arrangement was available. Here the company had been incorporated in the Cayman
Islands, but was running a power station in this country: clear evidence of a
sufficient jurisdictional link. A similar conclusion was arrived at in *Re The
Home Insurance Co*,[52] where a company incorporated in New Hampshire was
permitted by Mann J to exploit the scheme of arrangement procedure. To
permit this to happen did not infringe the concept of comity. In *Re La Mutuelle
de Mans Assurance*,[53] Pumfrey J followed this line of authority and held that,
as the French insurer was not covered by the jurisdictional rules in the EC
Regulation on Insolvency Proceedings (1346/2000), it could in theory be
wound up under English law and, therefore, in fact was eligible for recon-
struction under ss. 425–7. This point at least therefore appears to be well
settled.

Issues of the applicability of English law to foreign companies have
cropped up with regard to the operation of director disqualification orders
handed down by the English courts. In *Official Receiver v Stern (No. 2)*,[54] the
Court of Appeal held the English courts, in spite of the uncertainty as to the
position, did indeed have the power to extend any disqualification of a director to his/her actions in respect of a foreign company operating here. Lloyd J
explained:[55]

> Nor do I accept that the public, with whose protection the court is concerned, is only
> the public in the UK, or for that matter, in England and Wales. The effect of a
> disqualification order is defined by the Act so as to extend to foreign companies and
> therefore it is clear that an effective order from which no relevant exception is made
> will have, or is capable of having, a protective effect in relation to some foreign
> classes of actual or potential creditors.

Like all presumptions, there is the possibility of rebuttal. Explicit provisions
in the Companies Act may encompass foreign companies. The clearest example here is afforded by Part XXIII of the 1985 Act, which provides a detailed
set of rules regulating companies which establish a place of business or branch
in Great Britain. Under the 2006 Act, this regime is to be found in Part 34. This
matter has been considered above in this chapter. Overseas companies may be

---

[51]   [2004] 1 BCLC 10. See also *Re DAP Holdings* [2006] BCC 22 and *Re
Sovereign Marine and General Insurance Co Ltd* [2006] EWHC 1335 (Ch), [2006]
BCC 774.
[52]   [2005] EWHC 2485 (Ch), [2006] BCC 164.
[53]   [2005] EWHC 1599 (Ch), [2006] BCC 11.
[54]   [2001] BCC 305.
[55]   Ibid at 358.

the subject of DTI investigation (see CA 1985, s. 453, as substituted by CA 1989, s. 70), though the powers of the state are more limited than those available when investigating domestic companies. The explicit jurisdiction to wind up overseas companies (found in the Insolvency Act 1986, s. 221) may also be noted here. This particular jurisdiction will be considered fully in Chapter 8. The Enterprise Act 2002 also contains measures applying English law to foreign companies.[56] These instances are relatively clear; what is more of a problem is where it is suggested that *implied* inclusion of foreign companies has taken place. It is clear from the review of cases above that this remains a vexed issue.

A distinct jurisdiction which indirectly justifies the winding up of foreign companies in the public interest[57] deserves mention here. The point to note is that it can be exercised in respect of solvent companies incorporated abroad, but only if a sufficient link with the English jurisdiction can be established. As Peter Gibson J in *Re Titan International Inc*,[58] explained:

> To arrogate to the English court jurisdiction to wind up a foreign company merely because of its association as an investment vehicle outside the jurisdiction with another foreign company that has been active within the jurisdiction would be in my view to make a giant, impermissible and unjustified extension of the jurisdiction of the English court.[59]

It should be apparent to all that the position is unsatisfactory. What is needed is a clear legislative steer on this increasingly important issue. A short statute would prove useful; it would also serve to excise peripheral provisions from our present Companies Acts which have no relevance to domestic companies. Such a slimming-down exercise for the Companies Acts would be seen as welcome in many quarters.

Unfortunately, the Companies Act 2006 does not change the position for the better. We are wedded to the approach of a random scattering of provisions made applicable to overseas companies – for example, s. 1120, which applies Part 35 of the 2006 Act to overseas companies. An opportunity to enhance the law has therefore been lost. The courts can consequently look forward to further litigation on this vexed matter of statutory construction.

---

[56]   Enterprise Act 2002, s. 254.
[57]   See *Re Titan International Inc* [1998] 1 BCLC 102 (winding-up refused on the facts), *Re Normandy Marketing* [1993] BCC 879.
[58]   [1998] 1 BCLC 102.
[59]   [1998] 1 BCLC 102 at 108–9.

6   FOREIGN COMPANIES AND LISTING RULES

Many securities issued by foreign companies are listed on the London Stock Exchange, as they are keen to raise capital through the opportunities offered by the London market. Cross-listing or secondary listing is not discouraged. However, a light touch[60] is often offered to such companies, possibly as a result of a desire to get such issuers participating in the London market and thereby boosting its status as a world capital markets hub. Compare this with the position in the USA under the Sarbanes-Oxley Act 2001, where the full gamut of disclosure and governance requirements is applied to foreign issuers.[61] This has not improved the attractiveness of the New York Stock Exchange and has provoked some soul-searching in the US. Where a primary listing is sought in the UK, the foreign issuer is generally subject to the same rules as a domestic company.

7   FOREIGN COMPANIES IN LITIGATION

7.1   Foreign Company as Claimant

At the beginning of this chapter, we noted the desire of the English legal system to attract foreign parties to litigate in this country. However, there is a catch – where an overseas non-resident party wishes to commence litigation in the English courts, it runs the risk of being required to pay a deposit in the form of security for costs.[62] This risk existed for all limited liability companies, no matter where resident, as section 726 of the Companies Act 1985 made clear. Under s. 726 (now conflated within CPR, r. 25.13),[63] any corporate claimant that appears to be unlikely to meet an adverse costs award can be required to provide security for costs. However, the risk is exacerbated for non-residents, because under Civil Procedure Rule 25.13, the court may require such security to be furnished irrespective of the financial standing of the company in question. Under Rule 25.13, security may be ordered in the case of a company not resident in a Brussels/Lugano Convention territory,

---

60   See I. MacNeil and A. Lau (2001) 50 ICLQ 787 for a lucid analysis.

61   For discussion of the position of foreign issuers in the US, see M.J. Lunt [2006] JBL 249.

62   See D. Milman in B. Rider (ed.), *The Realm of Company Law* (Kluwer) (1998) 167–81. For an up to-date review of the subject, see J. Ching (2009) 28 CJQ 89. A defendant who is raising substantial counterclaims may be treated as a claimant for these purposes – *Thistle Hotels Ltd v Orb Estates plc* [2004] 2 BCLC 174.

63   See *Jirehouse Capital v Beller* [2008] EWCA Civ 908, [2008] BPIR 1498 for analysis of CPR 25.13.

even if there are no questions about its ability to meet the costs of the proceedings. How has that jurisdiction been exercised?

In *Little Olympian Each-Ways Ltd (No. 2)*,[64] the position was that a Jersey company was treated as ordinarily resident overseas with the result that it became susceptible to a security for costs order. It is difficult to see how Lindsay J could have come to any other conclusion on the particular facts of this case.

Attitudes in this area are changing. Within the EU, it is not possible by virtue of Art 12 EEC to impose national[65] discriminatory requirements and indirectly this would cover discrimination based upon residence. Moreover, Art 14 of the European Convention on Human Rights, with its prohibition on discrimination, should also be noted in this context. In *Texuna International Ltd v Cain Energy plc*,[66] the court indicated that to order security for costs simply because the claimant was non-resident might well infringe the fundamental expectations embodied in Art 14. On the facts of this case, Gross J ordered security for costs to be paid; the company was incorporated in Hong Kong and although its directors were resident here, the evidence suggested that it had not paid tax in this country and so must be deemed to be non-resident. The additional expense in enforcing a costs order abroad was a relevant consideration when considering an order for security for costs.

At the end of the day, all factors need to be evaluated by the court before making an order for security for costs in such circumstances. Non-residence is a factor, but is no longer a major consideration in its own right.[67] The making of security for costs orders against foreign or non-resident companies as a knee-jerk response looks to be a thing of the past.[68] Companies litigation is thus evolving in this respect in reflection of a changing world.

7.2 Service of Proceedings on Foreign Companies

Where a party wishes to commence proceedings against a foreign company in English law, a range of preconditions must be satisfied. Firstly, there is the jurisdictional issue – is the foreign company amenable to the jurisdiction of

---

[64]   [1995] 1 WLR 560.
[65]   *Data Delecta v MSL Dynamics (C43/95)* [1996] ECR I-4661.
[66]   [2005] 1 BCLC 579.
[67]   *Thistle Hotels v Orb Estates plc* [2004] 2 BCLC 174.
[68]   See the discussion in *Nasser v United Bank of Kuwait* [2001] EWCA Civ 556, [2002] 1 WLR 1868. Noted in (2002) 51 ICLQ 463 at 469 by P. McEleavy and W. Kennett. Although this case does not involve a corporate claimant, the observations made by Mance LJ are most instructive.

the English courts? This to a large extent depends upon principles of private international law.[69]

Even if the jurisdictional hurdle is overcome, there is the question of service of proceedings. Under current rules, if the intended defendant has established a place of business for the purposes of the Companies Act, then proceedings can be served at that location.[70] What constitutes 'establishing a place of business' has occupied much judicial effort. There is clearly some requirement for a substantial link,[71] but it does not have to be a company's main place of business. The occupation of premises for business purposes would suffice,[72] but this is not an absolute prerequisite. Merely having an agent (as opposed to having employees) located in the jurisdiction would not be viewed as sufficient.[73] Equally, if there is a branch, that can be an appropriate venue for service.[74] In *Saab v Saudi American Bank*,[75] the Court of Appeal held that if there was a place of business suitable for service within the terms of s. 694A of the Companies Act 1985, the fact that the litigation did not exclusively relate to matters carried on at that branch was immaterial.

The above rules have their flaws. So, in *Rome v Punjab Bank (No. 2)*,[76] a company established a place of business and gave an address for service. It then ceased to have an established place of business, but the court held that proceedings could still be served against it at the nominated address.

These dedicated company law solutions must now be viewed alongside the Civil Procedure Rules, which complicate matters further. Under CPR, r. 6.5(6), proceedings can be served at a place of business. The difference between this more relaxed test and the stricter criterion applied by s. 695 of the Companies Act 1985 was noted by the Court of Appeal in *Lakah Group v al-Jazeera Satellite Channel*.[77]

Under s. 1139(2) of the Companies Act 2006, a general provision which applies to overseas companies, the position will be that valid service is

---

[69]   On amenability of the jurisdiction of the English courts, see P. Rogerson [2000] 3 CFILR 272.
[70]   CA 1985, s. 695 (established place of business) or s. 694A (branch).
[71]   *South India Shipping Corp v Export-Import Bank of Korea* [1985] 2 All ER 219. See L.S. Sealy (1985) 6 Co Law 231.
[72]   *Cleveland Museum of Art v Capricorn Art International SA* (1989) 5 BCC 860.
[73]   *Rakusens Ltd v Baser Ambalaj Plastik Sanayi Tiscaret AS* [2002] 1 BCLC 104. See also *Matchmet plc v Wm Blair & Co LLC* [2003] 2 BCLC 195, where Ferris J concluded that a Delaware company had no established place of business nor indeed any link to the jurisdiction.
[74]   CA 1985, s. 694A.
[75]   [2000] BCC 466.
[76]   [1989] 1 WLR 1211. For a critique, see A. Lidbetter [1990] JBL 137.
[77]   [2003] EWCA Civ 1781.

effected by leaving the documentation at either the address of the nominated person or at any place of business which the overseas company maintains. The problem of companies ceasing to be present in the jurisdiction is addressed by s. 1058 which, as we have seen earlier in this chapter, provides that the departing company must notify the registrar.

Essentially, once again we see in these cases the characteristic desire of the English courts to capture litigation, notwithstanding its clear foreign component.

8 OBLIGATIONS TO REGISTER COMPANY CHARGES: PROBLEMS WITH OVERSEAS ASPECTS

One area where real difficulties have arisen is in the area of company charge registration. This should not have been a problem, because a discrete statutory provision has been on the books for many years, having first been introduced via s. 43 of the Companies Act 1928 in response to the recommendations of the Greene Committee.[78] The established provision was s. 409 of the Companies Act 1985. For historical reasons, it is worth replicating here:

> (1) This Chapter extends to charges on property in England and Wales which are created, and to charges on property in England and Wales which is acquired, by a company (whether a company within the meaning of this Act or not) incorporated outside Great Britain which has an established place of business in England and Wales.
> (2) In relation to such a company, sections 406 and 407 apply with the substitution, for the reference to the company's registered office, of a reference to its principal place of business in England and Wales.

Unfortunately, that provision, which sought to render Chapter 1 of Part 12 in CA 1985 on registration of charges in England and Wales applicable to an overseas company context, created a host of interpretative problems. In order to grasp the potential impact of this provision, two points need to be borne in mind. Firstly, companies that create charges can, and frequently do, move their place of business between jurisdictions. Secondly, the charged assets themselves may be mobile; security over ships, aircraft and even vehicles springs to mind. In order to guarantee the effectiveness of a charge in English law, the requirements in the Companies Act on charge registration must be complied with.

---

[78]   1926, Cmd 2657.

The first inkling of the problems to come was encountered in *NV Slavenburg Bank v Intercontinental Natural Resources*.[79] The issue here was quite simple; did the obligation to register details of charges apply only to those overseas companies registered under Part XXIII or was it a general requirement for all foreign companies where charged assets may find their way into the jurisdiction? Lloyd J favoured the latter expansive interpretation, notwithstanding the fact that for some time the Companies Registry had been refusing to register details of charges submitted by foreign companies that had not complied with Part XXIII. The outcome of this fiasco was the bureaucratic response of setting up the so-called 'Slavenburg' register,[80] designed to capture details of charges that had been submitted to, but then rejected by, the Companies Registry. The Companies Act 1989, Part IV contained provisions (s. 105 and Sched 15) which would have had the effect of reversing this inconvenient ruling, that reversal having been recommended by the Diamond Committee,[81] but those provisions, along with the entirety of Part IV, were never implemented and finally given a decent burial by the Companies Act 2006 (s. 1180).

A different issue arose in *Re Oriel Ltd*.[82] Here the question was whether the obligation to register would arise where a foreign company (originally outside Part XXIII) subsequently established a place of business some time *after* the creation of the charge. The Court of Appeal answered this question in the negative – the critical issue was whether there was an established place of business in England when the charge was created. The court concluded that for some of the charges this criterion had been met, but not in other cases. The fact that a director was personally resident in England did not mean that the company had established a place of business here.[83]

The Company Law Review investigated the problems arising in this area of law and corporate practice. In a consultative document in October 2000 enti-

---

[79] [1980] 1 WLR 1076 – see A. Boyle (1980) 1 Co Law 214, D. Milman (1981) 125 SJ 294.

[80] For details of the Slavenburg register, see Companies House website at www.companieshouse.gov.uk. Note also *Arthur D Little Ltd v Ableco Finance LLC* [2002] 2 BCLC 799 – noted by I. Fletcher [2004] 17 Ins Intell 61.

[81] *A Review of Security Interests in Property* (1989). For discussion of the report of the Diamond Committee, see M. Lawson [1989] JBL 287.

[82] [1986] 1 WLR 180. See also *Re Alton Corporation* [1985] BCLC 27.

[83] This distinction, which has been made in other cases such as *Stojevic v Komercni Banka AS* [2007] BPIR 141, reflects the orthodox legal distinction between the identity of the company and that of its controller. Where a director is present in a jurisdiction to attend to a company's affairs, this does not mean that the centre of main interests is also located there.

tled 'The Registration of Company Charges', it called for a simplification of the law along the lines of a more logical approach.[84]

The position has, of course, moved on with the enactment of the Companies Act 2006. As far as s. 409 of the 1985 Act is concerned, it is not restated in the 2006 Act. The position seems to be that the Secretary of State is empowered by s. 1052 to make secondary rules in this context. One can only hope that these new rules will be clearer than their predecessors.

Under Part 3 of the Draft Overseas Companies (Company Contracts and Registration of Charges) Regulations 2009,[85] published in 2008, the obligation to register will only apply to those overseas companies that have been registered as having an establishment and which then create a charge. We have thus reverted to the position pre-*Slavenburg*[86] – registration will only be required if the chargor company is registered as an overseas company. The *Slavenburg* register will become redundant.

In the long term, there is the possibility of fundamental reform of the charge registration system coming from proposals of the Law Commission,[87] though the timescale for implementation here is unclear.

---

[84] See paras 3.63–3.68.

[85] SI 2009/Draft.

[86] Above note 71.

[87] *Company Security Interests*, Law Commission Report No. 296 (Cm 6654) (2005) – see G. McCormack (2005) 18 Sweet & Maxwell's Company Law Newsletter 1. For an insider's account of the thinking behind the Law Commission's strategy here, see H. Beale, chapter 3 in J. Lowry and L. Mistellis (eds), *Commercial Law: Perspectives and Practice* (2006) (Butterworths).

6. Cooperation with foreign courts and overseas regulators

1 EXTRATERRITORIALITY

It is somewhat ironic, bearing in mind the constructive theme of this chapter, but we must first address the concept of the aggressive extraterritorial application of national law. In a globalised economy, domestic courts will increasingly be called upon to deal with parties or assets located in foreign jurisdictions. A range of strategies has emerged to combat this problem. One controversial methodology is to apply directly English law beyond the shores of this jurisdiction – that is, in an 'extraterritorial' fashion. This is a vexed issue in international law generally.[1] The legal device of extraterritoriality is used extensively by the US courts, but only where sanctioned by Act of Congress.[2] A few examples will show the potential for usage of this strategy in English law.

The general principle is that provisions in the Companies Acts do not apply extraterritorially.[3] This reflects the general stance of English law.[4] So, for

---

[1]   For general discussion of the problems associated with extraterritoriality, see A.V. Lowe [1988] RabelsZ 163 and S. Dutson (1997) 60 MLR 668.

[2]   The RICO (Racketeer-Influenced and Corrupt Organisations) Act is perhaps the most celebrated example of an Act of Congress that is used extraterritorially. On the extraterritorial effect of the Sarbanes-Oxley Act 2001, see J. Friedland (2004) 25 Co Law 162. The US courts will not, however, adopt an extraterritorial stance where the legislature has not given a lead – see *Maxwell Communications Corp v Société Générale* [2000] BPIR 764.

[3]   *Ex parte Blain* (1879) 12 Ch D 522, *Re Vocalion (Foreign) Ltd* [1932] Ch 196 (which dealt with the statutory predecessor of s. 130(2) of the Insolvency Act 1986). See K. Dawson [2000] Ins Law 81. In *Mazur Media Ltd v Mazur Media GmbH* [2004] 1 WLR 2966, Lawrence Collins LJ held that the bar on proceedings imposed by s. 130(2) of the Insolvency Act 1986 could not be applied extraterritorially to stop overseas legal proceedings against a foreign company being wound up here. On the other hand, in *Holis Metal Industries v GMB* [2008] IRLR 187, the Employment Appeal Tribunal (HHJ Ansell sitting alone) has apparently held that the TUPE regulations dealing with protection of employee rights on a business transfer can apply where the business is transferred overseas – for a note on this case see (2008) 118 NLJ 42.

[4]   See *Clarke v Oceanic Contractors Inc* [1983] 2 AC 130 at 145 per Lord Scarman and *Serco Ltd v Lawson* [2006] UKHL 3.

instance, in *Mitchell v Carter*,[5] the Court of Appeal refused to accept an argument that the restrictions upon executions imposed by s. 183 of the Insolvency Act 1986 could operate in an extraterritorial fashion by frustrating garnishee proceedings in Florida.

But that aforementioned starting principle admits of exceptions. So, therefore, in *Re Paramount Airways Ltd (No. 2)*,[6] the administrators of an insolvent airline sought to exercise their statutory power to recover assets now located out of the jurisdiction (in Jersey), where those assets had allegedly been disposed of by the company at an undervalue. The court held that this particular statutory transactional avoidance provision, namely Insolvency Act 1986, s. 238, was capable of having such an extended compass. To hold otherwise would be to severely inhibit its utility by opening up safe havens for exploitation by asset strippers. As Jersey was a friendly jurisdiction, leave was given to serve the proceedings in that legal jurisdiction.[7] This case was followed in *Re Unigreg Ltd*,[8] where HHJ Weeks indicated that, in principle, where a director of a company had removed assets of the company by placing them in the hands of a foreign party, then an order could be made for recovery under s. 238 of the Insolvency Act 1986 against that foreign party, notwithstanding the fact that the foreign party in question was outwith the jurisdiction. The case of *Jyske Bank (Gibraltar) v Spjeldnaes (No. 2)*[9] provides yet another example of a statutory transactional avoidance power being accorded extraterritorial effect. The provision in question here was s. 423 of the Insolvency Act 1986, which allows the court to avoid transactions entered into by insolvents with a view to defeating creditors. Evans-Lombe J made such an avoidance order, even though it affected property located in Ireland. Critically, all of the parties were before the court and none of these had raised jurisdictional concerns. The order would operate *in personam* so far as parties before the English courts were concerned, but it would need the leave of the Irish courts in order to be effective in that jurisdiction.

Perhaps the most significant discussion of this issue is found in *Re Mid East Trading Ltd*.[10] Amongst the several issues to be determined here was whether

---

5 [1997] BCC 907. Having so decided, the court affirmed its inherent jurisdiction to prevent creditors from retaining the benefits of a foreign execution by granting what was in effect an anti-suit injunction, though such a power was to be exercised sparingly.

6 [1992] 3 WLR 690.

7 Compare *BNC v Cosmos Trading Corp* [2000] BCC 90 – refusal to make an s. 238 order because of the protective effect of state immunity.

8 [2005] BPIR 220.

9 [1999] 2 BCLC 101 – for comment, see K. Dawson in [2000] Ins Law 81 and (2000) 21 Co Law 132.

10 [1998] BCC 726.

the English courts, in exercising their jurisdiction to wind up an overseas company, could make an order under s. 236 of the Insolvency Act 1986 directing the delivery up of documents held in a foreign jurisdiction. Chadwick LJ, reading the composite judgment of the Court of Appeal, had no doubts:

> In our view there is force in the submission that, in so far as the making of an order under s. 236 of the Insolvency Act 1986 in respect of documents which are abroad does involve an assertion of sovereignty, then that is an assertion which the legislature must be taken to have intended the courts to make in an appropriate case.[11]

Having made that point, it was conceded that at the end of the day, the court must conduct a balancing exercise and will take account of the fact that compliance with the s. 236 order may expose a party abroad to criminal liability for breach of confidentiality in that foreign jurisdiction.

The use of extraterritoriality inevitably involves service of process out of the jurisdiction. The general rules are now found in Civil Procedure Rules (SI 1998/3132 as amended) (in particular CPR 6.21).[12] For insolvency cases in particular, it is Insolvency Rules 1986 (SI 1986/1925) r. 12.12 which determines the appropriate procedures and requires the leave of the court before insolvency proceedings can be served out of the jurisdiction.[13] There are limits to the ambit of Insolvency Rule 12.12. For instance, it only covers the service of 'proceedings'; not the serving of notice of creditors' meetings. This point was emphasised by David Richards J in *Re T & N Ltd*,[14] where it was held that the leave of the court was not required to give notice of a CVA creditors' meeting to foreign creditors and this conclusion will do much to reassure practitioners, who increasingly these days are faced with foreign creditors of English businesses. Any additional procedural burdens would be most unwelcome because of their attendant cost implications.

2   JUDICIAL COMITY

Asserting extraterritorial jurisdiction is hardly a diplomatic or constructive way forward in the modern world. Fortunately, for many years a principle of judicial comity between courts of different nations has emerged as an alternative way forward. Comity has many aspects to it. Clearly, there is an element of reciprocity involved; and therefore comity will only be extended to the

---

[11]   Ibid at 754.
[12]   See *Re Krug International (UK) Ltd* [2008] EWHC 2256 (Ch), [2008] BPIR 1512.
[13]   A. Walters, I.G. Williams and H.M. Marsh [2006] (19) Ins Intell 58.
[14]   [2006] EWHC 842 (Ch).

courts of those foreign jurisdictions that in turn extend their comity to the UK courts. The comity approach might result in the recognition of foreign entities, a process described in Chapter 5. It could more often feature practical cooperation between courts in particular cases. It might lead to a policy of non-intervention in foreign legal processes.[15] It could involve the enforcement of foreign judgments.[16]

One formal legal instrument used to access judicial comity is the letter of request.[17] This is a procedure whereby a foreign court at the behest of an applicant seeks the assistance of the English courts. In the specific area of insolvency law, s. 426 of the Insolvency Act 1986 provides an opportunity for the English courts to support requests for assistance from foreign courts based in specified jurisdictions.[18] This procedure has its origins in s. 122 of the Bankruptcy Act 1914.[19] The Cork Committee on Insolvency Law and Practice[20] recommended that this facility should be further developed. Essentially, the procedure under s. 426 involves a party applying to their local court in order to get that local court to request assistance in an insolvency matter. The assistance sought must be particularised. There is no direct right of application to the English courts; the existence of this local judicial filter is therefore significant. Another restriction imposed on the jurisdiction is that it is only available if the request is made from a court in a scheduled territory – various statutory instruments[21] have been made identifying these territories and they are essentially countries that were at some stage former British colonies. This makes practical sense, as the insolvency laws of such countries will often embody familiar basic legal principles. If the application is procedurally well founded, the English courts have a range of options at their

---

[15] See *Mitchell v Carter* [1997] BCC 907 at 913 per Millett LJ. Note *New Hampshire Insurance Co v Rush & Tompkins Group* [1998] 2 BCLC 471, where the English courts refused to wind up a foreign company that was already undergoing insolvency proceedings in the Netherlands. The creditors would be adequately protected under Dutch law.

[16] Under the Foreign Judgments (Reciprocal Enforcement) Act 1933 – for the relevance of this legislation in determining forum, see *Konamaneni v Rolls Royce Industrial Power (India) Ltd* [2002] 1 BCLC 336 at 370 [para 131].

[17] On the limitations of letters of request (or letters rogatory), see *Re International Power Industries NV* [1985] BCLC 128.

[18] The jurisdictions are specified by statutory instrument (see SI 1986/2123, SI 1996/253, SI 1998/2766) – essentially they are a selection of common law jurisdictions – see L.S. Sealy and D. Milman, *Annotated Guide to Insolvency Legislation* (11th edition, 2008) (Sweet & Maxwell) at 476 for the full list of jurisdictions falling within the ambit of s. 426.

[19] For discussion, see *Al Sabah v Grupo Torras* [2005] BPIR 544.

[20] Cmnd 8558, Chapter 49.

[21] See SI 1986/2123, SI 1996/253, SI 1998/2766.

disposal, which include applying English insolvency law (whether based in statute or common law) to the scenario.

A substantial body of case law on s. 426 has emerged over the past 20 years and that in turn has generated a considerable amount of published scholarship.[22] The leading case for many years was *Hughes v Hannover-Rucksversicherungs AG*,[23] where the Court of Appeal was at pains to stress that the English courts enjoy a discretion whether or not to offer assistance to the foreign requesting court. Assistance was refused in this instance because of a change in circumstances between the date of the issue of the letter of request and the final hearing in the English courts. This point was reinforced a decade later by the Court of Appeal in *Re HIH Casualty and General Insurance Co*,[24] where again assistance in the form of a request that English provisional liquidators hand over funds to Australian liquidators was refused. The reason for this apparent lack of comity on the part of the Court of Appeal lay in a curiosity in Australian law, whereby the pari passu rule of distribution was displaced for winding up of insurance companies, so as to enable policy-holders protective rights. The members of the English Court of Appeal felt that this could have a negative effect upon English creditors who were not policy-holders. This case then progressed on appeal to the House of Lords where their lordships, sub nomine *McGrath v Riddell*,[25] came to a very different conclusion. The judgment, which is a milestone in the law, is not easy to decipher because of a significant difference of opinion between Lords Hoffmann and Scott as to the relationship between the statutory power of the court to assist under s. 426 and the inherent jurisdiction of the court.[26] Nevertheless, the outcome is very much in favour of extending comity wherever possible.

Notwithstanding these cautionary tales, the utility of s. 426 was revealed in the early case of *Re Dallhold Pty Ltd.*[27] Here a company, which had been incorporated in Western Australia but which owned assets located in England, needed protection from its creditors. As English law stood then, it was not possible for a foreign company to exploit the administration order regime

---

22   See P. Smart (1996) 112 LQR 397, (1998) 114 LQR 46, I. Fletcher [1997] JBL 471, P. Omar [2003] Ins Law 74, W. Trower [2004] 17 Ins Intell 136.

23   [1997] BCC 921.

24   [2006] EWCA Civ 732. See also *Re Focus Insurance Co Ltd* [1996] BCC 659 for a similar refusal of comity.

25   [2008] UKHL 21, [2008] BCC 349.

26   See G. Moss [2008] 22 Ins Intell 145 and J. Bannister [2008] (232) SMCLN 1.

27   [1992] BCC 394. Compare *Re Maxwell Communications Corp (No. 3)* [1995] 1 BCLC 501, where Vinelott J refused to let a US attorney conduct an s. 236 interrogation. This case did not involve a request for assistance under s. 426 and turned rather upon the interpretation of s. 236.

because the relevant statutory provisions did not automatically apply to foreign companies. To get around this apparent obstacle, an application was made to the English courts to persuade them to apply the administration order facility to this situation. This request was successful before Chadwick J.

In *England v Smith (Re Southern Equities)*,[28] the assistance sought was designed to permit an Australian judge to sit in this country to take evidence from a party who might have useful information about the background to a corporate collapse. The Court of Appeal, stressing the need for comity, allowed the request for assistance. The fact that the English courts might not have permitted such an examination to take place was not decisive; the interviewee could be adequately protected by safeguards found in Australian law that did not exist in English law. To grant assistance would not be oppressive. A similar scenario arose in *Re Duke Group Ltd*,[29] where Jonathan Parker J acceded to a request from the liquidator of a South Australian company to enable an Australian judge to come to this country to interrogate an official of the company. These decisions very much indicate a pro-comity trend.

In *Re Television Trade Rentals Ltd*,[30] the s. 426 judicial assistance procedure was used to permit a company incorporated in the Isle of Man to enter into a company voluntary arrangement in this country. This conclusion was arrived at because the company effectively operated within this jurisdiction and the bulk of its creditors were located here.

It is apparent therefore that this comity jurisdiction has been embraced by the English courts, though not to the extent that they feel obliged to exercise it in every case where assistance is sought. Balanced decisions turning on the facts of each individual case have to be reached.

The English courts are not unique in their constructive approach towards judicial comity. Comparable examples can be found in many a jurisdiction. Indeed, the practice is so widespread that it is the cases where comity is refused that attract press attention. Witness the furore over the *Bear Stearns* case,[31] where Judge Burton Lifland in the US Bankruptcy Court (Southern District of New York) refused to make Chapter 15 US Bankruptcy Code assistance

---

28   [2000] 2 WLR 1141.
29   [2001] BCC 144.
30   [2002] BCC 807. See also the CVA case involving a BVI company in liquidation which is discussed by M. Rutstein in [1999] 12 Ins Intell 57. For a comparable case, see *Re Business City Express Ltd* [1997] BCC 826 where the assistance offered by Rattee J facilitated an Irish business rescue plan.
31   See J. Marshall [2007] (Winter) Recovery 9 and G. Moss [2007] 21 Ins Intell 157 for comment on this affair. See also S. Moore (2007) 23 IL & P 178 for further discussion. On Chapter 15 assistance generally, see *Re Loy* [2008] BPIR 111.

available to hedge funds[32] based in the Cayman Islands. The decision appears to turn on a lack of COMI. An appeal in this high profile case was heard by District Judge Sweet, who upheld the first instance ruling.[33]

3   PROTOCOLS

Another device that has evolved is the use of a judicial protocol or concordat between courts. An early example of its usage is found in the aftermath of the Maxwell Communications Corporation collapse.[34] Although welcome, such concordats smack of ad hoc solutions brought about by the lack of a more formal framework.

Advances in communications technology have opened up further avenues for collaboration. For example, video conferencing between courts located in different jurisdictions is now a real option. The courts will not, however, always embrace new technology if there are concerns that it will be detrimental to the administration of justice in English law. In *Re T & N Ltd*,[35] David Richards J refused to agree to a conference call arrangement with a US court in the context of resolving the affairs of companies which were undergoing Chapter 11 bankruptcy proceedings in the US and administration under English law. A protocol had already been agreed between the courts of the two jurisdictions, but David Richards J refused to comply with the request for a conference call because the matters which it was intended to discuss (determination of quantum of asbestos-related liabilities) were so controversial as to require careful handling. These contested issues were likely to be addressed in the English courts. Where a matter was so much in dispute between the parties, it would not be appropriate for a conference call to make binding rulings on the issue. The request to use this facility was viewed as premature. In commenting *ex cathedra* on this type of scenario, Mr Justice Lightman has gone on record as stating that telephone conferences with foreign courts are acceptable provided adequate safeguards are put in place. These safeguards

---

[32]   For the problems of regulating hedge funds, see J. Harris (2007) 28 Co Law 277 and H. McVea (2007) 27 Leg Studs 709. See also Chapter 9.

[33]   See G. Moss [2008] 22 Ins Intell 27 and [2008] 22 Ins Intell 118 for critique – 'Bitter Pill is Delivered by Judge Sweet'.

[34]   For discussion of the Maxwell concordat, see Glidewell LJ in *Barclays Bank v Homan* [1992] BCC 757 at 769. See also chapter 5 in J. Flood and E. Skordaki, *Insolvency Practitioners and Big Insolvencies* (1995) (ACCA Research Report No. 43). Mark Homan in [2002] 15 Ins Intell 60 at 62 points out the limitations of such concordats.

[35]   [2004] EWHC 2878 (Ch), [2005] BCC 982.

require all parties to participate in the telephone conference and for that conference to be transcribed.[36]

4 REGULATORY AUTHORITIES WORKING TOGETHER

Relying on the courts exclusively to enhance cooperation is not a panacea. In an era where corporations are regulated more and more by national legislatures, it is important that the regulatory authorities operating in different countries work together for their mutual benefit.

The significance of such constructive cooperation is best exemplified in the field of insider trading/market abuse. This is a good example to choose because the development of a bar on such behaviour is a prime illustration of a global response to what is now generally perceived to be an unacceptable practice in the securities markets. It is unacceptable because it is seen as damaging the reputation of particular markets. The market is thus seen as the victim and the argument that insider dealing is a victimless crime is thereby rebutted. Although the scope of English law and its criminal prohibition is territorial,[37] there are many indications of a recognition of the need for regulators to work together. The Council of Europe Convention on Insider Trading[38] provides an early manifestation of this spirit of cooperation. On a global level, the Airlie House Declaration[39] of September 1990 shows a willingness on the part of regulators in the US, Japan and UK to work together to protect their financial markets. More recently, the Insider Dealing Directive (1989/592) and its successor, the Market Abuse Directive (2006/3), have provisions promoting cooperation between Member State supervisory bodies. So, for example, in Art 16 of the Market Abuse Directive, we find a standard set of cooperation provisions based on the need to cooperate, but paying respect to national sovereignty.

---

[36]   [2005] (19) SMCLN 1. Sir Gavin Lightman's comments relate to an actual case where he engaged in a telephone conference with a US Bankruptcy Court judge – for background, see G. Moss [2003] 16 Ins Intell 47.

[37]   See Criminal Justice Act 1993, s. 62.

[38]   See J. Lowry [1990] JBL 460.

[39]   For this Declaration, which was signed in Virginia, see Hansard, HoC Debates, 31 October 1990, col 612.

Cooperation provisions are also found in the area of DTI investigations.[40] Where cross-border criminality is suspected, agreements on extradition may come to the fore. The Extradition Act 2003, s. 137(2) also facilitates extradition in such instances. The US and UK have such an extradition agreement, which was exploited recently in the extradition of the so-called 'Nat West Three'.[41] The Attorney General has issued Guidelines on the appropriate approach to extradition where an alleged offence might be tried either in the UK or in the USA. Needless to say, this is controversial territory, but such cooperation is surely the only way forward where commercial activities and business malpractices cross national borders.

5   RECOGNITION OF FOREIGN DISQUALIFICATIONS

We have asserted that the regulatory tool of disqualification of unfit directors plays an important part in UK company law, by offering protection to the public against future abuse of limited liability. We have also noted that there is no bar upon a foreign individual being registered as a director under English law. Foreign directors of foreign companies that are being wound up here may be the subject of English disqualification procedures.[42] But what of unfit/ undesirable foreign directors who might flit from jurisdiction to jurisdiction, exploiting the advantages offered by limited liability companies and wreaking havoc in the process? The law must address this scenario.

New provisions introduced in Part 40 of the Companies Act 2006 (ss. 1182–91) will enable recognition to be given to foreign director disqualifica-

---

40   Overseas companies operating in Great Britain are subject to DTI investigation – see CA 1985, s. 453. See CA 1989, ss. 82 et seq. for the cooperation provisions with regard to assisting overseas regulators. These appear unaffected by CA 2006. See also FSMA 2000, ss. 47, 169, 195.

41   See R. Burger (2007) 157 NLJ 354. This case, celebrated as the 'Nat West Three' (Bermingham, Darby and Mulgrew), was linked to the ENRON collapse. For the refusal of the English courts to block the extradition, see *R (Bermingham) v Director of the SFO* [2007] 1 WLR 362. Eventually the Nat West Three, having been extradited to the USA, entered a plea bargain in exchange for a reduced sentence. Details of 37-month sentences of imprisonment are to be found in the *Times*, 23 February 2008 at p. 55. For discussion of another case involving the Extradition Act 2003 against a businessman alleged to have been involved in anti-competitive practices, see A. Stanic (2007) 157 NLJ 396. As it happened, in this particular case the House of Lords later found good reasons for not allowing extradition without the clarification of certain issues – see *Norris v Government of the USA* [2008] UKHL 16, [2008] 2 WLR 673. On extradition in commercial matters generally, see C. Bamford (2007) 28 Co Law 97.

42   See *Re Eurostem Maritime Ltd* [1987] PCC 190.

tion and similar restriction orders (such as those used in Ireland). Such orders will prevent individuals who are subject to foreign disqualification from accepting directorships in companies in this country. Severe consequences will flow from a breach of such foreign disqualification orders. These adverse consequences might involve the commission of a criminal offence (s. 1186) or a director being made personally liable for business debts, as is made clear by s. 1187 of the 2006 Act. Mandatory disclosure of any foreign restrictions may also be imposed (ss. 1188–9) and such information can be made public (s. 1190). The full operational details are Part 40 are not fully spelled out in the Act; secondary legislation, which is not yet available, will be critical, as s. 1185 makes clear. What we do know is that this type of mechanism is in operation in other jurisdictions (for example in Ireland[43]).

---

[43] For discussion of of s. 42 of the Company Law Enforcement Act 2001, see A. O'Neill (2007) 18 ICCLR 166.

7. Corporate law and conflict of laws

We have already encountered a number of instances where corporate law comes into contact with the rules of private international law, a scenario commonly called 'conflicts of laws'. We now need to examine the relevant issues more closely.

1 ESSENTIAL PROPOSITIONS

Certain fundamental building blocks should first be established. So, for instance, it is well settled that a parent company is not to be treated as present in a jurisdiction merely because of the presence of a subsidiary.[1] This principle is of great significance when considering the prevalence of multinationals with subsidiaries scattered across the globe. Companies interacting with each other may identify a legal jurisdiction by which their relationship is to be determined; but such a choice of law provision cannot exclude a jurisdiction from determining rights under its own system of property law.[2] The lex situs is the dominant determinant here.

2 PLACE OF INCORPORATION V REAL SEAT

One fundamental problem encountered in this field is that there are two radically different traditions at work in the treatment of corporations in private international law.[3] Under the place of incorporation theory (which is favoured

---

[1] *Adams v Cape Industries* [1990] 1 Ch 433.

[2] *Re Weldtech Ltd* [1991] BCC 16 – but compare *Re Leyland DAF Ltd* [1994] 2 BCLC 106. See C.G.J. Morse [1993] JBL 168 for a general discussion of title retention and private international law. This article provides a helpful analysis of how the choice of law clause in a title retention arrangement has been analysed in the courts in Scotland.

[3] On this issue in general, see *Dicey, Morris and Collins on the Conflict of Laws* (14th edition, 2006) chapter 30, S.G. Rammeloo, *Corporations in Private International Law: A European Perspective* (2001) (OUP), J.J. Fawcett (1988) 37 ICLQ 645 and R.R. Drury [1998] 57 CLJ 165. Amongst the earlier literature worth consulting is the piece by T.C. Drucker in (1968) 17 ICLQ 28.

by most common law jurisdictions – for example, USA, UK, Canada, Australia, New Zealand, Japan (post-1945), Denmark, Finland, Ireland, the Netherlands, Switzerland, Norway and Sweden), the governing law of corporation is the law of the place of original incorporation/registration. This approach is simple but provides predictability, an essential quality for the conduct of modern commerce. The place of incorporation will determine the domicile of the company, which in turn determines its powers and status.[4] Residence of a company is a different matter: here the crucial criterion is the location of the central management.[5] A company may therefore be foreign but resident in the UK.[6] The dichotomy between place of incorporation and residence is very much the downside of this common law model.

A continental tradition, favoured in major jurisdictions such as France and Germany, argues that the governing law of a corporation is the law of the place where its 'real seat' of management is based.[7] This approach has the merit of realism and avoids the dichotomy noted above, but it does engender some uncertainty in terms of locating the place of the real seat. Indeed, it can lead to a situation where a corporation having its real seat in a jurisdiction which is not a place of incorporation might be treated as a nullity or a non-person for certain purposes.

These traditions in private international law predate the formation of the European Union. That latter regime has had a profound effect upon the relative status of these competing models.[8] If the real seat doctrine were to be transplanted into English law, it could have significant implications for UK company law. With our corporate law increasingly influenced by Europe, there may have been concerns that such a development was a distinct possibility. However, those concerns have been allayed by securing comfort from an unexpected source. In *Centros (Case C212/97)*,[9] two Danish entrepreneurs, being unable or unwilling to provide the minimum share capital needed to establish a company in Denmark (a substantial sum), decided instead to incorporate a private company in England. There was no intention to trade in England; the aim was to use the English company to set up a branch in Denmark, trading with the benefit of limited liability. The Danish authorities took a dim view of this opportunism and refused to register the branch.

---

  [4]   *First Russian Insurance Co v London and Lancashire Insurance Co Ltd* [1928] Ch 922, *Gasque v CIR* [1940] 2 KB 80.
  [5]   *De Beers Consolidated Mines* [1906] AC 455.
  [6]   See *Unit Construction Co v Bullock* [1960] AC 351.
  [7]   This is the *siège réel* or *sitzholie*. For French perspectives here, see H. Xanthaki (1996) 17 Co Law 28.
  [8]   Though this divergence of perspectives was one of the factors behind the failure of the European Convention on the Mutual Recognition of Companies 1968 to be adopted – see B. Goldman (1968–9) 6 CMLRev 104.
  [9]   [2000] Ch 446.

Litigation ensued and a reference was made to the European Court of Justice, seeking clarification as to whether freedom of establishment had been infringed. The Court of Justice, came down in favour of the interpretation favoured by the entrepreneurs. Where a company had been validly incorporated in one Member State, it had a right to establish branches in any other Member State. There was no evidence of fraud here and the argument put by the Danish authorities that the minimum share capital requirement offered an essential safeguard to creditors was treated with considerable scepticism by the European Court of Justice.

This development has thrown open many opportunities for UK corporate law. It is estimated that hundreds of EC firms have relocated here by incorporating under English law. It is estimated that some 20,000 German firms have used the *Centros*[10] loophole by incorporating as a private company under English law with the sole intention of trading with limited liability in Germany. There are plans afoot to reduce the minimum share capital of the GmbH from 25,000 to 10,000 euros.[11] In response to this migration of enterprises, France in 2003 reduced its minimum share capital requirement for its private company (SARL) to one euro! For dyed-in-the-wool share capital maintenance lawyers this is a race to the bottom with a vengeance!

Centros[12] has generated a huge amount of academic controversy.[13] Some continental corporate lawyers[14] see it as the beginning of the emergence of a 'Delaware syndrome' in the EU. Certainly, it has serious implications for the real seat tradition, because the tenor of the judgment suggests support for the place of incorporation model. That interpretation has been challenged,[15] but subsequent rulings from the European Court of Justice indicate that it is a reasonable analysis. *Centros*[16] has also been followed by the Supreme Court in Austria in *Graz*.[17]

---

[10]   Ibid.

[11]   See C. Jaehne and J. Henning (2007) 28 Co Law 34, J. Schmidt (2007) 18 ICCLR 306. Sweden is moving towards a reduction of its minimum share capital for private companies, but the new figure will still be comparatively high – see C. Svernlow and T.L. Dozet (2008) 19 ICCLR 379.

[12]   Ibid.

[13]   For articles on *Centros*, see, for example, T. Tridimas (1999) 48 ICLQ 708, P. Cabral and P. Cunha (2000) 25 ELR 157, V. Edwards [2000] CFILR 342, E. Micheler (2000) 21 Co Law 179, W.-H. Roth (2000) 37 CMLRev 147, H. Xanthaki (2001) 22 Co Law 2, J. Lowry [2004] CLJ 331, M. Gelter (2005) 5 JCLS 247, M. Andenas (2006) 27 Co Law 1.

[14]   On the Delaware syndrome generally, see the discussion in Chapter 1 and the references cited therein.

[15]   S. Rammeloo (op. cit. note 3) at 85.

[16]   [2000] Ch 446.

[17]   [2001] 1 CMLR 38 – discussed by I. Rappaport in [2000] JBL 628. This case

As indicated above, the European Court of Justice followed up with the ruling in *Uberseering (Case C208/00)*.[18] Here a Dutch company had its real seat in Germany. This company wished to pursue proceedings in Germany, but under the real seat theory it was treated as a nullity. This again was challenged under EU law by invoking the argument that the right to litigate to protect one's rights was an integral aspect of freedom of establishment. The Court of Justice agreed, thereby dealing a mortal wound to the real seat theory.

Another ECJ case worthy of scrutiny is *Inspire Art (C167/01)*.[19] The point at issue here concerned Dutch share capital curbs on the establishment of branches by English companies. The ECJ ruled that additional constraints not envisaged by the 11th Company Law Harmonisation Directive (89/666) were not permitted.

The latest case in this procession of consistent ECJ rulings is *Re SEVIC Systems AG (Case C411/03)*.[20] Here the European Court of Justice ruled that a German law that effectively placed barriers in the way of cross-border mergers involving German companies infringed the right of establishment. In paragraph [19] of its ruling, the Court made an important statement of principle:

> Cross-border merger operations, like other company transformation operations, respond to the needs for co-operation and consolidation between companies established in different member states. They constitute particular methods of exercise of the freedom of establishment, important for the proper functioning of the internal market, and are therefore amongst those economic activities in respect of which member states are required to comply with the freedom of establishment laid down by art 43 EC.[21]

The Court noted that this prohibition in German law was general in nature and lacked exceptions. The Court indicated that focused restrictions on cross-border mergers that were intended to protect shareholder interests or the integrity of revenue collection might be justified.

The pattern of these three rulings is thus consistent. The conclusion therefore that can be drawn from these rulings of the European Court of Justice is that the place of incorporation model stands firm both in English and EU law. Having said that, however, the real seat doctrine is not dead for all purposes.

---

is particularly interesting, in that the Austrian corporate law system applies the real seat concept.

  [18]   [2005] 1 WLR 315. See T. Bachner [2003] CLJ 47. For comment, see also D. Robertson (2003) 24 Co Law 184, E. Micheler (2003) 52 ICLQ 521, D. Griffiths and F. Tschentscher [2004] 17 Ins Intell 57.

  [19]   [2003] ECR I 10155 or 10195. See W.-H. Roth (2003) 52 ICLQ 177, J. Lowry [2004] CLJ 331.

  [20]   [2006] 2 BCLC 510. See M. Andenas (2006) 27 Co Law 1.

  [21]   Ibid, para [19].

Ironically, it is arguable that the 'centre of main interests' (or 'COMI') concept, which is used to determine jurisdiction for the purposes of the EC Regulation on Insolvency Proceedings (1346/2000), is an evolution of that basic idea.[22] Place of incorporation merely creates a presumption of COMI (see Art 3(1) of the EC Regulation) and, on the evidence of cases coming before the English courts, that presumption is frequently rebutted. Further discussion of this issue is to be found in Chapter 8.

3   GOVERNING LAW OF CORPORATIONS

English courts have in recent years been invited to assume jurisdiction in cases where a foreign law of corporations might appear to be more appropriate. In such instances, the English courts may have the right to decline jurisdiction by recourse to the notion of forum non conveniens.[23] A few illustrations of this manifestation may aid the discussion.

An aggrieved shareholder approached the English courts in *Re Harrods (Buenos Aires) Ltd*,[24] seeking either relief under CA 1985, s. 459 (the unfair prejudice remedy[25]) or a winding-up on the just and equitable ground (under s. 122(1)(g) of the Insolvency Act 1986). This solicitation was not inappropriate in this instance, as the company in question was incorporated in this country. However, the company had always been effectively controlled and managed in Argentina. Indeed, that was where all of the crucial documents (which were written in Spanish) were located. Taking an overview, the Court of Appeal held that Argentina would be the preferable location for the litigation and accordingly, the English proceedings were stayed on the basis of forum non conveniens. In so deciding, the court took the opportunity to examine the Argentinian law of shareholder protection and, having noted the differences with English protection, concluded that there was an equivalent level of protection available. There are questions as to whether this authority can stand today as authority for a general proposition, when set against the later ruling of the European Court of Justice in *Owusu v Jackson (C281/02)*.[26]

---

[22]   See P. Omar [2002] Ins Law 122 – 'Cross Border Allocation of Jurisdiction and the European Insolvency Regulation'.

[23]   On the doctrine generally, see *Spiliada Maritime Corp v Cansulex Ltd* [1987] AC 460. Note D.W Robertson (1987) 103 LQR 398. See also *Cleveland Museum of Art v Capricorn Art International* (1989) 5 BCC 860.

[24]   [1991] BCC 249. For comment, see A.J. Boyle [2000] 11 EBLR 130.

[25]   Now CA 2006, s. 994.

[26]   [2005] QB 801 at paras [37]–[46] – for analysis, see C. Hare [2006] JBL 157 and A. Briggs (2005) 121 LQR 535. The background issues are admirably reviewed by W. Kennett [1995] CLJ 552.

Although this case is not a ruling specifically on company law, it suggests that to deny a party access to the legal system of a Member State by invoking forum non conveniens where that party (as opposed to the defendant) was domiciled in the jurisdiction was to be seen as unacceptable.

The case of *Lubbe v Cape (No. 2)*[27] represents a significant milestone in the evolving picture. The case is interesting in that it ostensibly says little about corporate law and is more concerned with private international law. Its implications for corporate lawyers are profound. Here South African miners and their families wished to sue for wrongful exposure to asbestos. The most likely defendant was the South African subsidiary company that employed them. However, they decided to pursue the UK parent. The House of Lords ruled that the proceedings could be heard in London. In so deciding, they took into account the availability of litigation support in English law that would not be available if the proceedings took place in South Africa.

The issue before Lawrence Collins J in *Konamaneni v Rolls Royce Industrial Power (India) Ltd*[28] was whether a derivative claim brought by minority shareholders on behalf of an Indian company could be heard in this country or whether it should be tried in India. The judge noted that the procedural foundation for a derivative claim (CPR, r. 19.9[29]) was not limited to derivative claims with respect to English companies but adopted the position that in general shareholder rights should be determined by the place of incorporation. Although the exceptional situations where a shareholder could bring a derivative claim might be characterised as 'procedural' (and therefore governed by the lex fori), it would be wrong to ignore the fact that the basic rule relating to derivative claims was governed by the law of the place of incorporation. Here, even taking into account that point, the links with India were so overwhelming that the case should be tried there on the basis of forum non conveniens.

---

[27]   [2000] 1 WLR 1545. The issue of pursuing MNEs to the courts of their home jurisdiction is controversial. There have been particular problems in the US, particularly with regard to the Alien Tort Claims Act 1789 and more recently in regard to the Racketeer Influenced and Corrupt Organisations ('RICO') Act 2002 – see S. Joseph, *Corporations and Transnational Human Rights Litigation* (2004) (Hart).

[28]   [2002] 1 BCLC 336 – discussed by A.J. Boyle (2002) 23 Co Law 263. This decision was followed by Lewison J in *Reeves v Sprecher* [2007] EWHC 117 (Ch), [2007] 2 BCLC 614, where the judge held that the place of incorporation was the proper place for the determination of shareholder disputes. Investors who incorporate overseas can hardly complain if the English courts adopt this stance.

[29]   See now CPR, r. 19.9A etc.

> In my judgment the courts of the place of incorporation will almost invariably be the most appropriate forum for the resolution of the issues which relate to the existence of the right of shareholders to sue on behalf of the company. [para 128][30]

Lawrence Collins J weighed up a number of factors before coming to this conclusion. In particular, he noted the adequacy of the remedies available to the disgruntled shareholders under Indian Company Law.

In *Banco de Bilbao v Sancha*,[31] the Court of Appeal ruled that the place of incorporation determines matters of the interpretation of the articles of association and in particular issues concerned with the appointment of directors. The place of incorporation will also determine issues concerned with restrictions relating to share capital maintenance, unless there are rules of English law specifically addressing this matter.[32]

In *Base Metal Trading Ltd v Shamurin*,[33] the question was where to locate the governing law of directors' duties. The company here was incorporated in Guernsey, but carried on business in Russia. The Court of Appeal ruled that the law of Guernsey should be applied to determine what duties a director owed to this company. Arden LJ declared at [75]

> Companies are increasingly trading across national borders and moving their trading operations from country to country. They must not by so doing escape proper regulation or otherwise creditors and shareholders will suffer. The only system of law that can consistently and effectively regulate such multinational companies is the law of the place of incorporation. Accordingly, I would strongly disagree with any suggestion that the duties imposed on directors . . . by the law of the place of its incorporation should be regarded as irrelevant or 'mechanistic'.[34]

Arden LJ explained that the merit in this solution was the resulting certainty and the benefit for corporate governance generally.

In *Macmillan Inc v Bishopsgate Investment Trust (No. 3)*,[35] a question arose as to whether a dispute over title to a block of shares should be heard under English law or under the law of New York. The English Court of

---

[30]   [2002] 1 BCLC 336 at 370.

[31]   [1938] 2 KB 176. The company's powers are determined also by place of incorporation – *First Russian Insurance Co v London and Lancashire Insurance Co Ltd* [1928] Ch 922 at 935 per Romer J.

[32]   On this conundrum, see *Arab Bank v Mercantile Holdings* [1993] BCC 816.

[33]   [2005] 1 WLR 1157. See B. Jones [2005] 18 Ins Intell 29.

[34]   Ibid at [75]. Note also CA 2006, s. 259, which seems to confirm a similar approach.

[35]   [1996] 1 WLR 387. See J. Stevens (1996) 59 MLR 741 and J. Bird [1996] LMCLQ 57. See also *Re Harvard Securities* [1998] BCC 567, which is discussed by R. Stevens in [1999] CFILR 138 and by P. Eden in (2000) 16 IL & P 134 and 175.

Appeal favoured New York as the more appropriate forum because the shares were issued by a company incorporated in New York. That was also the appropriate lex situs here. Had the shares in question been viewed as negotiable instruments, a different conclusion might have ensued. Had the share registers been kept in England, that might also have been an influential factor.

4   CHOICE OF LAW AND CORPORATE DISPUTES

English corporate law can also be given a role to play in commercial disputes where the contracting parties include a choice of law clause[36] and that clause explicitly incorporates English law. Such clauses are common fare in commercial precedents and are generally enforced by the courts by means of an anti-suit injunction.[37] However, if the dispute properly falls outside the ambit of the clause, then the English courts will not restrain foreign litigation.[38] Conversely, a foreign bond issuer may by explicit provision seek to prevent disputes being litigated under English law, though the efficacy of such a ploy can be a matter of contention.[39]

Setting aside issues of insolvent companies,[40] the key European measure here for many years was the Brussels Convention,[41] which was implemented in English Law by the Civil Jurisdiction and Judgments Act 1982. This contained a number of provisions dealing with corporate issues. So for example Art 16.2 conferred exclusive jurisdiction on the law of the place of domicile where a dispute centred on the validity of a corporate constitution or a decision of a company's organs. Domicile was under Art 53 to be determined

---

[36]   See S.G. Rammeloo [1994] MJ of Euro and Comp Law 426.

[37]   See Look Chan Ho (2003) 52 ICLQ on anti-suit injunctions.

[38]   *AWB (Geneva) SA v North America Steamships Ltd* [2007] EWCA Civ 739.

[39]   See Jacob J in *Colt Telecom Group plc (No. 2)* [2002] EWHC 2815 (Ch), [2003] BPIR 324. Note also the comments of Peter Smith J in *Music Sales Ltd v Shapiro Bornstein & Co Inc* [2006] 1 BCLC 371, distinguishing the question of choice of applicable law from the issue of forum in which that law is to be applied. Note also *Re Leyland DAF Ltd* [1994] 2 BCLC 106, where receivers were bound by a choice of law clause entered into by the company prior to the receivership.

[40]   Insolvency proceedings fell outwith the scope of the Brussels Convention. However, insolvency proceedings were narrowly defined – see *Gourdain v Nadler (C133/78)* [1979] ECR 733. Having said that, winding-up proceedings featuring solvent companies could fall under the Brussels Convention – *Re Cover Europe Ltd* [2002] BPIR 1. Insolvency proceedings are now covered by the EC Regulation on Insolvency Proceedings (1346/2000) (as amended).

[41]   The Brussels Convention applied to EU states. The Lugano Convention operated a parallel system for EFTA states.

by place of seat, which in turn depended upon rules of private international law. Disputes as to public registers were under Art 16.3 to be resolved in the jurisdiction where the register was kept. Art 17 permitted the parties by contract to agree their own exclusive jurisdiction for the resolution of disputes.

Case law has added a gloss to this legislative regime. In *Sar Schotte Gmbh v Parfums Rothschild (C218/86)*,[42] the European Court of Justice ruled that a company was present in a jurisdiction, where it traded not through a branch but through an independent firm using the same name and a common management. In *Re Fagin's Bookshop Ltd*,[43] the case concerned the question whether an application by a company pursuant to what is now CA 2006, s. 125 (formerly CA 1985, s. 359) to change its register of members could be heard in England or whether under the Brussels Convention, it must be heard at the place where the shareholder affected was domiciled. Harman J opted for the former conclusion, on the grounds that as the register was open to public inspection and the proceedings were intended to test the accuracy of that register, the application fell within the exception envisaged in Art 16(3) of the Convention. In *Powell Duffryn plc v Petereit*,[44] the European Court of Justice confirmed that provisions in the constitution of a company determining the place of resolution of internal disputes constituted an agreement for the purposes of Art 17 of the Convention and therefore achieved their intended purpose.

The EC Judgments Regulation (44/2001) is now the significant measure here, in that it has superseded the Brussels Convention to all intents and purposes (see Art 68). Many of the principles embodied in the Brussels Convention and case law thereunder, however, remain apposite. Insolvency proceedings are specifically excluded from the ambit of this Regulation (Art 1.2(b)). Under Art 2.1 of this measure, domicile will normally determine jurisdiction, subject to a number of exceptions. One of these is prescribed by Art 22.2, which states that disputes which have as their object the validity of the constitution or the nullity or dissolution of companies or the validity of the decisions of their organs should be heard within the Member State in which the company has its seat (as determined by private international law). In *Speed Investments v Formula One Holdings (No. 2)*,[45] the Court of Appeal was faced with a dispute over the interpretation of a shareholders' agreement relating to the composition of the board of directors of a Jersey company. In particular, the dispute centred upon the appointment of two Swiss residents to the board. Although the Swiss courts had first been seized of the proceedings, it was felt

---

42 [1992] BCLC 235.
43 [1992] BCLC 118.
44 The *Times* 15 April 1992.
45 [2004] EWCA Civ 1512.

that under both the Lugano Convention 1988 and under Art 22.2 of the EC Judgments Regulation (44/2001), the proceedings should be heard in England because they related to a constitutional issue relating to a Jersey company, even though the agreement was stated to be subject to determination in the courts in Switzerland.

Other important provisions in the Judgments Regulation are: Art 5.5, which allows branches to be sued in the place where the branch is situated; Art 22.3, which deals with disputes involving the validity of public registers; Art 23, which retains the right of parties to make an agreement on exclusive jurisdiction; and Art 60, which in effect determines the domicile of a company by reference either to the real seat or place of incorporation.

5 APPLICATION OF THE TAKEOVER CODE

Jurisdictional issues can arise in the context of the regulation of takeovers, where there is a cross-border element involved. For instance, it used to be the case that the UK Takeover Code applied to takeovers effected on the Irish Stock Exchange in Dublin, but in 1997 the Irish developed their own statutory-based takeover code,[46] thereby removing this curious arrangement. Looking at takeovers from our domestic perspective, the critical criterion which governs the application of the UK Code generally today is the location of the real seat of management of the target company. If it is in the UK (no matter where the target company is incorporated), then the Code will apply.[47] The position is not changed by Part 28 of the Companies Act 2006 which gives statutory effect to the Takeover Code. Interestingly, Part 28 extends to the Channel Islands and the Isle of Man,[48] which again represents the continuance of the former position.

---

[46] For background, see B. Clarke, *Takeovers and Mergers Law in Ireland* (1999) (Round Hall Press) at 35 et seq.

[47] For enlightenment, see T. Ogowewo (2002) 23 Co Law 216.

[48] See CA 2006, s. 965 and SI 2008/3122.

8. Dealing with transnational corporate collapse

Transnational business failure is not a new phenomenon,[1] but it is much more common these days and the economic disruption caused and the legal problems generated can be immense. It is incumbent on any national system of corporate law to provide an effective working set of rules to manage such a crisis. Increasingly, it is seen as a necessity for the international corporate law community to contribute to providing effective working solutions.[2]

Recent examples of transnational collapses or comparable incidences of global/overseas firms' experiencing financial distress that have posed challenges for English law include BCCI (1991),[3] Maxwell Communications Corporation (1991),[4] Barings (1995),[5] Enron (2001),[6] Federal Mogul (2001)[7]

---

[1]   Historical examples of such cross-border insolvencies would include the Scali bankruptcy in 1326 – see D. Graham [2000] 13 Ins Intell 36.

[2]   For scholarly analysis of the problems associated with cross-border insolvency, see P. St J. Smart, *Cross-border Insolvency* (1992) (Butterworths), K.H. Nadelmann (1944) 93 Univ of Penn L Rev 58, P. St J. Smart [1999] Ins Law 12, P. Omar (2006) 22 IL & P 132. For an historial perspective, see D. Graham (2001) 10 Int Ins Rev 153.

[3]   BCCI was a bank whose activities spanned the globe. See N. Kochan and B. Whittington, *Bankrupt: The BCCI Fraud* (1991) (Victor Gollancz Ltd) for the essential details of this unprecedented financial scandal, which produced a huge volume of reported litigation. See also A. Arora [2006] JBL 487 for the regulatory lessons.

[4]   The *Maxwell Communications* case, which is a story of a massive fraud spanning several jurisdictions perpetrated by the late Robert Maxwell, is fully described in the 2001 DTI Inspectors Report on Mirror Group Newspapers, a Maxwell subsidiary. Again, a voluminous body of case law resulted.

[5]   On the circumstances leading to the demise of Barings, see S. Fay, *The Collapse of Barings* (1996) (Arrow Books). The watershed events, of course, occurred in Singapore as a result of the unauthorised trading activities of Nick Leeson, who was working for a Barings subsidiary. For Leeson's own interpretation, see *Rogue Trader* (1996) (Little Brown & Co).

[6]   For Enron, see J. Armour and J.A. McCahery, *After Enron* (2006) (Hart). Note also S. Griffin [2003] Ins Law 214. For the response to Enron, see P. Davies, chapter 8 in J. Lowry and L. Mistelis, *Commercial Law: Perspectives and Practice* (2006) (Butterworths).

[7]   The difficulties of Federal Mogul owe much to the crippling costs associated

130

and most recently, Lehman Bros (2008).[8] In each of these cases, many of the critical events leading to corporate failure arose outside the jurisdiction of English law, but the consequences for creditors and other stakeholders were felt acutely in this country. These are the most obvious examples in recent memory; other modern instances can be cited to complete the overall picture.[9]

1 COMMON LAW SOLUTIONS

Companies have operated across national borders since the dawn of corporate law. Companies have suffered financial collapse since those early days. Initially, it was left to common law to resolve the legal difficulties posed by collapse of transnational business. As might be expected, various pragmatic rules and principles emerged.

1.1 Principles

One fundamental rule favoured by the English courts is the principle of universality. This, in effect, states that the assets and liabilities of an insolvent company are all one, no matter where located in the world.[10] It also encompasses the idea that all creditors, no matter where located, should be treated equally, subject to accepted priorities determined by English law.[11] Debts

---

with asbestos liability. This led to the interminable T&N litigation, the burden of which has been shouldered by David Richards J.

8   The Lehman collapse is already generating litigation in the English courts – see, for example, *Re Lehman Bros International (Europe) Ltd* [2008] EWHC 2869 (Ch).

9   Barlow Clowes (1988) (an offshore investment scheme whose collapse led to an official inquiry) – see L. Lever, *The Barlow Clowes Affair* (1992) (Macmillan) for an intimate day-by-day account of the affair and the official Le Quesne Report, which was summarised by D. Milman in (1989) 10 Co Law 113; Polly Peck (1990) (whose high profile controller left these shores for Northern Cyprus); HIH Casualty and General Insurance (2001) (an Australian insurance company whose difficulties led to the setting up of a Royal Commission in Australia and have generated litigation before the English courts) – for background, see M. Murray [2002] Ins Law 223; WorldCom (2002) (a US Chapter 11 bankruptcy case).

10   See *Cambridge Gas Transport Corp v Official Committee of Unsecured Creditors of Navigator Holdings* [2006] UKPC 26 and the analysis offered by Sir Donald Nicholls VC in *Re Paramount Airways Ltd (No. 2)* [1992] 3 WLR 690 at 699–700.

11   On this, see the comments of Millett LJ in *Mitchell v Carter* [1997] BCC 907 at 912. Foreign creditors (for example, those claiming under a foreign judgment) are to be treated with respect – on this, see *Re Shruth Ltd* [2005] EWHC 1293 (Ch), [2007] BCC 960. Foreign governments have no special rights of preference – *Re Rafidain*

owed in a foreign currency are provable in an English liquidation.[12] English law does not accept the idea of a liquidation limited to national assets solely for the benefit of local creditors; rather it takes the view that a winding-up order granted by the English courts has universal effect. This is commendable in its simplicity, but is a legal approach which is not above criticism.[13] Having said that, English law does recognise the idea of an ancillary liquidation governed by English law, which is subordinate to the main winding-up.[14]

The 'hotchpot' rule[15] is a useful illustration of the common law at work. Under this principle of distributive justice, which was delineated by a number of 19th-century bankruptcy cases,[16] if a creditor of an insolvent debtor being liquidated under English law has received a dividend in respect of a foreign liquidation, then that dividend has to be surrendered before the foreign creditor can benefit from a dividend under English winding-up procedures.[17] Surrender of the foreign benefit is the price of admission to the English distribution and in some cases it may not be a rational decision to participate in the English distribution process. This rule, which may be rationalised by reference to the pari passu principle of distributive justice, was considered most recently by the Privy Council in *Cleaver v Delta Reinsurance*.[18] Whilst upholding the relevance of the rule in modern commerce, the Privy Council held that it did not apply to funds received by a creditor in a foreign liquidation where that realisation was the product of security rights, because secured creditors were not subject to the pari passu principle. The rule should not be extended simply because one creditor might be said to be behaving in an unfair fashion.

A different type of conflicts of law issue arose in *Wight v Eckhardt Marine*.[19] Here the question was whether a creditor could prove in a Cayman

---

Bank Ltd [1992] BCC 376. In *MG Rover Belux SA/NV* [2007] BCC 446, administrators were authorised to make payments to foreign creditors for the good of the administration, even though such payments were not strictly in accordance with English law.

[12]   *Re Dynamics Corp of America* [1976] 2 All ER 669.

[13]   See the comments of Scott VC in *Banco Nacional de Cuba v Cosmos Trading Corp* [2000] 1 BCLC 813 at 820.

[14]   See *Re BCCI (No. 10)* [1997] Ch 213, *English, Scottish and Australian Chartered Bank* [1893] 3 Ch 385 at 394 per Vaughan Williams J. For a strong statement to the effect that the English courts must apply English law in an ancillary liquidation, see *Re BCCI (No. 11)* [1997] 1 BCLC 80 – but this must now be viewed in the light of the range of views expressed by the Law Lords in *McGrath v Riddell* [2008] UKHL 21.

[15]   On the origins of the hotchpot rule, see the bankruptcy cases of *Selkrig v Davis* (1814) 2 Rose 291 and *Banco de Portugal v Waddell* (1880) 5 App Cas 161.

[16]   *Banco de Portugal v Waddell* (1880) 5 App Cas 161.

[17]   *Re Oriental Steam Co* (1874) LR 9 Ch App 557.

[18]   [2001] 2 WLR 1202.

[19]   [2003] UKPC 37 – see P. Smart and C. Booth (2004) IL & P 147, Look Chan Ho [2003] LMCLQ 95.

Islands liquidation in respect of a debt which had been extant at the time of entry into liquidation, but which had been discharged by a statutory recon-struction scheme in Bangladesh. The Privy Council advised that the pari passu rule did not require the liquidators to admit proof of such a claim.

Another common law rule concerns the treatment of foreign revenue authorities seeking to prove as creditors under English law. In spite of the general trend in English corporate law not to discriminate against foreign stakeholders, the traditional approach here is to deny this possibility of foreign revenue authorities proving as creditors. In *Government of India v Taylor*,[20] this discriminatory attitude was all too apparent. The thinking here is that foreign revenue laws are viewed as akin to penal laws and therefore do not fall within broad principles of comity. This House of Lords authority was followed (and extended) by the Court of Appeal in *QRS 1 Aps v Frandsen*,[21] where the disqualification on proof was applied to the indirect enforcement of foreign revenue laws. The point was noted that the Brussels Convention had not modi-fied the position at common law. The status of this rule today is changing. As far as revenue laws of EU Member States are concerned, it no longer applies, as Art 39 of the EC Regulation on Insolvency Proceedings (1346/2000) specif-ically displaces it. In the wider global community, the common law rule may still have been regarded as valid. However, with the UNCITRAL Model Law on Cross-border Insolvency being brought into effect in English law in April 2006 through the making of the Cross-border Insolvency Regulations[22] (SI 2006/1030), we may safely assume that this common law rule has now been superseded. Under Art 13 of the 2006 Regulations, foreign revenue debts are not automatically to be disqualified, but may be challenged if characterised as penal. The twin forces of globalisation and the need for greater judicial comity have rendered the unthinking discriminatory approach at common law inap-propriate in modern commercial conditions.

1.2   Attitudes – Common Law Assistance

The courts in the exercise of their inherent jurisdiction and armed with notions of comity have on occasions exercised discretion to facilitate the handling of cross-border insolvencies. What might comity involve? It could encompass

---

[20]   [1955] AC 491 – see K. Dawson [2000] Ins Law 81 and P. Fidler [2000] Ins Law 219. Note also *Re Norway's Application (Nos 1 and 2)* [1990] 1 AC 723 – see J.G. Miller [1991] JBL 144.

[21]   [1999] 1 WLR 2169. See P. St J. Smart (2000) 116 LQR 360. The Australian courts were less keen on the bar – *Ayres v Evans* (1981) 39 ALR 129.

[22]   SI 2006/1030.

the recognition of a foreign insolvency practitioner[23] or some other form of assistance to such a party. So, for example, in *Barclays Bank v Homan*,[24] English administrators of one of the Maxwell companies were in effect allowed by the Court of Appeal to forum shop in order to instigate transactional avoidance litigation in the most favourable jurisdiction for the creditors who stood to benefit if the claim succeeded. It is common knowledge that litigation commenced in the US is likely to attract premium compensation awards, but here the attraction was that the prospects of challenging a suspect transaction were enhanced because of differences in the substantive law. In refusing to grant an anti-suit injunction, Leggatt LJ commented:

> In the insolvency of MCC in which both assets and creditors are distributed worldwide, it cannot sensibly be suggested that any one forum is the natural forum, that is, the forum in which exclusively proceedings should be brought . . . The very fact that the foreign court constitutes a natural forum usually means that the institution of proceedings in it is not unconscionable[25]

Again, in *Re MG Rover Espana SA*,[26] His Honour Judge Norris allowed an appendix to be added to his judgment, ordering the administration of a company to explain to a foreign audience exactly what the administration process under English law involved. This was innovative, but a clear indication of the English courts recognising their responsibilities in a shrinking world of commerce. In *Re Daewoo*,[27] provisional liquidators were authorised by Lewison J to hand over funds collected in this country to Korean receivers. This was not a difficult decision to reach, because the English provisional liquidation had been initiated for that very purpose and the English creditors did not object.

However, to be set against these authorities is the basic principle that the powers of a liquidator do not automatically extend overseas.[28]

In *Cambridge Gas Transport Corp v Official Committee of Unsecured Creditors of Navigator Holdings*,[29] the Privy Council broke new ground in offering common law assistance in an insolvency matter. Here the question

---

23   For insolvency practitioner recognition in New Zealand, see *Turners and Growers Exporters Ltd v The Ship Cornelis Verolme* [1997] 2 NZLR 110.
24   [1992] BCC 757. For subsequent resulting litigation in the US courts, see *Maxwell Communications Corporation v Société Générale* [2000] BPIR 764. See A. Henshaw [1997] (July) Ins Law 5.
25   Ibid at 778.
26   [2006] BCC 599.
27   [2006] BPIR 415. See also *Re Collins & Aikman* [2006] EWHC 1343 (Ch).
28   *Hibernian Merchants* [1958] Ch 76, *Re BCCI* [1994] 1 WLR 708.
29   [2006] UKPC 26, [2006] BCC 962. For a critique, see Look Chan Ho (2006) 22 IL & P 217, G. Moss [2006] 19 Ins Intell 123, A. Walters (2007) 28 Co Law 73.

was whether the Manx courts could assist a Chapter 11 reorganisation in New York. In deciding that assistance was possible in this instance, Lord Hoffmann explained:

> The English common law has traditionally taken the view that fairness between creditors requires that, ideally, bankruptcy proceedings should have universal application. There should be a single bankruptcy in which all creditors are entitled and required to prove. (para [16])[30]

Of course, there is no obligation imposed on the courts to offer assistance at common law. Discretion is the order of the day, though there may be an obligation at common law to consider whether that discretion be exercised.[31] We have encountered this principle in the context of s. 426 of the Insolvency Act 1986. So, for instance, in *Schemmer v Property Resources Ltd*,[32] Goulding J refused to recognise the title of a US-appointed receiver over the assets of a company incorporated in the Bahamas, because the circumstances of the appointment were unusual and there was no evidence that the company had submitted to the jurisdiction of the US courts.

1.3 Common Law Remedies of Potential Use in Transnational Insolvency

A common law remedial device that has proved its worth in the context of insolvency is the asset-freezing order. Although not restricted to the insolvency scenario, the prevention of assets leaving the jurisdiction clearly has added utility in that traumatic context. Developed by the Court of Appeal in *Mareva*,[33] the mechanism is now contained in the Civil Procedure Rules.[34] It is possible to obtain orders freezing assets in this jurisdiction and also

---

[30]   [2006] BCC 962 at 967. *Cambridge Gas* (above) was followed by Registrar Jaques in *Re Phoenix Kapitaldienst GmbH* [2008] BPIR 1086.
[31]   This, arguably, may be one consequence of the views expressed by certain of the Law Lords in *McGrath v Riddell* [2008] UKHL 21.
[32]   [1974] 3 All ER 451. See also *Fournier v The Ship Margaret Z* [1997] 1 NZLR 629.
[33]   [1980] 1 All ER 213. It should be noted that the grant of such an injunction does not create a security interest – *Cretanor Maritime Co Ltd v Irish Marine Management Ltd* [1978] 1 WLR 966.
[34]   See CPR, r. 25.1(1)(f). In Ireland, under s. 55 of the Company Law Enforcement Act 2001, there is a dedicated provision facilitating the grant of Mareva-type injunctions against company directors who may be tempted to transfer assets out of the jurisdiction. This is an important facility if there is the chance of personal recovery actions being brought against company directors.

worldwide freezing orders.[35] As a matter of judicial comity, interlocutory injunctive relief can be granted to aid a foreign court exercising insolvency jurisdiction.[36]

2 LEGISLATIVE RESPONSES

Clearly, the common law had its limitations in dealing with all of the ramifications of cross-border insolvencies. For example, there is no power at common law to wind up a foreign company; this is a wholly statutory jurisdiction. As was mentioned in Chapter 5, Parliament intervened and such explicit power now exists in the form of s. 221 of the Insolvency Act 1986, which permits the winding-up of unregistered companies. This statutory jurisdiction specifically states (see s. 225) that it can be used, notwithstanding the fact that the foreign company may have been dissolved in its home jurisdiction.[37] Where the jurisdiction is invoked, the winding-up will be carried out according to the requirements of English law.[38] Let us examine how this jurisdiction has been exercised by the English courts. There is a respectable corpus of case law to note.[39]

The original view, as exemplified by Lord Evershed MR in *Banque de Marchands de Moscou Koupetchesky v Kindersley*,[40] was that this jurisdiction could only be exercised if the foreign company had assets in the jurisdiction. There was a presumption that the English courts would not interfere in the administration of a winding-up properly afoot abroad.

In *Re Compania Merabello San Nicholas S*,[41] the court moved towards the modern position. Megarry J indicated that six factors needed to be taken into account. Although there is some repetition involved in this exposition, those factors included a recognition of the fact that there was no need to establish

---

[35]   See *Derby & Co v Weldon* [1990] Ch 48. For recent guidelines on worldwide injunctions, see *Dadourian Group International Inc v Simms* [2006] EWCA Civ 399.

[36]   Discussed by T. Rutherford (2006) 156 NLJ 837, F. Meisel (2007) 26 CJQ 176, K. Qureshi and T. Sprange (2007) 157 NLJ 1958. On anti-suit injunctions in an insolvency context, see Look Chan Ho (2003) 52 ICLQ 697. See also the comments of Hoffmann J in *Banque Indosuez v Ferromet Resources* [1993] BCLC 112 at 117–18.

[37]   On this possibility, see *Re Russian Bank for Foreign Trade* [1933] 1 Ch 745 and *Russian and English Bank v Baring Bros* [1936] AC 405.

[38]   *Re Suidair International Airways* [1951] 1 Ch 165.

[39]   See *Re Normandy Marketing Ltd* [1993] BCC 879, where this jurisdiction was used to wind up a company incorporated in Northern Ireland. See generally, I.J. Dawson [1995] (October) Ins Law 3. For a review of a comparable jurisdiction in Australia, see P. Omar [1999] Ins Law 69.

[40]   [1951] Ch 112.

[41]   [1972] 3 All ER 448. See also *Eloc* [1981] 3 WLR 176, where a Dutch company was wound up here in order to trigger a strategic advantage for employees.

that the foreign company had ever carried on business here and that there was no need to show the presence of hard assets. What did need to be shown was the reasonable possibility of a benefit accruing to creditors if a winding-up was ordered.

The leading modern case is the Court of Appeal ruling in *Stocznia v Latreefers*,[42] where the Court of Appeal indicated three prerequisites that must be satisfied before the winding up jurisdiction could be exercised against a foreign company – a sufficient link to the English jurisdiction, potential benefit to creditors and the creditors should be subject to the English jurisdiction. A potential benefit to creditors might exist where a liquidator could bring a recovery action against directors or seek the setting aside of a transaction.

Conversely, in *Re Real Estate Development Co*,[43] jurisdiction was declined by Knox J, because the connection with the English jurisdiction was deemed insufficient. Here there was an allegation that assets had been transferred into this country under a transaction that was voidable under French law.

With the advent of the EC Regulation on Insolvency Proceedings (1346/2000), these rules allocating insolvency jurisdiction require a rethink. The ability of the English courts to wind up a foreign company having its COMI in another participating Member State[44] will be limited to territorial or secondary proceedings (Arts 3(2) and 3(3)). Winding up of foreign companies where there is no COMI located within a participating Member State remains unaffected. The above principles therefore still have value.

Another statutory provision worthy of a footnote is s. 72 of the Insolvency Act 1986, which permits a receiver appointed under Scottish law to exercise powers of realisation of a floating charge in England and vice versa. There is, however, little evidence of this provision (which ultimately can trace its origins back to s. 7 of the Administration of Justice Act 1977 and then s. 724 of the Companies Act 1985) being engaged in practice.[45]

Section 426 of the Insolvency Act 1986 is the most apparent manifestation of the need to have legislative mechanisms to enhance judicial comity. This has been considered above in Chapter 6 and requires no further comment.

---

[42]   [2001] 2 BCLC 116. See K. Dawson [2000] Ins Law 173 and [2005] JBL 28.

[43]   [1991] BCLC 210. For further discussion, see *Jubilee International Inc v Farlin Timber Pte Ltd* [2005] EWHC 765 (Ch), [2005] BPIR 765. Jurisdiction was also refused by Clarke J in *Re OJSC ANK Yugraneft* [2008] EWHC 2614 (Ch), partly because the court felt that the petitioners had not made full disclosure

[44]   Denmark has opted out of the Insolvency Proceedings Regulation – for discussion of the implications, see *Re Arena Corp* [2004] BPIR 375 (Lawrence Collins J) and [2004] BPIR 415 (CA), which involved analysis of whether an Isle of Man company with its COMI in Denmark could be subject to the English winding-up jurisdiction.

[45]   For a rare example of the usage of s. 72, see *Norfolk House v Repsol Petroleum* [1992] SLT 235.

There are provisions in the Enterprise Act 2002 that take matters further. For example, under s. 254 the Secretary of State for Trade and Industry is empowered to make regulations to extend insolvency legislation to companies incorporated outside Great Britain. This power has not yet been exercised.

3   MULTILATERAL APPROACHES

3.1   EC Level

As we have stated above, the EC Regulation on Insolvency Proceedings (ECRIP) (1346/2000)[46] has had a major impact since taking effect in English law on 31 May 2002.[47] From the viewpoint of UK corporate law, the impact has been wholly beneficial.

The EC Regulation is all about identifying jurisdiction in cases involving collective insolvency proceedings.[48] Central to this methodology is the idea that primary jurisdiction to deal with a corporate collapse is to be determined by identifying where the 'centre of main interests' (or COMI) lies. The centre of main interests is the place where the company is effectively managed from. In effect, it is a concept equivalent to the 'real seat' doctrine of private international law. We have already seen that this doctrine is not part of the English law tradition and increasingly it is being marginalised in European law. It is therefore ironic that its near relative, COMI, is playing such a prominent role across Europe. Indeed, once again, UK corporate law appears to be a beneficiary. English law has captured foreign liquidations through the COMI concept, though there are clear signs of an increased sensitivity to the legitimate expectations of foreign creditors.[49]

In order to determine the COMI of a company, the presumption is that the place of its registered office is the key determinant (Art 3(1)). However, that

---

[46]   As amended by EC Regulations 603/2005, 694/2006 and 1791/2006. For background, see H. Rajak [2000] CFILR 180, P. Omar [2000] Ins Law 211, K. Gaines [2001] Ins Law 201, K. Dawson [2003] Ins Law 226, C. Campbell and Y. Sakkas (2003) 19 IL & P 48. The Regulation has flaws, only some of which have been addressed by the amending Regulations – see G. Moss and C. Paulus [2006] 19 Ins Intell 1, P. Omar [2007] 20 (1) Ins Intell 7.

[47]   ECRIP does not apply if the insolvency proceedings were commenced before 31 May 2002 – see *Oakley v Ultra Vehicle Design Ltd* [2006] BPIR 115.

[48]   The regulation does not apply to public interest winding-up cases as the company in question may be solvent – *Re Marann Brooks CSV Ltd* [2003] BCC 239. Such cases are also outwith the Brussels Convention because they involve the exercise of a public power – *Re Senator Hanseatische* [1996] 2 BCLC 562.

[49]   See, for example, *Re MG Rover Belux SA/NV* [2007] BCC 446.

presumption can be, and frequently is, rebutted, as we shall see illustrated below.

Re BRAC Rent-a-Car International Inc,[50] a company incorporated in Delaware was placed in administration in this country, because its COMI was located here. This was the first reported case on ECRIP in English law and in his judgment, Lloyd J set the tone for future developments. Similarly, in *Re Ci4net.com Inc*,[51] the existence of COMI within the English jurisdiction enabled the English court to place a Jersey company in administration and a Delaware company into liquidation.

In *Re Enron Directo SA*,[52] it was held that a company which had been incorporated in Spain (where it also traded) in fact had its COMI in England and so could be placed in administration here. Similar conclusions were arrived at in *Re Sendo Ltd*[53] (in respect of a Cayman Islands company), *Re Parkside Flexibles SA*[54] (which involved a Polish company) and *Re 3 Tel Ltd*[55] (where the company had been incorporated in Northern Ireland). This impressive stream of authority shows how frequently the presumption that COMI is located at the place of incorporation can be rebutted.

The *Daisytek-ISA Ltd* case[56] well illustrates the modern position. Here we were dealing with a large business group ultimately controlled from the USA, but having an intermediate parent company based in Bradford, which ran its European operations. The Bradford parent company controlled the finance and marketing activities of various European subsidiaries located in France and Germany. Judge McGonigle (sitting as a Deputy Judge of the High Court) concluded that all of these European subsidiaries had their COMI in England and so could be placed in administration here. This conclusion met with initial opposition from first instance courts in both France and Germany who objected to loss of control of insolvency proceedings featuring 'their' companies. However, on appeals, both the French[57] and German appellate courts

---

50   [2003] BCC 248. There is a marked similarity between the factors relevant for COMI and those used under conflict of laws to determine presence in the jurisdiction – see *Adams v Cape Industries* [1990] BCLC 479 at 506–7 per Slade LJ.

51   [2005] BCC 277.

52   Unreported, Lightman J, 4 July 2002 – but see the note of this case in [2002] 15 Ins Intell 64.

53   [2006] 1 BCLC 396.

54   [2006] BCC 589.

55   [2006] 2 BCLC 137.

56   [2003] BCC 984. The group implications of this case are evaluated by I. Mevorach [2006] JBL 468. See also *Energotech SARL* [2007] BCC 123 – French courts finding that COMI of Polish company was in France. Key factors underpinning this decision were location of board meetings, governing law of contracts, situs of creditors and place where commercial policy was determined.

57   *Klempka v ISA Daisytek SA* [2003] BCC 984.

adopted a communitaire perspective and concluded that COMI was indeed located in England. By way of comparison, in *Hans Brochier Holdings Ltd v Exner*,[58] the initiation of administration proceedings in England was held by Warren J to be misguided. Although the company had been incorporated here, its business operations had been controlled from Germany, most of its employees were based there and the major contractual relationships were governed by German law. Main proceedings in Germany was the only sensible outcome. This case provides a welcome reminder that the COMI concept can be a double-edged sword for those practitioners concerned with 'capturing' insolvency litigation.

In *Re TXU German Finance*,[59] Chief Registrar Baister held that the EC Regulation permitted the English courts to confirm the validity of a foreign company being placed into creditors' voluntary liquidation in this country. This, in many quarters, represented an unexpected extension of the English winding-up jurisdiction, which previously was believed to be limited to compulsory liquidation.

If COMI exists, it seems that the fact that it took root in this country late in the day is no bar to the exercise of insolvency jurisdiction.[60]

Where there is no COMI but the existence of an establishment can be proved, secondary proceedings may be a possibility.[61] However, the presence of the establishment cannot be taken for granted merely because the company has premises[62] or a registered office within the jurisdiction. This point was emphasised in the High Court by Warren J in *Hans Brochier Holdings Ltd v Exner*,[63] where attempts to establish first COMI and then jurisdiction to open territorial proceedings failed; the COMI of this English company was in Germany and there was no establishment to justify the opening of territorial proceedings. This case is interesting in that it may deter the large numbers of distressed German companies seeking to move their COMI to the UK at the 11th hour to exploit our more flexible restructuring models (particularly the CVA).

Cases involving the impact of the EC Regulation in other Member States[64] have progressed to the European Court of Justice. The most significant of

---

58   [2007] BCC 127. For background, see S. Moore [2009] 22 Ins Intell 9.

59   [2005] BCC 90.

60   *Re Collins and Aikman* [2006] BCC 606. But see *Staubitz-Schreiber (C1/04)* [2006] BCC 639, where COMI is moved after commencement of insolvency proceedings, but before the court opens proceedings.

61   *Telia AB v Hilcourt (Docklands) Ltd* [2003] BCC 856.

62   Ibid.

63   [2007] BCC 127 – noted by R. Rose in (2006) 22 IL & P 225.

64   Information on how the Regulation has fared in the national courts of other member states can be obtained from the website – www.eir-database.com.

these is *Eurofood IFSC Ltd (C341/04)*,[65] which involved a jurisdiction contest between Ireland and Italy in the aftermath of the Parmalat collapse. Here the Irish courts permitted a company (an Irish Parmalat subsidiary) to be placed into provisional liquidation under Irish law, notwithstanding the fact that it was already undergoing special administration under Italian law. The Italian administrator objected to this exercise of jurisdiction by the Irish courts, but the European Court of Justice ruled that the COMI of this subsidiary was indeed in Ireland. The existence of a large degree of control by the Italian parent did not rebut the presumption that the place of incorporation determined the matter. A crucial fact was that creditors viewed this company as an Irish concern. More generally, the ECJ ruled that the courts of one Member State could not review the opening of main insolvency proceedings in another Member State, unless the case fell within Art 26 (that is, where there were public policy grounds).[66] This conclusion will promote certainty and improve the working of ECRIP.

One consequence of this Regulation is, as we have seen above, that the common law principle of discrimination against foreign revenue authorities is no longer permitted, as Art 39 implies.

Where the Regulation is engaged, there are mechanisms set in place for the compulsory cooperation between insolvency practitioners operating within different Member States.[67]

A side issue that is of interest to our broader study is the fact that the doctrine of COMI looks suspiciously like the concept of 'real seat', which was discussed above. Those companies that have incorporated in England but intend to operate in other Member States may therefore find that insolvency proceedings will be governed by the law of the host state and not by English law.

One significant practical problem with the Regulation is that there is no central registry within the EU indicating the opening of proceedings in any particular Member State. This seems an alarming omission and may well lead to the opening of main proceedings in one Member State in ignorance of the fact that such proceedings have already been initiated in another Member State.[68] This systemic flaw is already manifesting itself.

---

[65] [2006] BCC 397. See G. Moss [2006] 19 Ins Intell 97, J. Armour [2006] CLJ 505 and C. Rapinet [2006] (10) SMCLN 1 for comment.
[66] See ibid at para 67 for discussion of the public policy angle.
[67] See ECRIP Art 31.
[68] There are instances where this systemic fault is already creating problems – see *Stojevic v Komercni Banka AS* [2007] BPIR 141, where this led to recriminations between the national courts in England and Austria, partly due to a fundamental misunderstanding of the role of the English courts in processing insolvency petitions. For general discussion of the problems, see G. Flannery (2005) 21 IL & P 57.

The EC Regulation on Insolvency Proceedings is not the only measure relevant to cross-border insolvency. Mention should also be made of the rules relating to the operation of state guarantee funds, where an employing company becomes insolvent, leaving arrears of wages due to its employees unpaid. In such instances, the state is obliged to guarantee that the arrears will be met. These protective measures, which were contained in EC Directive 1980/987 (as amended by Directives 1987/164 and 2002/74), have been consolidated in Directive 2008/94. They are implemented in English law via the Employment Rights Act 1996, s. 182.[69] In *Regeling (C125/97)*,[70] the ECJ set its face against national laws intended to undermine these guarantees. One difficult issue that can arise here is to determine which state guarantee fund should bear the cost, where the insolvent business was operating across national boundaries. The case law here is instructive.

The position in *Danmarks (C117/96)*[71] was that an English company had one employee based in Denmark. It had no substantial presence in that jurisdiction and was undergoing solvency proceedings under English law. Bearing in mind that combination of factors, it was hardly surprising that the European Court of Justice ruled that the UK state guarantee fund should meet the commitments to the employee in question. Again, in *Everson v Secretary of State for Trade and Industry (C198/98)*,[72] the case involved the employment commitments of an English branch of a foreign company. The ECJ ruled that the claim for arrears which was made by a number of employees should be made against the UK Redundancy Fund and not against the comparable institution where the company was incorporated. The link with the English jurisdiction here was substantial.

In response to this burgeoning case law, the Directive was amended by EC Directive 2002/74. Art 8a of the amended Directive states that, where an undertaking has activities in more than one Member State, the state guarantee fund of the state in which they habitually work is responsible for arrears of wages on the insolvency of the undertaking.

Further consideration to the state guarantee system in the cross-border context in the light of Art 8a was given by the ECJ in *Svenska Staten v Anders*

---

[69]   It must be remembered that the state liability principle in EC Law emerged from the non-transposition of this Directive – *Francovich v Italy (C6 and 9/90)* [1991] ECR I-5537. Similar state guarantee funds designed to protect employees in the event of employer insolvency operate outside the EU – for the position in Australia, see A. Keay [2000] Ins Law 137.

[70]   [1999] 1 CMLR 1410. See also the view expressed in *Wagner Miret (C334/92)* [1995] 2 CMLR 49 that higher management staff can enjoy the protection of the state guarantee fund.

[71]   [1998] 2 BCLC 395.

[72]   [2000] 1 CMLR 489.

Holmqvist (Case C310/07).[73] The point at issue here was whether an employee of a Swedish transport company, which was carrying out operations in other Member States without establishing a branch or establishment in such states, could claim against the Swedish guarantee fund. The Court ruled that, although a branch or establishment was not required, there must be evidence of a stable economic presence featuring human resources which enable it to perform its activities there. In the case of a transport company delivering to businesses in other Member States, that criterion would not normally be met, so the home guarantee fund should remain responsible. As Art 8a is replicated by Art 9 of the consolidated EC Directive 2008/94, this preliminary ruling should remain valuable for the foreseeable future.

3.2   International Level

The importance of providing effective legal rules to minimise national conflicts where a transnational corporation collapses was quickly recognised by UNCITRAL (a UN-sponsored body set up in 1966). In 1997, UNCITRAL promulgated its Model Law on Cross-border Insolvency.[74] The Model Law has been widely adopted – by Ethiopia, Mexico, Serbia, Montenegro, South Africa, New Zealand[75] and most recently the USA.[76] Australia is in the process of adopting this Model Law.[77] This law was adopted by the UK with effect from 2007 (power to adopt was allocated to the Secretary of State for Trade and Industry by the Insolvency Act 2000, s. 14). This power was exercised in 2006 through the Cross-border Insolvency Regulations.[78] These

---

73   Unreported

74   For analysis, see I. Fletcher [2000] 13 Ins Intell 57, P. Omar [2000] Ins Law 211, K. Dawson [2000] 4 RALQ 147, P. Omar [2002] Ins Law 228. The Model Law is reproduced in Volume 2 of Sealy and Milman, *Annotated Guide to Insolvency Legislation* (11th edition, 2008). See also Look Chan Ho (ed.), *Cross Border Insolvency* (2006) (Globe Law and Business), which offers an excellent multi-jurisdictional study by expert authors.

75   See Insolvency (Cross-border) Act 2006 – for comment, see D. Brown and T.G.W. Telfer, *Personal and Corporate Insolvency Legislation* (2007) (LexisNexis) at 105 et seq.

76   The US have adopted the Model Law by introducing via the Bankruptcy Abuse Prevention and Consumer Protection Act 2005 a new Chapter 15 into their US Bankruptcy Code to replace the widely used mechanism in s. 304 of the Code – for explanation, see J. Tovrov (2006) 22 IL & P 17, T. Zink and F. Vazquez [2007] 20 Ins Intell 17. For discussion of Chapter 15 in the US bankruptcy courts, see *Re Loy* [2008] BPIR 111.

77   See D. Emmett (2005) 21 IL & P 199.

78   SI 2006/1030. See I. Fletcher [2006] 19 Ins Intell 86, L.S. Sealy [2006] 7 SMCLN 1, L. Verrill (2006) 22 IL & P 155.

Regulations adopt the Model Law (which is reproduced in Schedule 1), subject to minor modifications. The Regulations do not apply to Northern Ireland, for which separate provision was made by the Cross-border Insolvency Regulations (Northern Ireland) 2007 (SR 2007/115), which implemented the Model Law in the Province with effect from 12 April 2007.

The Model Law and implementing Regulations work in much the same way as the EC Regulation by determining jurisdiction. The device of using the concept of centre of main interests to determine primary jurisdiction is also employed for these purposes (see Art 2(b)). Place of incorporation creates only a rebuttable presumption of COMI (art 16(3)). Although foreign revenue claims may be proved in a liquidation, Art 13(3) of the adopted Model Law reserves the right to refuse proof where the claim may be viewed as a penalty.

Disputes as to the applicability of the Regulations will be determined by the English courts.[79] Unlike the procedures under s. 426 of the Insolvency Act 1986, there is a direct right of access to the English courts and no filtering out of applications by foreign courts.

These Cross-border Insolvency Regulations and the Model Law should help, but problems remain. As the Model Law is not formally regarded as a treaty, states can cherry pick when implementing it. Practitioners need to be cautious about making assumptions – recourse to national implementing measures will therefore be required.

---

[79]   Cases are beginning to surface – see *Re Rajapakse (Note)* [2007] BPIR 99 – discussed by N. Griffiths in (2007) 23 IL & P 6. For later proceedings in this personal insolvency case, see *C. Brooks Thurmond III v Rajapakse* [2008] BPIR 283.

9 The future of national corporate law systems

1 CONVERGENCE

Any astute observer of the development of company law across the globe could not fail to pick up on the fact that national systems of corporate law are *converging*.[1] In chapter 9 of *The Anatomy of Corporate Law*, Paul Davies, Gerard Hertig and Klaus Hopt assert:

> Our analysis clearly establishes that corporate law has converged significantly across our benchmark jurisdictions over the past two decades. Jurisdictions are under pressure to adopt uniform 'best practices' to facilitate the cross border tapping of investors by their publicly-traded companies. In addition, national lawmakers have come to realise that a modernised framework of company law can provide even their closely held companies with a competitive advantage.[2]

Taking convergence to its logical extreme, are we about to see a version of 'The End of History' in corporate law?[3] Accepting this as an instructive starting point, this summative chapter will seek to bring together some of the reasons for this pattern of evolution and consider where it will end up as far as English law is concerned.

---

[1]   On convergence in corporate law generally, see J.A. McCahery (ed.), *Corporate Governance Regimes: Convergence and Diversity* (2002) (OUP), J. Gordon and M.J. Roe (eds), *Convergence and Persistence in Corporate Governance* (2004) (CUP), M.M. Siems, *Convergence in Shareholder Law* (2007) (CUP), L.A. Cunningham [2004] 1 Int Jo of Discl and Gov 269. For a strong counter-thesis, see D. Branson (2001) 34 Cornell Jo of Int Law 321.

[2]   (2004) (OUP) at p. 218.

[3]   The commentator Francis Fukuyama coined this phrase most famously in his text *The End of History and the Last Man* (1992) (Penguin), which further considered the thesis raised in his 1989 paper that, with the victory of Western market liberalism over communism, world political orders were becoming indistinguishable. Events over the intervening decade have shown that History is remarkably robust and that new religious and political theories are always on hand to divide mankind.

2 FACTORS PROMOTING FURTHER CONVERGENCE

2.1 Capitalism and Consensus

The idea of the limited company with shareholder owners and managed by directors is now standard fare in every developed legal jurisdiction.

Having made that point, the modern large corporate enterprise has its critics.[4] That is not surprising, because it is an easy target that often conspires with the forces of capitalism to produce a negative impact. Joel Bakan, in his polemic *The Corporation*,[5] attacks many of the aspects of its operation. Noreena Hertz is equally scathing in her monograph, *The Silent Takeover*.[6] In response to such impressive voices of dissent, one could argue that, although there is no doubt that corporations can provide the basis for inappropriate behaviour, equally, they can be forces of progress by encouraging economic development. Commentators such as Bakan and Hertz are still in a minority and, more significantly, foreign governments are voting with their feet. Even in countries where a socialist tradition has held sway, the adoption of the Western corporate law paradigm seems inexorable. China, the fastest growing economy in the world, appears firmly committed to a Western-style capitalist structure, based upon the limited liability corporation. With its recent corporate law revisions of 1993 and 2005, China has shown a willingness to take on board ideas from a range of cultures. The original 1993 law was heavily influenced by continental corporate law traditions, with a strong liking for the discipline of share capital maintenance and a two-tier board structure.[7] In its 2005 corporate law revision, there has been a definite move towards the Anglo-American model, with the share capital maintenance doctrine being watered down to a considerable extent.[8]

Even the most hard-line of capitalists accept that some concession needs to be made to a wider group of stakeholders – hence the rise to prominence of the somewhat cosmetic campaign for 'corporate social responsibility'.[9] Attempts

---

[4] For an extreme vision of the stakeholder-oriented company and how the law might help to attain that vision by moving corporate law into the sphere of public law, see K. Greenfield, *The Failure of Corporate Law* (2006) (University of Chicago Press).

[5] (2004) (Constable).

[6] (2002) (Arrow).

[7] See P.C. Ann (1996) 17 Co Law 199. On shareholder rights in China, see L. Miles and M. He (2005) 16 ICCLR 275.

[8] For the 2005 China Company Law Revision, see A.Y.S. Li and S.S.M. Ho (2006) 27 Co Law 311, A. Lau (2006) 27 Co Law 376. For the cultural background of Chinese company law, see T. Ruskola (2000) 52 Stan L Rev 1599.

[9] On the Corporate Social Responsibility debate, see W. Wedderburn (1985) 15 Melb Univ L Rev 4, B. Pettet [1997] CLP 279, C.M. Slaughter (1997) 18 Co Law 313

to produce a firmer basis on which shareholder wealth maximisation impera-tives have been subordinated to the needs of wider stakeholders have met with limited success in English law – one need look no further than the final compromise wording of s. 172 of the Companies Act 2006 to confirm this crit-icism.[10] The global financial crisis will put this new statement of responsibil-ities to a severe test, as the need to survive takes centre stage and will be prioritised over social responsibilities.

2.2 Globalisation

One consequence of globalisation, with its emphasis on interlocking economies, is the domino effect where a financial crisis hits a region. Witness the Asian financial crisis of 1997 which forced many jurisdictions in South East Asia to hurriedly introduce/remodel corporate rescue regimes based upon Western precedents.[11] A decade later, we witnessed the US sub-prime lending fiasco sending shockwaves through both public stock markets and private financial institutions around the globe.[12]

What globalisation has done is to neuter the power of the nation state.[13] Inevitably, corporate law, as part of the trappings of national sovereignty, has surrendered to international influences. This survey of how English law has adapted to global influences should attest to that truism.

2.3 Legal Scholars as Agents of Convergence

Academics increasingly conduct comparative research to test their hypotheses. They have always been inclined towards that method, but it is much easier to conduct legal scholarship on that basis these days, with unlimited access to the resources of the internet and the growth of legal publishing.

In the early days of post-colonialism, it was not unusual for newly inde-pendent states to draw upon the expertise of English academics to model their

---

and I. Lynch-Fannon (2007) 58 NILQ 1. For an Australian perspective, see H. Anderson (2007) 7 Ox Univ Comm LJ 93.

[10] See A. McBeth (2004) 33 CLWR 222 on abortive legislation designed to include extraterritorial curbs on multinational behaviour.

[11] See R. Tomasic (ed.), *Insolvency Law in East Asia* (2006) (Ashgate). In 1998, Indonesia, Thailand and South Korea revised their corporate insolvency regimes to facilitate rescue.

[12] For an illuminating account of the sub-prime crisis, see G. Walker (2008) 29 Co Law 22.

[13] We are not merely talking about developing countries here. See D. Korten, *When Corporations Rule the World* (1995) (Kumarian Press), G. Monbiot, *Captive State: The Corporate Takeover of Britain* (2000) (Macmillan).

shiny new corporate law models. One could cite here the work of Professor Jim Gower in devising the revolutionary Ghana Company Law[14] and the contribution of Professor Robert Pennington in advising governments on corporate law reform in both the Seychelles and Trinidad and Tobago.[15] Such scholars do not simply transport in an uncritical way the existing system of corporate law from their home jurisdiction to the host country. Cherished reforms unimplemented in the home jurisdiction can be introduced into the host jurisdiction. They may thus be forces for reform.

On a more subtle level, through the natural processes of academic debate (which is increasingly internationalised), scholars raise awareness of the good and bad points of their native system of corporate law, thereby enabling foreign policymakers to adopt solutions seen to be working overseas. The boom in international conference activity has also contributed to a broader knowledge of corporate law models across the globe.

The influx of foreign academic corporate lawyers into the English legal faculty, whether they be Jewish refugees from Nazi Germany (such as Clive Schmitthoff[16]), academics dissatisfied with the apartheid system in South Africa or simply scholars looking to broaden their intellectual horizons (or enhance their salaries), has heightened our awareness of comparative solutions to common problems affecting the operation of limited liability companies. Globalisation is very much in evidence in the international market for the services of legal academics.

The employment of academics, with their comparative insights, by law reform bodies is becoming marked.[17] It is the norm for any review panel in the UK to include at least one academic, and not merely in a token role. In recent decades, one could cite the Gower Report[18] and the Prentice Report[19] as examples of this reform process at work, with academics leading from the front.

---

[14]   Gower basically constitued a one-man committee reviewing Ghana Company Law in the years 1958–61. On the story of Ghana company law reform, see O. Kahn-Freund (1962) 25 MLR 78.

[15]   See B. Rider (1983) 4 Co Law 47.

[16]   For an example of an evaluation of their contribution, see J. Beatson and R. Zimmerman, *Jurists Uprooted* (2004) (OUP).

[17]   The late Professor John Parkinson played a significant role in the Company Law Review – see the tribute to him by S. MacLeod in *Global Governance and the Quest for Justice – Volume 2: Corporate Governance* (2006) (Hart).

[18]   L.C.B. Gower, *Review of Investor Protection (Part 1)* (1984, Cmnd 9125) – this led to the ground-breaking Financial Services Act 1986. For Gower's own thoughts, see (1988) 51 MLR 1.

[19]   Professor Dan Prentice reviewed the law on ultra vires in 1986 and his proposals influenced reform in the Companies Act 1989 – see L.S. Sealy (1986) 7 Co Law 90, J. Birds (1986) 7 Co Law 203, B. Hannigan [1987] JBL 173.

One danger to note here is the growing tendency always to look primarily at US scholarship as an inspiration for theoretical debates in other jurisdictions. Ideas that work well in the US context may have less value in the diverse cultures in other parts of the world. One also detects an inward-looking perspective in some US scholarship, a mindset which often plays down academic work undertaken beyond the circuit of the leading US universities.[20] For academic discourse to operate at an optimum level in corporate debates, it must be bilateral. The need for a wider search for solutions to the conundrums of corporate law regulation is highlighted by the global financial crisis which has placed in jeopardy the assumed superiority of US regulatory ideas, with their emphasis on market supremacy.

2.4 Law Reform Processes

Increasingly, all countries have reviewed the effectiveness of their current corporate law models. As part of this process, opportunities have been taken to consider corporate law mechanisms adopted abroad.

A few examples may serve to illustrate this. The Mercantile Law Commission of 1854 certainly took advantage of comparative data. The Jenkins Committee[21] took evidence from representatives of the Securities and Exchange Commission when considering appropriate rules for the disclosure of interests in shares.

The spread of corporate rescue mechanisms across the globe in the past 20 years typifies a trend towards mimicry. The Cork Committee (Cmnd 8558) was undoubtedly influenced by developments abroad and, in particular, by the mystique surrounding the Chapter 11 bankruptcy reorganisation procedure in the USA.

More recently, both the Law Commission and the Company Law Review came down strongly in favour of adopting the Canadian statutory derivative action as an effective means of protecting minority shareholders.[22] This reform has now materialised in English law in the shape of the Companies Act 2006 (Part 11), which came into effect on 1 October 2007.

Looking further afield, in Ireland,[23] the adoption of pooling orders and contribution orders in cases of group insolvency can, as we saw in Chapter 3 above, be traced back to New Zealand influences. More recently, the use of

---

[20] A point made forcefully by D. Branson in (2001) 34 Cornell Jo of Int Law 321.

[21] Cmnd 1749, paras 142 and 228.

[22] See LC Report No. 246, Cm 3769 (1997), *Shareholder Remedies* and URN (01/942) (2001) respectively.

[23] See Companies Act 1993 (Ireland) ss. 140–41 (pooling).

comparative research is evident in the First Report of the Company Law Review Group.[24]

Comparative research therefore has informed corporate law reform processes. But the following warning from Sealy is worthy of record: 'We should look at developments abroad; not to copy what others have done, but to jolt our preconceptions and stimulate in ourselves a fresh and questioning approach.'[25]

2.5   International Law Firms and Accountancy Practices

These professional firms, increasingly dominated by US players, serve as agents through which corporate law ideas are transmitted across the developed world. Precedents and other standard documents used within the firm at its many offices are significant here, as is the role played by such firms in policy debates. Such global law firms and accountancy practices have considerable resources at their disposal and are quite capable of mounting effective campaigns to change the law.[26] The speedy introduction of the Insolvency Act 1994 and the enactment of the Limited Liability Partnerships Act 2000 confirm this point in the context of English law. In spite of their 'clout', the performance of these huge audit firms in discharging their responsibilities as 'gatekeepers'[27] with regard to a number of high profile collapses has been poor. Ironically, this evidence of professional underperformance has triggered a new round of convergence in the field by extending both the powers and duties of auditors.

2.6   Higher Education

The emergence in UK universities over the past 20 years of an LLM in International Business will have a long-term impact. Tens of thousands of overseas students have had the opportunity to study Western Corporate Law and to discuss corporate law ideas with their fellow postgraduates. On their return to their home jurisdiction, such individuals will invariably occupy key positions of influence within the legal, commercial and political elite, thereby affording themselves the opportunity to influence the future direction of

---

[24]   (2001) para 1.8.2.

[25]   See *Company Law and Commercial Reality* (1984) (Sweet & Maxwell) at 87. See also A. Boyle (2000) 21 Co Law 308.

[26]   For comment on this phenomenon, see J. Flood and E. Skordaki, *Insolvency Practitioners and Bi Corporate Insolvencies* (1995) (ACCA Research Report No. 43).

[27]   See J. Coffee, *Gatekeepers: The Role of the Professions in Corporate Governance* (2006) (OUP).

corporate law. This may be seen as a form of cultural imperialism, but with the decline of alternative models to capitalism, few criticisms are being raised.

2.7 Role of International Organisations

Bodies such as the World Trade Organization, the Organisation for Economic Cooperation and Development (OECD), the International Monetary Fund, the World Bank, the International Institute for the Unification of Private Law (UNIDROIT) and UNCITRAL have all contributed to the emergence of a common corporate structure and guiding principles, particularly in the developing countries. This may happen in a variety of ways. Such jurisdictions may be looking to borrow and changes in private law may be imposed as a precondition for lending. Alternatively, such countries may be in the market for a new corporate system and will naturally look to internationally favoured models. OECD has produced a model code of conduct for multinationals,[28] but the real utility of such voluntary codes or 'soft law' is open to question.[29]

2.8 Multinationals and International Joint Ventures

Transnational businesses have always been a force to be reckoned with in terms of their impact on local commercial law.[30] It is believed that the Dutch East India Company (which was incorporated in 1602) 'introduced' the common Roman/Dutch law into the Cape Colony in 1652.[31] Parallel examples can be drawn from the operation of businesses linked to the rise of the British Empire, particularly in India, where the separation of powers between commercial enterprise (that is, the East India Company) and lawmaking was blurred.

In more recent times it has also been argued by scholars[32] that multinational enterprises (MNEs) and other large commercial organisations are themselves creators of a form of 'law'.

---

[28] The first OECD Code dates back to 1976. For the 2000 version, see the note in (2000) 21 Co Law 306, A. Dignam and M. Galanis [1999] EBLR 396, S. Tully (2001) 50 ICLQ 394. For later developments, note F. Macmillan (2003) 24 Co Law 355. See now Annual Report on OECD Guidelines for MNEs (2004). In the UK, see DTI Press Notice, 13 July 2006 for details of the UK National Contact Point for the implementation of the OECD Guidelines

[29] For a lucid analysis, see S. Picciotto (2003) 42 Col Jo of Transnat Law 131. See also S. Wheeler, *Corporations and The Third Way* (2002) (Hart) at 126.

[30] See D. Branson (2001) 34 Cornell Jo of Int Law 321.

[31] See generally S.D. Girvin (1992) 13 Jo of Leg Hist 63.

[32] For a consideration of the issues here see the essays in G. Teubner (ed.), *Global Law without a State* (1997) (Ashgate).

The fact that many businesses operate transnationally either by means of a multinational group structure or possibly through the medium of a joint venture means that there is a vested commercial interest in standardising rules of corporate law, because this can reduce transaction costs.

2.9   Race to the Bottom

This manifestation of regulatory competition is not simply restricted to Delaware and the USA. The *Centros (C212/97)*[33] ruling of the ECJ and its subsequent pronouncements (considered in Chapter 7 above) have exposed the possibilities for the emergence of this syndrome within the context of the EU. It has been suggested that the reduction of the minimum share capital for private companies in France to a single euro is a manifestation of this responsive syndrome at work. The GmbH in Germany is being forced to adapt or risk facing extinction. As the EU family expands, those possibilities are accordingly magnified. Offshore jurisdictions compete fiercely in order to attract international business and a key element in that competitive process is the design of the corporate law regime.

2.10   Harmonisation Processes

These have been discussed at length in Chapter 1 and require no further comment. Their contribution to convergence is self-evident and measurable.

2.11   Converging Capital Markets

This economic phenomenon has played a role in producing common rules in the area of market abuse. Certainly, the increasing competitiveness of capital markets is one factor behind the spread of the insider dealing prohibition beyond the US and EU into leading share market jurisdictions such as Japan, Hong Kong and Singapore.

The move towards a single global capital market has been aided by the advent of investors' information tools such as Deminor ratings,[34] which are used to evaluate the effectiveness of corporate governance regimes in issuers by applying no less than 300 indicators. This global measuring standard compels issuers to adopt governance regimes that tick the right boxes and in particular mirror the Anglo-American model.

---

[33]   [2000] Ch 446.
[34]   Deminor ratings originated in the 1990s. For comment on this and other rating systems, see H. Sherman [2004] 12 Corp Gov 5.

2.12 Foreign Players

This factor is to some extent a by-product of the previous element. As capital markets become more open to foreign entrants, so those entrants will begin to play a more active role in corporate law systems. For example, the arrival of US and offshore 'vulture funds'[35] in the UK secondary market for distressed debt has generated much litigation as such funds tend to favour the use of aggressive litigation in workout situations over the traditional British compromise (such as the London Approach[36]). Having said that, one detects a certain disquiet on the part of the English courts towards such aggressive tactics – the opinions expressed by Jacob J in *Re Colt Telecom Group plc (No. 2)*,[37] a case involving an abortive attempt by a vulture fund to have a company placed into administration against its wishes, being just one example of this hostility being voiced.

In Germany, the entrance of US institutional investors (such as CalPERS[38]) into its previously sedate corporate governance world has shaken things up. Germany will not be the only jurisdiction to feel this institutional investor flexing its muscles. It was estimated by Gilson[39] that more than 20 per cent of the holdings of CalPERS are in foreign securities.

2.13 New Technology

The influence of new communications technology is pervasive.

Firstly, it has enhanced awareness of foreign legal systems. We can all now quickly access both legislation and case law emanating from a host of foreign jurisdictions. Tools such as LEXIS and Westlaw are in wide usage and with the advent of the internet, both primary and secondary sources on corporate law regimes across the globe can be easily accessed.

---

[35] On vulture funds see J. Flood in chapter 12 of D. Nelken and J. Feest (eds), *Adapting Legal Cultures* (2001) (Hart) at 270 et seq. Vulture funds operate internationally in the field of distressed sovereign debt – see the recent case involving Zambia discussed in the *Times* 15 February 2007. There is a question as to whether vulture funds are the same as hedge funds, but the better view is that they represent a sub-species of hedge fund – for discussion see *Re Colt Telecom Group plc (No. 1)* [2003] BPIR 311 at 313 per Lawrence Collins J and *Re Colt Telecom Group plc (No. 2)* [2003] BPIR 324 at 329 per Jacob J (judge refuses to be drawn on this distinction).

[36] See Chapter 2 above.

[37] [2002] EWHC 2815 (Ch), [2003] 1 BCLC 290.

[38] The California Public Employees Retirement Systems fund has investments worth some $256 billion. The fund was established in 1932 – its website www.calpers.ca.gov is particularly informative. See M.P. Smith (1996) 51 Jo of Fin 227.

[39] See R.J. Gilson, chapter 4 in J.N. Gordon and M.J. Roe, *Convergence and Persistence in Corporate Governance* (2004) (CUP) at 146.

It has also necessitated change in national corporate rules to reflect new technologies. This has been necessary to maintain the competitive edge of national systems. If virtual shareholders meetings are permissible in jurisdictions such as Delaware, Canada and Australia, why not in our home jurisdiction? Websites will be used increasingly to communicate news to shareholders, once the Companies Act 2006 is fully in force. The new EC Directive 2007/36 will undoubtedly accelerate moves towards constructive uses of technology to empower shareholders.

2.14   The Common Law

Although operating at greatly attenuated levels these days, the common law can still promote convergence. Some of its vigour has been lost through greater usage of legislation at a local level, but it still has a role to play. This is particularly evident with the importation of principles developed in Commonwealth courts into English Company Law (discussed in Chapter 1). The *Cambridge Gas Transport* case[40] shows the continued inventiveness of the common law in areas where specific legislative models have been introduced but may not be available to particular applicants (see Chapter 8).

2.15   The Role of Language and Corporate Discourse

Convergence can be promoted by the simple device of everyday discourse between corporate law players. Certain phrases become common fare when practitioners, academics and policymakers meet to discuss corporate law. For more than a generation, we have been familiar with the phrase, 'lifting the veil' of corporate personality.[41] The 'Berle and Means thesis'[42] is a common starting point for any analysis of corporate governance. Much discussion has been devoted to the 'race to the bottom'[43] in the context of corporate regulatory competition. More recently, phrases such as 'Chinese walls',[44] 'hedge

---

[40]   [2006] UKPC 26 – see G. Moss [2006] 19 Ins Intell 123.

[41]   This phrase of lifting the veil probably originated in the US. In Germany, they talk of breaching the wall of the corporation. Linguistic analysis can produce interesting insights – see S. Ottolenghi (1990) 53 MLR 338.

[42]   *The Modern Corporation and Private Property* (1932) (Macmillan).

[43]   See Brandeis J in *Liggett v Lee* (1933) 288 US 517 at 557–60.

[44]   On Chinese walls (a term which incidentally is viewed as politically incorrect in many quarters), see L. Herzel and D.E. Colling (1983) 4 Co Law 14, N. Poser (1988) 9 Co Law 120 and 165 and G. McCormack (1999) 1 ICCLJ 5. For judicial comment, see Lord Millett in *Prince Jefri v Bolkiah* [1999] 1 BCLC 1 at 59. See generally H. McVea [2000] CLJ 370, H. McVea, *Financial Conglomerates and the Chinese Wall* (1993) (Clarendon Press).

funds'[45] and 'poison pills' have become prominent and such concepts have therefore become the subject of regulatory attention in a number of jurisdictions at the same time. The characterisation of the final period of a company's existence as the 'twilight zone'[46] is well recognised in corporate law discourse. A common language of corporate law is being created. That language is indisputably American in character.[47] That said, the English courts have cautioned practitioners about using metaphors (no matter what their origin) to draw legal conclusions as a substitute for following clear legislative provision.[48]

2.16 Convergence through Paralysis

Convergence may already exist in certain fields of corporate law, but in theory it could disappear, as new solutions to age-old problems emerge. Very often, that novelty fails to materialise because a nation state is reluctant to break ranks. It may be that it supports an extant legal principle because it is efficient. But it may also do this in order not to offend the international business constituency upon which the well-being of its economy depends. The failure to tackle multinationals and, in particular, to make them responsible for the actions of their subsidiaries, may be a manifestation of this malaise at work.[49]

Paralysis may be voluntary or it may be enforced. The best illustration of this is the inability of Member States within the EU to change outmoded corporate law models because they are locked into the harmonised structure. Much work has to go on behind the scenes to convince European partners of the need for change. However, this is not a futile exercise – witness the adoption of Directive 68/2006, which introduces much-needed flexibility into share capital maintenance regimes.

---

[45] On the regulation of hedge funds, see H. McVea (2007) 27 Leg Studs 709 and T.R. Hurst (2007) 28 Co Law 228.

[46] The term is universally recognised – see *Directors in the Twilight Zone* (INSOL, 2001). For discussion see D. Milman [2004] JBL 493.

[47] Thus the English term 'book debts' increasingly gives way to the US phrase 'receivables'. Had the Company Law Review been set up a decade later, it probably would have been labelled the 'Corporate Law Review'. Perhaps the only surprise is that the Companies Act 2006 was so entitled.

[48] See the comments of Lewison J in *First Independent Factors v Mountford* [2008] BPIR 515 on the phoenix syndrome and its relevance to the interpretation of ss. 216 and 217 of the Insolvency Act 1986.

[49] See A.J. Boyle (2002) 23 Co Law 35, P. Muchlinski (2002) 23 Co Law 168.

3 OTHER LIKELY TRENDS IN UK CORPORATE LAW

If we accept the inevitability of convergence, is that the sole future development we may expect? The short answer is no.

3.1 Corporate Mobility

Corporate mobility will be very much part of the future of UK corporate law. The presumptive 14th EC Harmonisation Directive, if it had ever been adopted, would have permitted the moving of registered offices within the EC.[50] This initiative, first floated in 1997, is important because, at present, if a company wishes to move its legal home from one Member State to another, it will have to be dissolved in the first state and reincorporated in its new host. This is profoundly disruptive in commercial terms. The discussion of this issue is to be found in Chapter 5. As it happens, the future of the proposed 14th Directive is now unclear partly because of general developments in the area of freedom of establishment producing a view at Commission level that there is no need for an explicit Directive.[51]

The UK government appears committed to change here. It has supported the proposals of the Company Law Review[52] designed to facilitate redomestication. The Company Law Review favoured opening up migration avenues for companies to move within Great Britain and to and from Great Britain, provided adequate safeguards for creditors were put in place.[53] However, a perusal of the Companies Act 2006 will find no such provisions.

As rules develop to iron out the inevitable difficulties of cross-border commerce, this pattern will become more evident.

---

[50]　Thereby neutralising *R v HM Treasury ex parte Daily Mail and General Trust (C81/87)* [1989] 1 All ER 328. For comment, see C. Schmitthoff [1988] JBL 454.

[51]　The Commission announced in March 2008 its present intention not to proceed with this Directive – see G.-J. Vossestein (2008) 4 Utrecht Law Review 53. This decision to pull back from reform may have influenced the views expressed by the Advocate General in *Cartesio Oktato as Szolgaltato bt (C210/06)* [2008] BCC 745. For comment on the Advocate General's opinion, see S. Moore [2009] 22 Ins Intell 9. Surprisingly, when *Cartesio* came before the ECJ, on the preliminary ruling the Court did not follow the opinion of the Advocate General. We may therefore wonder whether the Commission might look to revert to the proposal for a 14th Directive. See generally S. Rammeloo (2008) 15 MJ of Euro and Comp Law 359.

[52]　URN 01/942. See *Gower and Davies: The Principles of Modern Company Law* (7th edition, 2003) (Sweet & Maxwell) chapter 6.

[53]　Companies have to be solvent and movement restricted to scheduled jurisdictions. Ibid at paras 14.3 et seq.

3.2 Supranational Companies

The emergence of the 'societas europea', or European Company (which was first mooted in 1958), points to the possibilities here. This model was introduced into the UK system with effect from October 2004.[54] Its take-up has been minimal, with figures for 2005/6 disclosing only one such company being registered in Great Britain. The prospects here do not look good.[55]

Could a uniform corporate entity be developed at global level? The challenge here would be immense, but not insurmountable, particularly as many of the fundamentals are now common fare. UNCITRAL or OECD would appear to be the most likely progenitors of such an ambitious initiative.

3.3 A Twin Track System

Historically, UK corporate law has been monolithic in legislating for companies. Our awareness of foreign systems shows that this is unusual; separate legal regimes for public and private companies is quite a common phenomenon. Having said that, the Irish Company Law Review Group, in its First Report,[56] rejected the idea of separate statutes, though it did favour greater differentiation within a single statute, with the private company being given pride of place. This policy has been taken further in Ireland, with their forthcoming putative Companies Bill 2009.[57] One can safely predict that the divergence between company law for large and small firms will continue apace and one might reasonably expect a separate legislative basis to be formalised. At the moment, there is fresh impetus being given to the idea that there should be a model private company statute for the EU.[58]

4 OVERVIEW

How has English law fared in respect of convergence?

The drive towards convergence in the UK and other national systems is clear and the reasons for it are compelling. Since the millennium, we have

---

54   EC Regulation 2157/2001 – implemented in English law by SI 2004/2326. See J. Rickford (ed.), *The European Company* (2003) (Intersentia).
55   See J. McCahery and E. Vermeulen [2005] ELJ 785.
56   (2001) para 1.8.2.
57   At the time of writing, a timescale for the enactment of the Irish reform proposals was unclear.
58   This idea is not new – see R. Drury and A. Hicks [1999] JBL 429.

admitted into our corporate law system treasury shares,[59] abolished financial assistance bars for private companies,[60] introduced statutory derivative claims[61] and allowed both LLPs and the Societas Europa (SE) to be set up in this country. In the decades before 2000, title retention clauses and shareholders' pre-emption rights[62] made their entrance onto our local scene. Convergence in corporate governance regimes (which does not necessarily require legislative action) has been more marked. We thus have in this aspect a form of what has been labelled as 'functional convergence'.[63]

But one must not assume that complete convergence is inevitable[64] or that there will not be setbacks on the way. Looking at the history of UK corporate law, we have steadfastly refused to admit the US 'business judgment rule' to protect directors.[65] Perversely, for no apparent reason we have held out against the idea that preincorporation contracts may be ratified, when that solution has been universally adopted elsewhere.[66] Our refusal to accept the possibility of a fifth exception[67] to *Foss v Harbottle*[68] has been robust,[69] though with the

---

[59]   See G. Morse [2004] JBL 303. Singapore introduced treasury shares in 2005 – see H. Tijo (2006) 21 BJIBFL 316.

[60]   The financial assistance bar was removed from private companies in the UK with effect from October 2008. For an impressive review of the financial assistance bar in Pacific rim jurisdictions, see K. Fletcher (2006) 6 Ox Univ Comm LJ 157.

[61]   See A. Keay and J. Loughrey (2008) 124 LQR 469. Hong Kong has recently introduced statutory derivative claims – see P. von Nessen, S.H. Goo and C.K. Low [2008] JBL 627.

[62]   Pre-emption rights were a feature of US law, but were actually introduced into English Law in 1980 via the Second EC Company Law Harmonisation Directive (77/91) – see Art 29. The ECJ reviewed this Article in *Siemens AG v Nold (C42/95)* [1997] BCC 759. For general background, see I. MacNeil [2002] JBL 78.

[63]   Coffee stresses this in his piece in (1999) NwUL Rev 641 at 679.

[64]   Once again I commend D. Branson (2001) 34 Cornell Jo of Int Law 321. E. Micheler makes a similarly cautious observation in (2007) 123 LQR 251.

[65]   For the business judgment rule, see M.R. Pasban, C. Campbell and J. Birds (1997) 26 Anglo-Am L Rev 461, M.R. Pasban [2001] JBL 33, M. Hemraj (2003) 24 Co Law 218, D. Arsalidou (2003) 24 Co Law 228. A revised version of the business judgment rule was recently introduced for German public companies – see T. Naruisch and F. Liepe [2007] JBL 225 at 238.

[66]   See, for example, the acceptance of ratification of preincorporation contracts in Singapore (*Cosmic Insurance Corp v Khoo Chiang Poh* (1981) 131 NLJ 286), which is discussed by W. Woon in (1983) 25 Mal L Rev 399. Ratification is accepted in Malaysia, India and New Zealand. Nigeria accepts this posibility – see L.O. Okeke (2000) 21 Co Law 320. The Isle of Man accepted the idea most recently in s. 87(1)(b) of its Companies Act 2006. The Jenkins Committee (Cmnd 1749, para 54) called for a ratification facility to be adopted by English law. Indeed, the First Company Law Harmonisation Directive (66/151) seems to assume that ratification is permitted.

[67]   The fifth exception, which is open ended and based on the interests of justice, is recognised in jurisdictions such as Australia, Israel and Nigeria – see K.D. Barnes

advent of statutory derivative claims, that now may only be of historical relevance. Most recently of all, the Privy Council[70] has made it clear that the Australian *Gambotto* principle,[71] which seeks to protect minorities when articles of association are varied, has no place in English law. The idea pioneered in North America of an appraisal remedy for shareholders in a private company, guaranteeing exit rights in defined circumstances, has not found favour.[72] No par value shares have not been accepted in English law, though one suspects that it is the EU factor that is preventing that.[73] In the corporate insolvency arena, we have refused to introduce an explicit facility offering super-priority for business rescue funding.[74] Attempts to introduce a security registration scheme based upon Art 9 of the US Uniform Commercial Code have come to nothing.[75]

Looking at matters from the other side of the fence, we have not been particularly successful in selling the floating charge to those jurisdictions that have enjoyed choice in the matter of corporate law reform.[76] It is hardly coincidental that the private receiver is also largely unique to the followers of English law.[77] Only offshore jurisdictions find our flexible approach to 'corporate directors' attractive. By way of balance, we have been successful in

(1987) 8 Co Law 93, O.A. Osunbor (1987) 36 ICLQ 1, L.S. Sealy (1989) 10 Co Law 52, A. Reisberg (2003) 24 Co Law 250.

68   (1843) 2 Hare 461.

69   See *Prudential Assurance v Newman Industries (No. 2)* [1982] Ch 204.

70   *Citco Banking Corp v Pussers Ltd* [2007] UKPC 13 – see R. Williams [2007] CLJ 500.

71   *Gambotto v WCP Ltd* (1995) 182 CLR 432 – see M. Whincop (1995) 23 ABLR 276.

72   See *O'Neill v Phillips* [1999] 1 WLR 1092. Hong Kong is considering adopting this idea – R. Cheung (2008) 19 ICCLR 325.

73   The Jenkins Committee (Cmnd 1749, para 34) favoured no par value shares, as had the Gedge Committee (Cmd 9112, para 11) previously.

74   This idea was dismissed in the policy discussions leading up to the Enterprise Act 2002. With the poor record of rescue mechanisms in English law, it is likely to return to the agenda – see G. McCormack [2007] JBL 701. For cultural differences between the US and the UK on corporate rescue, see G. McCormack (2007) 56 ICLQ 515.

75   See the Law Commission Report No. 296 (2005) (Cm 6654) and the background analysis of G. McCormack in chapter 5 of J. de Lacy (ed.), *The Reform of UK Company Law* (2002) (Cavendish).

76   Notable exceptions of non-common law jurisdictions where the floating charge has found favour abroad are to be found in Scotland (1961) (where it was recognised by legislation) and Mauritius (1969). On the floating charge in Mauritius, see *Aquachem Ltd v Delphis Bank* [2008] UKPC 7. Surprisingly, Denmark introduced a variant of the floating charge in 2006.

77   See I. Macdonald and D. Moujalli (2001) 14 Ins Intell 76. Note also F. Dahan (1996) 17 Co Law 181.

exporting the idea that company accounts should present a true and fair picture of a company's finances[78] and corporate governance standards.[79] We have also exported the idea of a takeover code, with its underlying philosophy of protecting the interests of the shareholders in the target company as the main priority.[80] Our preference for the place of incorporation principle in private international law has attracted widespread support.[81]

What these examples show us is that English law, like all other systems, is not going to be rushed into harmonising in every instance. This reality has been recognised in the European Union, with its political doctrine of 'subsidiarity'[82] now driving forward harmonisation in a more culturally sensitive manner. This pattern of selective adoption of ideas is practised in most jurisdictions, with few legal systems surrendering completely to foreign corporate law influences.[83]

Why is there opposition to convergence when it may appear to be the only rational option? Fundamental cultural heritage may offer an explanation,[84] as may naked self-interest on the part of those who would stand to lose out in the event of corporate law reform.[85] Lawyers can be influential figures here.

---

[78]   See K.P.E. Lasok and E. Grace (1989) 10 Co Law 13.

[79]   See A. Dignam (2000) 21 Co Law 70. For a critique of the practice of importing Western-style corporate governance regimes without regard to the underlying culture, see L. Miles [2007] JBL 851 (discussing the position in South Korea).

[80]   See A. Dignam (2008) 28 Leg Studs 96 for discussion.

[81]   See Chapter 7.

[82]   The doctrine was developed in the 1980s. It is reflected in Art 5(2) of the EC Treaty. Its influence on Company Law Harmonisation Directives since then has been all too apparent, in that it has speeded up the adoption process by allowing for some local flexibility.

[83]   This selective approach may exacerbate transplantation problems if the non-adopted element is critical to the whole. On the other hand, cultural differences may justify selective adoption.

[84]   See D.M. Branson again (2001) 34 Cornell Jo of Int Law 321. See also T. Ruskola (2000) 52 Stan L Rev 1599. In (2002) 50 Am Jo of Comp Law, K. Pistor makes the point that harmonising substantive law in a developing jurisdiction is no panacea; much more needs to be done to the underlying culture.

[85]   See L.A. Bebchuk and M.J. Roe, chapter 2 in J.N. Gordon and M.J. Roe, *Convergence and Persistence in Corporate Governance* (2004) (CUP). On the evolution of the idea of path dependence, see M.J. Roe (1996) 109 HLR 641. How this can happen is illustrated by the ending of the bar on financial assistance in private company share acquisitions in UK law (effective from 1 October 2008). This might be seen as a cause for universal joy, but it now transpires that many smaller law firms which have made a nice living from 'whitewashing' transactions that would otherwise breach the prohibition will suffer financially – see D. Jordan, *The Lawyer*, 4 November 2002. There is no evidence of lawyers in the UK using their influence to block reform in this area, but in Germany lawyers have been stout defenders of share capital maintenance – F. Kubler (2004) 15 EBLR 1031.

Countries whose entire economies depend on having a more deregulated system of corporate law will never be satisfied with a uniformity that destroys their competitive advantage. Finally, one must never underestimate pure chauvinism, in the sense of a deep-seated reluctance to be seen to be surrendering a native legal rule (no matter how obsolete) to external influences.

Notwithstanding these glitches, convergence is occurring in many areas of corporate law, but is it a panacea or an unqualified blessing? Substantive convergence that takes no account of enforcement possibilities, cultural heritage or wider institutional issues will be destined to achieve only limited success.[86] Economic advantages may undoubtedly flow from the associated reduction in transaction costs where convergence occurs,[87] but will the fountain of corporate law novelty dry up if it becomes entirely dependent on one source, namely US corporate law philosophy, with its obsessional focus on widely held public corporations?

It has been suggested that the credit crunch might trigger a new round of convergence in corporate regulation, with US models again leading the field. But as the credit crunch originated in the US, those market-based models might themselves be seen as tarnished goods. What the world financial crisis may do is to change the path of convergence towards a common model using a wider range of regulatory tools. Those tools may not necessarily be American-designed.

In summary, therefore, we can safely assert that convergence in corporate law is a real phenomenon,[88] but we cannot say that its total victory is assured (or even desirable). Dissent and diversity are ideals that corporate lawyers should not surrender simply on the grounds of supposed economic efficiency.

---

[86] See K. Pistor (2002) 50 Am Jo of Comp Law 97 and also K. Pistor et al. (2003) 31 Jo of Comp Econ 674 (where the importance of the ability of host nations to innovate is emphasised). Further discussion of these issues can be found in G. Hertig, chapter 10 in J.N. Gordon and M.J. Roe, *Convergence and Persistence in Corporate Governance* (2004) (CUP).

[87] See J.C. Coffee (1999) 93 NwULRev 641 at 705.

[88] Convergence is occurring in many other legal areas, including constitutional law.

Appendix

THE COMPANIES ACT 2006: A NOTE FOR READERS

The Companies Act 2006 received the Royal Assent in November 2006. Weighing in on enactment at a massive 1300 sections and 16 schedules it represents the longest statute ever enacted by the UK Parliament. This legislation is partly consolidatory and partly reforming; the consolidation element being an afterthought once the full implications of the Company Law Reform Bill (the precursor to the 2006 Act) became apparent to all. The Bill thus changed its legislative character in a fundamental way during its Parliamentary passage. Having made that point, it needs to be noted that the 2006 Act is not a full consolidation of all UK companies legislation – a feature most readily apparent from the fact that some provisions in the Companies Act 1985 survive (for example, those relating to DTI investigations and Community Interest Companies). The Financial Services and Markets Act 2000 is amended, but not replaced. The Insolvency Act 1986 and Company Directors Disqualification Act 1986 remain largely untouched.

The Companies Act 2006 will be brought into effect in stages with full implementation being scheduled for 1 October 2009. Only one or two provisions will be commenced at a later date (yet to be determined).

For a useful guide to the thinking behind the many provisions in the Act, see Explanatory Notes to Companies Act 2006, available on the Department of Business, Enterprise and Regulatory Reform website – http://www. berr.gov.uk. Generally, the website of the Department of Business, Enterprise and Regulatory Reform provides a valuable source of intelligence. The government has also produced an invaluable guide showing how provisions in the 1985 and earlier legislation have been restated in the 2006 Act, but this tool needs to be treated with caution as the new restated provision may contain subtle changes.

The following Commencement Orders should be consulted when considering whether particular provisions mentioned in the text are in force.

The Companies Act 2006 (Commencement No. 1, Transitional Provisions and Savings) Order 2006 (SI 2006/3428, C. 132)

The Companies Act 2006 (Commencement No. 2, Consequential Amendments, Transitional Provisions and Savings) Order 2007 (SI 2007/1093, C. 49)

The Companies Act 2006 (Commencement No. 3, Consequential Amendments, Transitional Provisions and Savings) Order 2007 (SI 2007/2194, C. 84)

The Companies Act 2006 (Commencement No. 4, and Commencement No. 3 (Amendment)) Order 2007 (SI 2007/2607, C. 101)

The Companies Act 2006 (Commencement No. 5, Transitional Provisions and Savings) Order 2007 (SI 2007/3495, C. 150)

The Companies Act 2006 (Commencement No. 6, Saving and Commencement Nos 3 and 5 (Amendment) Order 2008 (SI 2008/674, C. 26)

The Companies Act 2007 (Commencement No. 7, Transitional Provisions and Savings) Order 2008 (SI 2008/1886, C. 83)

At the time of going to press the major substantive Parts of the legislation *not fully* commenced include elements of:

Part 1 (introductory)
Part 2 (formation)
Part 3 (constitution)
Part 4 (capacity)
Part 5 (name)
Part 6 (registered office)
Part 7 (re-registration)
Part 8 (members)
Part 10 (directors)
Part 12 (secretaries)
Part 17 (share capital)
Part 18 (financial assistance)
Part 24 (annual return)
Part 25 (company charges)
Part 31 (dissolution)
Part 33 (companies not formed under companies legislation)
Part 34 (overseas companies)
Part 35 (registrar of companies)
Part 36 (offences)
Part 40 (foreign disqualifications)
Part 41 (business names)
Part 45 (Northern Ireland)

There are literally dozens of discrete pieces of delegated legislation clarifying and supplementing the primary statutory provisions. These are not listed here, but may be referred to in the main text where relevant. Readers should, however, note The Companies (Model Articles) Regulations 2008 (SI 2008/3229), which will provide model sets of articles for private and public companies with effect from 1 October 2009.

Bibliography

BOOKS

Addo, M.K. (ed.), *Human Rights Standards and Responsibilities of Transnational Corporations* (1999) (Kluwer)

Andenas, M., Hopt, K., and Wymeersch, E., *Free Movement of Companies in EC Law* (2003) (OUP)

Andenas, M., and Wooldridge, F., *European Comparative Company Law* (2006) (CUP)

Armour, J., and McCahery, J.A. (eds), *After Enron: Reforming Corporate Governance and Capital Markets in Europe and the US* (2006) (Hart)

Bakan, J., *The Corporation* (2004) (Constable)

Balen, M., *A Very English Deceit* (2002) (Fourth Estate)

Bates, J., *The Isle of Man Companies Act 1992* (1992) (Sweet & Maxwell)

Baylis, T., and Smith, S., *The Globalization of World Politics* (3rd edition, 2005) (OUP)

Beatson, J. and Zimmermann, R., *Jurists Uprooted: German-speaking Emigré Lawyers in Twentieth Century Britain* (2004) (OUP)

Berle, A.A., and Means, G.C., *The Modern Corporation and Private Property* (1932) (Macmillan)

Beveridge, F., *Globalisation and International Investment* (2005) (Ashgate)

Blumberg, P.I., *The Multinational Challenge to Corporate Law* (1993) (OUP)

Bridge, M. and Stevens, J. (eds), *Cross-border Security and Insolvency* (2001) (OUP)

Broc, K.G. and Parry, R. (eds), *Corporate Rescue: An Overview of Recent Developments from Selected Countries in Europe* (2004) (Kluwer)

Brown, D., and Telfer, T.G.W., *Personal and Corporate Insolvency Legislation* (2007) (LexisNexis NZ)

Clark, G.L., and Wojcik, D., *Geography of Finance: Corporate Governance in a Global Marketplace* (2007) (OUP)

Clarke, A. (ed.), *Current Issues in Insolvency Law* (1991) (Stevens)

Clarke, B., *Takeovers and Mergers Law in Ireland* (1999) (Round Hall Press)

Coffee, J., *Gatekeepers: The Role of the Professions in Corporate Governance* (2006) (OUP)

Cooke, Lord, *Turning Points of the Common Law* (1997) (Sweet & Maxwell Hamlyn Lectures)

Cordingly, D., *Cochrane the Dauntless* (2007) (Bloomsbury Publishing)
Courtney, T.B., *The Law of Private Companies* (2nd edition, 2002) (Butterworths)
Cowles, V., *The Great Swindle* (1960) (Collins)
Dale, R., *The First Crash: Lessons of the South Sea Bubble* (2004) (Princeton University Press)
Dale, R., *Napoleon is Dead: Lord Cochrane and the Great Stock Exchange Scandal* (2007) (Sutton Publishing)
Dam, K.W., *The Law-growth Nexus: The Rule of Law and Economic Development* (2006) (Brookings Institute Press)
de Koker, L., 'The Limited Liability Act of 1855' (2005) 26 Co Law 130
de Lacy, J. (ed.), *The Reform of UK Company Law* (2002) (Cavendish)
De Schutter, O., *Transnational Corporations and Human Rights* (2006) (Hart Publishing)
Diamond, A.L., *A Review of Security Interests in Property* (1989) (DTI)
Dicey, Morris and Collins on the Conflict of Laws (L. Collins, ed.) (14th edition) (2006) (Sweet & Maxwell)
Dignam, A.J., and Allen, D., *Company Law and the Human Rights Act 1998* (2001) (Butterworths)
di Luigi, M.C., 'An Invasive Top-down Harmonisation or a Respectful Framework Model for National Law? A Critique of the SE Model' (2008) 19 ICCLR 58
Dine, J., *Companies, International Trade and Human Rights* (2005) (CUP)
Dine, J., *International Trade and Human Rights* (2005) (CUP)
Dine, J., *Company Law* (6th edition, 2007) (Palgrave Macmillan)
Dine, J., Koutsias, M. and Blecher, M., *Company Law in the New Europe* (2007) (Edward Elgar)
Directors in the Twilight Zone (2001) (INSOL)
Dragneva, R. (ed.), *Investor Protection in the CIS: Legal Reform and Voluntary Harmonization* (2007) (Martinus Nijhoff)
Dunning, J., *Multinational Enterprises and the Global Economy* (1993) (Addison-Wesley)
Easterbrook, F., and Fischel, D., *The Economic Structure of Corporate Law* (1991) (Harvard University Press)
Edwards, V., *EC Company Law* (1999) (OUP)
Emberland, M., *Human Rights of Companies: Exploring the Structure of ECHR Protection* (2006) (OUP)
Erleigh, Viscount, *The South Sea Bubble* (1933) (Peter Davies)
Farrar, J.H., and Hannigan, B.M., *Farrar's Company Law* (4th edition, 1998) (Butterworths)
Fay, S., *The Collapse of Barings* (1996) (Arrow Books)
Feldman, D., and Meisel, F. (eds), *Corporate and Commercial Law: Modern Developments* (1996) (Lloyd's of London Press)

Fifoot, C.H.S., *Lord Mansfield* (1936) (Clarendon Press)

Fletcher, I., *Insolvency in Private International Law* (2nd edition, 2005) (OUP)

Flood, J., and Skordak, E., *Insolvency Practitioners and Big Insolvencies* (1995) (ACCA Research Report No. 43)

Fukuyama, F., *The End of History and The Last Man* (1992) (Penguin)

Fuller, L., *The Morality of Law* (1964) (Yale University Press)

Gordon, J.N., and Roe, M.J. (eds), *Convergence and Persistence in Corporate Governance* (2004) (CUP).

Gower and Davies: The Principles of Modern Company Law (P. Davies, ed.) (7th edition, 2003) (Sweet & Maxwell)

Grantham, R., and Rickett, C., *Corporate Personality in the 20th Century* (1998) (Hart Publishing)

Greenfield, K., *The Failure of Corporate Law* (2006) (University of Chicago Press)

Guinness, J., *Requiem for a Family Business* (1997) (Pan Books)

Hansmann, H. et al. (eds), *The Anatomy of Corporate Law* (2004) (OUP)

Hertz, N., *The Silent Takeover* (2002) (Arrow)

Ho, L.C. (ed), *Cross-border Insolvency* (2006) (Globe Law and Business)

Howells, G.G. (ed.), *European Business Law* (1996) (Dartmouth)

Johnston, A., *The City Takeover Code* (1980) (Clarendon Press)

Joseph, S., *Corporations and Transnational Human Rights Litigation* (2004) (Hart)

Keay, A., *Insolvency: Personal and Corporate Law and Practice* (3rd edition, 1998) (John Libbey)

Keay, A., *Company Directors' Responsibilities to Creditors* (2006) (Routledge-Cavendish)

Kochan, N., and Whittington, B., *Bankrupt: The BCCI Fraud* (1991) (Victor Gollancz Ltd)

Korten, D., *When Corporations Rule the World* (1995) (Kumarian Press)

Kraakman, R., et al. (eds), *The Anatomy of Corporate Law* (2004) (OUP)

Leeson, N., *Rogue Trader* (1996) (Little Brown & Co)

Lever, L., *The Barlow Clowes Affair* (1992) (Macmillan)

Likosky, M.B., *The Silicon Empire: Law, Culture and Commerce: Global Perspectives* (2005) (Ashgate)

Lowry, J., and Mistelis, L., *Commercial Law: Practice and Perspectives* (2006) (Butterworths)

McCahery, J.A. (ed.), *Corporate Governance Regimes: Convergence and Diversity* (2002) (OUP)

MacLeod, S. (ed.), *Global Governance and the Quest for Justice – Volume 2: Corporate Governance* (2006) (Hart Publishing)

Macmillan, F., *International Corporate Law Annual Volume 1* (2000) (Hart)

Macpherson, B.H., *The Reception of English Law Abroad* (2007) (Supreme Court of Queensland Library)

McVea, H., *Financial Conglomerates and the Chinese Wall* (1993) (Clarendon Press)

Michie, R.C., *The London Stock Exchange: A History* (1999) (OUP)

Micklethwait, J., and Wooldridge, A., *The Company* (2003) (Weidenfeld and Nicolson)

Milman, D. (ed.), *Regulating Enterprise* (1999) (Hart)

Mokal, R.J., *Corporate Insolvency Law* (2005) (OUP)

Monbiot, G., *Captive State: The Corporate Takeover of Britain* (2000) (Macmillan)

Morse, G. et al. (eds), *Palmer's Limited Liability Partnership Law* (2002) (Sweet & Maxwell)

Muchlinski, P., *Multinational Enterprises and the Law* (1979) (Blackwell)

Muchlinski, P., *Multinationals and the Law* (1999) (Blackwell)

Muller, K., *The GmbH: A Guide to the German Limited Liability Company* (3rd edition, 2006) (Kluwer)

Nelken, D., and Feest, J. (eds), *Adapting Legal Cultures* (2001) (Hart Publishing)

Ogus, A., and Rowley, C.K., *Prepayments and Insolvency* (1984) (OFT)

Orhnial, T. (ed.), *Limited Liability and the Corporation* (1982) (Croom Helm)

Palmer, F., *Private Companies and Syndicates* (1877) (Stevens)

Patfield, F. (ed), *Perspectives on Company Law* (I) (1995) (Kluwer)

Perry, A., *Legal Systems as a Determinant of FDI: Lessons from Sri Lanka* (2001) (Kluwer)

Rajak, H., *Insolvency law, Theory and Practice* (1993) (Sweet & Maxwell)

Rammeloo, S., *Corporations in Private International Law: A European Perspective* (2001) (OUP)

Rickford, J. (ed.), *The European Company: Developing a Community Law of Corporations* (2003) (Intersentia)

Rider B. (ed.), *The Realm of Company Law* (1998) (Kluwer)

Rider, B., and Andenas, M. (eds), *Developments in European Company Law, Volume 1/96* (1997) (Kluwer)

Romano, R., *The Genius of American Corporate Law* (1993) (AEI Press)

Rungta, R.S., *The Rise of the Business Corporation in India* (1970) (CUP)

Sachs, J.D., and Pistor, K. (eds), *The Rule of Law and Economic Reform in Russia* (1997) (Westview Press)

Sampson, A., *The Seven Sisters* (1975) (Hodder and Stoughton)

Schmitthoff, C. (ed.), *Palmer's Company Law* (24th ed) (1987) (Stevens and Sons)

Sealy, L.S., *Company Law and Commercial Reality* (1984) (Sweet & Maxwell)

Sealy, L.S., and Milman, D., *Annotated Guide to Insolvency Legislation* (11th edition, 2008) (Sweet & Maxwell)

Siems, M.M., *Convergence in Shareholder Law* (2007) (CUP)

Sin, K.F., *The Legal Nature of the Unit Trust* (1997) (Clarendon Press)

Smart, P. St J., *Cross Border Insolvency* (1992) (Butterworths)

Smith, A., *The Wealth of Nations* (1776) (Penguin Classics, 1968)

Stiglitz, J., *Globalization and its Discontents* (2001) (Penguin/Allen Lane)

Stiglitz, J., *Making Globalization Work: The Next Steps to Global Justice* (2006) (Penguin/Allen Lane)

Symes, C.L., *Statutory Priorities in Corporate Insolvency Law: An Analysis of Preferred Creditor Status* (2008) (Ashgate)

Teubner, G. (ed), *Global Law without a State* (1997) (Ashgate)

Tomasic, R. (ed.), *Company Law in East Asia* (1999) (Dartmouth)

Tomasic, R. (ed.), *Insolvency Law in East Asia* (2006) (Ashgate)

Trollope, A., *The Way We Live Now* (1875) (Chatto and Windus)

Trollope, A., *The Way We Live Now* (1982) (OUP)

Twining, W., *Globalization and Legal Theory* (2002) (Butterworths)

Watson, A., *Legal Transplants: An Approach to Comparative Law* (2nd edition, 1993) (University of Georgia Press)

Wheeler, S., *Corporations and the Third Way* (2002) (Hart)

Whincop, M., *An Economic and Jurisprudential Genealogy of Corporate Law* (2001) (Ashgate)

Wood, P., *Maps of World Financial Law* (3rd edition, 1997) (Allen & Overy Global Law Maps)

Worthington, S. (ed.), *Commercial Law and Commercial Practice* (2003) (Hart)

Ziegel, J.S. et al. (eds), *Partnerships and Business Corporations* (2nd edition, 1989) (Carswell)

ARTICLES

Aldred, A., 'Businesses Have Rights Too: The Human Rights Act 1998' (2002) 23 Co Law 241

Al-Rimawi, L.M., 'Corporate Financial and Investment Legislation in Jordan' (1998) 19 Co Law 28

Al-Rimawi, L.M., 'Middle East: Recent Reforms in Arab Companies Regulations and an Outline of Jordan's Recent Association Agreement with the EU' (1998) 19 Co Law 89

Al-Rimawi, L.M., 'Jordan's Recent Association with the EU and the Latest Reforms in Arab Company and Financial Law' (1998) 9 EBLR 30

Andenas, M., 'Free Movement of Companies' (2003) 119 LQR 221

Andenas, M., 'Member States, Courts and Free Movement of Companies' (2006) 27 Co Law 1

Andenas, M., 'Cross Border Establishment in the EU' (2006) 27 Co Law 33

Andenas, M., 'Free Movement of Companies and Special Interests of Companies' (2007) 28 Co Law 65

Anderson, G.M., and Tollison, R.D., 'The Myth of the Corporation as a Creation of the State' (1983) 3 Int Rev of Law and Econ 107

Anderson, H., 'Corporate Social Responsibility: The Case for Unsecured Creditors' (2007) 7 Ox Univ Comm LJ 93

Ann, P.C., 'Some Concerns about Chinese Company Law' (1996) 17 Co Law 199

Arden, M., 'Reforming the Companies Acts: The Way Ahead' [2002] JBL 579

Armour, J., 'Share Capital and Creditor Protection: Efficient Rules for a Modern Company Law?' (2000) 63 MLR 355

Armour, J., 'European Cross Border Insolvencies: The Race Goes to the Swiftest?' [2006] CLJ 505

Armour, J., and Deakin, S., 'Norms in Private Insolvency: The London Approach to the Resolution of Financial Distress' [2001] 1 JCLS 21

Armour, J., and Whincop M., 'The Proprietary Foundations of Corporate Law' (2007) 27 OJLS 429

Arora, A., 'The Statutory Scheme of the Bank Supervision and the Failure of BCCI' [2006] JBL 487

Arsalidou, D., 'Objectivity vs Flexibility in Civil Law Jurisdictions and the Possible Introduction of the Business Judgment Rule in English Law' (2003) 24 Co Law 228

Bachner, T., 'Freedom of Establishment for Companies: A Great Leap Forward' [2003] CLJ 47

Ballantine, H.W., 'Separate Entity of Parent and Subsidiary Companies' (1925) 14 Calif L Rev 12

Ballantine, H.W., 'Questions of Policy in Drafting a Modern Corporation Law: California General Corporation Law' (1931) 19 Calif L Rev 465

Bamford, C., 'Legislative Reform and the Legacy of the Civil War' (2006) 27 Co Law 161

Bamford, C., 'Extradition and the Commercial World' (2007) 28 Co Law 97

Bamford, C., 'Northern Rock and the Single Market' (2008) 29 Co Law 65

Bannister, J., 'Universality Upheld: The House of Lords' Decision in *McGrath v Riddell* Considered' [2008] 232 SMCLN 1

Barnard, C., 'Social Dumping and the Race to the Bottom: Some Lessons for the EU from Delaware' (2000) 25 ELR 57

Barnes, K.D., 'Justice Survives Foss v Harbottle Rule' (1987) 8 Co Law 93

Baughen, S., 'Multinationals and the Export of Hazard' (1995) 58 MLR 54

Baums, T., 'Company Law Reform in Germany' (2003) 3 JCLS 181

Bebchuk, L.A., 'The Debate on Contractual Freedom in Corporate Law' (1989) 102 HarvLR 1883

Bebchuk, L.A., 'Federalism and the Corporation: The Desirable Limits on State Competition in Corporate Law' (1992) 105 Harv LR 1435

Bebchuk, L.A. and Roe, M.J., 'A Theory of Path Dependence in Corporate Ownership and Governance' (1999) 52 Stan L Rev 127

Belcher, A., 'Regulation by the Market: The Case of the Cadbury Code and Compliance Statement' [1995] JBL 321

Belcher, A., 'The Boundaries of the Firm: The Theories of Coase, Knight and Weitzman' [1997] 17 Leg Studs 22

Berg, A., 'The Cuckoo in the Nest of Corporate Insolvency: Some Aspects of the *Spectrum* Case' [2006] JBL 22

Berry, E., 'The Partnership Bill 2003: Unnecessary Tinkering or Much-Needed Reform?' [2005] JBL 70

Bird, C., 'The London Approach' (1996) 12 IL & P 87

Bird, J., 'Choice of Law Rule for Priority Disputes in Relation to Shares' [1996] LMCLQ 57

Birds, J., 'The Demise of Ultra Vires?' (1986) 7 Co Law 203

Birds, J., 'The Deregulatory Provisions of the Companies Act 1989' (1990) 11 Co Law 142

Birds, J., 'The Companies Act 2006: Revolution or Evolution?' [2007] 49 Manag Law 13

Bolodeoku, I.O., 'Going Virtual: Using Some Common Law World Initiatives to Update the Nigerian Law on Corporate Democracy' (2007) 36 CLWR 106

Bott, B., and Rosener, W., 'The Groupement d'Intérêt Economique' [1970] JBL 313

Bottomley, S., 'Taking Corporations Seriously: Some Considerations for Corporate Regulation' [1990] 19 Fed L Rev 203

Bovey, P., 'A Damn Close Run Thing: The Companies Act 2006' (2008) 29 Stat L Rev 11

Bowles, R., and Phillips, J., 'Judgments in Foreign Currencies: An Economist's View' (1976) 39 MLR 196

Boyle, A.J., 'When Foreign Companies Must Register Charges' (1980) 1 Co Law 244

Boyle, A.J., 'The Shareholder's Derivative Action in the English Conflict of Laws' [2000] 11 EBLR 130

Boyle, A.J., 'Law Reform: The Use of Comparative Law in the Strategic Framework' (2000) 21 Co Law 308

Boyle, A.J., 'The Company Law Review and Group Reform' (2002) 23 Co Law 35

Boyle, A.J., 'Conflict of Laws and Derivative Actions' (2002) 23 Co Law 263

Bradley, C., 'Corporate Control: Markets and Rules' (1990) 50 MLR 171

Bradley, C., 'Twenty First Century Anglo-American Partnership Law?' [2001] 30 CLWR 330

Branson, D.M., 'The Very Uncertain Prospect of "Global" Convergence in Corporate Governance' (2001) 34 Cornell Jo of Int Law 321

Bratton, W., 'The Nexus of Contracts: A Critical Appraisal' (1989) 74 Cornell L Rev 407

Bratton, W., 'Does Corporate Law Protect the Interests of Shareholders and Other Stakeholders: Enron and the Dark Side of Shareholder Value' (2002) 76 Tul L Rev 1275

Bridge, M., 'Clearing Houses and Insolvency in Australia' (2008) 124 LQR 379

Briggs, A., 'The Death of *Harrods*: Forum Non Conveniens and the European Court' (2005) 121 LQR 535

Briggs, H., '*Barcelona Traction*: The Ius Standi of Belgium' (1971) 65 Am Jo of Int Law 327

Brudney, V., 'Corporate Governance, Agency Costs and the Rhetoric of Contract' (1985) 85 Col L Rev 1403

Bryer, R.A., 'The Mercantile Laws Commission of 1854 and the Political Economy of Limited Liability' (1997) 50 Econ Hist Rev 37

Burger, R., 'Transatlantic Guidance' (2007) 157 NLJ 354

Butler, H.N., 'General Incorporation in 19th Century England: Interaction of Common Law and Legislative Processes' (1986) 6 Int Rev of Law and Econ 169

Cabral, P., and Cunha, P., 'Presumed Innocent: Companies and the Exercise of the Right of Establishment under Community Law' [2000] 25 ELR 157

Campbell, A., and Garrett, K., 'The Irish Examiner and Proposals for Reform of the Companies (Amendment) Act 1990' [1996] (February) Ins Law 12

Campbell, C., and Sakkas, Y., 'Transnational Insolvencies and the Impact of the EC Regulation on Insolvency Proceedings' (2003) 19 IL & P 48

Campbell, D., 'The Role of Monitoring and Morality in Company Law: A Critique of the Direction of Present Regulation' (1993) 7 Aust Jo of Corp Law 343

Capper, D., 'Final Report of the Legal Risk Review Committee' (1993) 44 NILQ 71

Carey, N., and Sarchet A., 'Guernsey: Squeezing Out Minority Shareholders: Developments in Takeover Law and Practice' (2006) 27 Co Law 252

Carr, I., 'The Legal Personality of Government Companies in India: An Overview' (1991) 10 ICCLR 339

Cary, W., 'Federalism and Corporate Law: Reflections Upon Delaware' (1974) 83 YLJ 663

Cerioni, L., 'The Barriers to the International Mobility of Companies within the European Community: A Re-reading of the Case Law' [1999] JBL 59

Cerioni, L., 'The Approved Version of the European Company Statute in Comparison with the 1991 Draft: Some First Remarks from the General Provisions and From the Directive on Employee Involvement' (2004) 25 Co Law 228

Cerioni, L., 'The Approved Version of the European Company Statute in Comparison with the 1991 Draft: Some Critical Issues on the Formation and Working of the SE and Key Challenges' (2004) 25 Co Law 259

Chandran, R., 'Singapore: New Insider Trading Legislation' (2001) 22 Co Law 63

Cheffins, B., 'Using Theory to Study Law: A Company Law Perspective' (1999) CLJ 197

Cheffins, B., 'Does Law Matter? The Separation of Ownership and Control in the United Kingdom' (2001) 30 Jo of Leg Studs 459

Cheffins, B.R., 'Law, Economics and the UK's System of Corporate Governance: Lessons from History' (2001) 1 JCLS 71

Cheffins, B., 'Law as Bedrock: The Foundations of an Economy Dominated by Widely-Held Public Companies' (2003) 23 OJLS 1

Cheffins, B.R., 'The Trajectory of (Corporate Law) Scholarship' [2004] CLJ 456

Cheung, R., 'Statutory Appraisal Right: The American Experience and Hong Kong Prospects' (2008) 19 ICCLR 325

Cheyne, I., 'Status of International Organisations in English Law' (1991) 40 ICLQ 981

Cheyne, I., 'The Foreign Corporations Act' (1991) 40 ICLQ 983

Ching, J., 'Security for Costs and Foreign Resident Claimants' (2009) 28 CJQ 89

Clarke, B., 'The Irish Takeover Panel Act 1997: A Further Cutting of the UK Regulatory Ties' [1998] (1) Palmer's In Company 1

Clarke, B., 'Arts 9 and 11 of the Takeover Directive (2004/25) and the Market for Corporate Control' [2006] JBL 355

Clarke, B., 'Insider Dealing: Getting under the Skin of Fyffes plc v DCC plc' [2009] JBL 68

Clausen, N.L., 'The Monitoring Duty of the Danish Board of Directors' (1991) 12 Co Law 68

Clough, M., 'Trying to Make the Fifth Directive Palatable' (1982) 3 Co Law 109

Coffee, J., 'The Future as History: The Prospects for Global Convergence in Corporate Governance and its Implications' (1999) 93 NwULRev 641

Cohn, E.J. and Simitis, C., 'Lifting the Veil in the Company Laws of the European Continent' (1963) 12 ICLQ 189

Copp, S. 'Thinking Ahead: "Flexibilty and Accessibility"' (2004) 25 Co Law 291

Cross, S., 'Limited Liability Partnerships Act 2000: Problems Ahead?' [2003] JBL 268

Cunningham L.A., 'From Convergence to Comity in Corporate Law: Lessons from the Inauspicious Case of SOX' [2004] 1 Int Jo of Disc and Gov 269

Curran, C., 'Changes to the Irish Examinership Procedure' [2003] 16 Ins Intell 7

Daehnert, A., 'Lifting the Corporate Veil: English and German Perspectives on Group Liability' [2007] 18 ICCLR 393

Dahan, F., 'The European Convention on Insolvency Proceedings and the Administrative Receiver: A Missed Opportunity?' (1996) 17 Co Law 181

Darvas, P., 'Australia – Corporate Law – into the Next Millennium' (2000) 21 Co Law 101

Dawson, I.J., 'The Territoriality of the Insolvency Act 1986 Where An Overseas Company Has been Wound Up by the English Court' [1995] (October) Ins Law 3

Dawson, K, 'The Extraterritoriality of the Insolvency Act 1986 and Foreign Directors' [1999] Ins Law 67

Dawson, K., 'An Extraterritorial Dichotomy?' [2000] Ins Law 81

Dawson, K., 'Winding up Foreign Companies: *Stocznia Gdanska v Latreefers Inc* Considered' [2000] Ins Law 173

Dawson, K., 'The UNCITRAL Model Law on Cross Border Insolvencies: Will It Make A Difference?' [2000] 4 RALQ 147

Dawson, K., 'The Jurisdictional Limit of the Court' (2000) 21 Co Law 132

Dawson, K., 'Hotchpot – Equality Amongst Creditors: *Cleaver v Delta Reinsurance*' [2002] Ins Law 53

Dawson, K., 'The Jurisdiction of the English Courts under the EC Regulation on Insolvency Proceedings' [2003] Ins Law 226

Dawson, K., 'The Doctrine of Forum Non Conveniens and the Winding Up of Insolvent Foreign Companies' [2005] JBL 28

Dean, J., 'Corporate Mobility and Company Law Cultures in Europe' [2003] 14 ICCLR 196

Deards, E., 'Partnership Law in the 21st Century' [2001] JBL 351

Deards, E., 'Limited Partnerships: Limited Reforms?' [2003] JBL 435

de Lacy, J., 'Anglo-Irish Retention of Title: The Current Position' (1987) 22 Ir Jur 212

de Lacy, J., 'Corporate Insolvency and Retention of Title Clauses: Developments in Australia' [2001] Ins Law 64

Diamond, A., 'The Reform of the Law of Security Interests' (1989) 42 CLP 231

Dignam, A., 'Exporting Corporate Governance: UK Regulatory Systems in a Global Economy' (2000) 21 Co Law 70

Dignam, A., 'The Globalisation of General Principle 7: Transforming the

Market for Corporate Control in Australia and Europe?' (2008) 28 Leg Studs 96

Dignam, A. and Galanis, M., 'Governing the World: The Development of the OECD Corporate Governance Principles' [1999] EBLR 396

Dine, J., 'The Community Company Law Harmonisation Programme' (1989) 14 ELR 322

Dine, J., 'The Governance of Governance' (1994) 15 Co Law 73

Dobson, J.M., 'Lifting the Veil in Four Countries: The Law of Argentina, England, France and the US' (1986) 35 ICLQ 839

Drucker, T.C., 'Companies in Private International Law' (1968) 17 ICLQ 28

Drury, R.R., 'Nullity of Companies in English Law' (1985) 48 MLR 644

Drury, R.R., 'The Regulation and Recognition of Foreign Corporations: Responses to the "Delaware Syndrome" ' [1998] 57 CLJ 165

Drury, R.R., 'Migrating Companies' (1999) 24 ELR 354

Drury, R.R., 'A European Look at the American Experience of the Delaware Syndrome' (2005) 5 JCLS 1

Drury, R.R., ' "The Delaware Syndrome": European Fears and Reactions' [2005] JBL 709

Drury, R.R., and Hicks, A., 'The Proposal for a European Private Company' [1999] JBL 429

Dumonteil, V.B. and Bertagne, J.J., 'The Reform of Company Law' (1984) 5 Co Law 47

du Plessis, J.J., 'Some International Developments in Company Law: A South African Perspective' (1993) 14 Co Law 224.

du Plessis, J.J., and Dine J., 'The Fate of the Draft Fifth Directive on Company Law' [1997] JBL 23

Dutson, S., 'The Conflict of Laws and Statutes: The International Operation of Legislation Dealing with Matters of Civil Law in the United Kingdom and Australia' (1997) 60 MLR 668

Easterbrook, F., and Fischel, D., 'Contractual Freedom in Corporate Law: Articles and Comments: The Corporate Contract' (1989) 89 Col L Rev 1416

Eden, P., 'Beneficial Ownership of Shares: The Implications of *Re Harvard Securities*' (2000) 16 IL & P 134 and 175

Edgtton, V., 'Appointment of Proxies by Electronic Communication: Do Companies Have to Wait for Enabling Legislation?' (2000) 21 Co Law 294

Edwards, V., 'Freedom of Establishment under the EC Treaty and the Effect of *Centros*' [2000] CFILR 342

Edwards, V., 'The European Company: Essential Tool or Eviscerated Dream?' (2003) 40 CMLRev 443

Eisenberg, M.A., 'The Structure of Corporation Law' (1989) 89 Col L Rev 1549

Elboz, S., 'Exiting Administration: Railtrack and the Future' (2002) 18 IL & P 187

Emmett, D., 'Australian Corporate Insolvency Law Reform' (2005) 21 IL & P 199

Enonchong, N., 'Harmonisation of Business Law in Africa: Is Art 42 of the OHADA Treaty a Problem' [2007] 51 JAL 95

Fabricius, F., 'The Private Company in German Law' [1970] JBL 229

Farnsworth, A., 'The Enemy Character of Corporations' (1944) 7 MLR 80

Farrar, J.H., 'Corporate Insolvency and the Law' [1976] JBL 214

Fawcett, J.J., 'A New Approach to Jurisdiction over Companies in Private International Law' (1988) 37 ICLQ 645

Fealy, M., 'Debt Subordination: Has the Eagle Landed?' [1993] CLJ 396

Ferran, E., 'The Decision of the House of Lords in *Russell v Northern Bank Development*' [1994] CLJ 343

Ferran, E., 'Corporate Law, Codes and Social Norms – Finding the Right Regulatory Combination and Institutional Structure' [2001] JCLS 381

Ferran, E., 'Simplification of European Company Law on Financial Assistance' [2005] 6 EBOLR 93

Fidler, P., 'The Foreign Tax Man Cometh: Or Does He?' [2000] Ins Law 219

Finch, V., 'Board Performance and Cadbury on Corporate Governance' [1992] JBL 581

Finch, V., 'Is Pari Passu Passé?' [2000] Ins Law 194

Finch, V., and Freedman, J., 'The Limited Liability Partnership: Pick and Mix or Mix-up?' [2002] JBL 475

Fitzgerald, N., 'Treatment of Directors of Insolvent Companies under Irish Law' (2004) 20 IL & P 108

Flannery, G., 'Registration and Publication of Judgments Opening Insolvency Proceedings under the EC Regulation (With Particular Reference to the Crisscross Communications case)' (2005) 21 IL & P 57

Fletcher, I., 'The Ascendance of Comity from the Ashes of Felixstowe Dock' [1993] 6 Ins Intell 10

Fletcher, I., 'International Insolvency Issues: Recent Cases' [1997] JBL 471

Fletcher, I., 'A New Type of International Insolvency – The Countdown Has Begun' [2000] 13 Ins Intell 57

Fletcher, I., 'Registration of Charges and the Conflict of Laws' [2004] 17 Ins Intell 61

Fletcher, I., 'Better Late than Never: The UNCITRAL Model Law Enters into Force in Great Britain' [2006] 19 Ins Intell 86

Fletcher, I., 'UNCITRAL Model Law in the UK' [2007] 20 Ins Intell 125

Fletcher, K., 'Financial Assistance around the Pacific Rim' (2006) 6 Ox Univ Comm LJ 157

Floyd, R.E., 'Corporate Recovery: The London Approach' (1995) 11 IL & P 82

Freedman, J., and Finch, V., 'Limited Liability Partnerships: Have Accountants Sewn up the Deep Pockets Debate' [1997] JBL 387

Frenkel, W.G., 'Russia's New Company Law' (1996) 7 ICCLR 175

Friedland, J., 'The Sarbanes-Oxley Act: Corporate Governance, Financial Reporting and Economic Crime' (2002) 23 Co Law 384

Friedland, J., 'Sarbanes-Oxley Makes Waves in the UK' (2004) 25 Co Law 162

Gaines, K., 'Appyling the May 2002 Insolvency Regulation on Insolvency Proceedings' [2001] Ins Law 201

Garoupa, N., and Ogus, A., 'A Strategic Interpretation of Legal Transplants' (2006) 35 Jo of Leg Studs 339

Gates, S., 'Disregarding the Corporate Entity in Favour of Beneficial Ownership and Control' (1984) 12 ABLR 162

Gelter, M., 'The Structure of Regulatory Competition in European Corporate Law' (2005) 5 JCLS 247

Getz, L., 'Annual Survey of Canadian Law: Corporate Law' (1971) 5 Ottawa L Rev 154

Girvin, S., 'The Antecedents of South African Company Law' (1992) 13 Jo of Leg Hist 63

Goddard, R., 'Modernising Company Law: The Government's White Paper' (2003) 66 MLR 402

Goddard, R., 'Disqualifying the Directors of a Corporate Director: *Secretary of State for Trade and Industry v Hall and Nuttall*' (2007) 28 Co Law 281

Goff, Lord, 'The Future of the Common Law' (1997) 46 ICLQ 745

Goldman, B., 'The Convention between Member States of the EEC on the Mutual Recognition of Companies and Legal Persons' (1968–9) 6 CMLRev 104

Goldson, S.F., 'The Commonwealth Caribbean Territories: The Reform of the Law Relating to the Duties of Directors' (2003) 24 Co Law 378

Goode, R., 'Rule, Practice and Pragmatism in International Commercial Law' (2005) 54 ICLQ 539

Gordon, J., 'The Mandatory Structure of Corporate Law' (1989) 89 Col LR 1549

Gower, L.C.B., 'A South Sea Heresy?' (1952) 68 LQR 214

Gower, L.C.B., 'Some Contrasts between British and American Corporate Law' (1956) 69 Harv L Rev 1369

Gower, L.C.B., 'Company Law Reform' (1962) 4 Mal L Rev 36

Gower, L.C.B., 'Reforming Company Law' (1980) 14 Law Teach 111

Gower, L.C.B., ' "Big Bang" and City Regulation' (1988) 51 MLR 1

Graham, C., ' "All that Glitters" . . . Golden Shares and Privatised Enterprises' (1988) 9 Co Law 23

Graham, C., and Prosser, T., 'Privatising Nationalised Industries: Constitutional Issues and New Legal Techniques' (1987) 50 MLR 16

Graham, D., 'Shakespeare in Debt: English and International Insolvency in Tudor England' [2000] 13 Ins Intell 36

Graham, D., 'Discovering Jabez Henry: Cross Border Insolvency Law in the 19th Century' [2000] 10 Int Ins Rev 153

Grantham, R., 'The Judicial Extension of Directors' Duties to Creditors' [1991] JBL 1

Grantham, R., 'The Unanimous Consent Rule in Company Law' [1993] CLJ 245

Greenwood, C., 'The Tin Council Litigation in the House of Lords' [1990] CLJ 8

Griffin, S., 'Corporate Collapse and the Reform of Boardroom Structures: Lessons from America' [2003] Ins Law 214

Griffin, S., 'Limited Liability: A Necessary Revolution?' (2004) 25 Co Law 99

Griffith, R., 'The Rusia Company – 439 Years Not Out!' (1994) 15 Co Law 105

Griffiths, A., 'Professional Firms and Limited Liability: An Analysis of the Proposed Limited Liability Partnership' [1998] CFILR 157

Griffiths, D., and Tschentscher, F., 'The Straw Dogs of Europe' [2004] 17 Ins Intell 57

Griffiths, N., 'The Cross Border Insolvency Regulations 2006' (2007) 23 IL & P 6

Haines, J.D., 'The Markets in Financial Investments Directive (MIFID): Investor Protection Enhanced by Suitability Requirements' (2007) 28 Co Law 344

Halbhuber, H., 'National Doctrinal Structures and European Company Law' (2001) 38 CMLRev 1385

Halstead, R., and Magee, S., 'A Government Takeover Panel: The Australian Experience' [2005] (14) SMCLN 1

Halstead, R., and Magee, S., 'Australian Takeovers Panel in Legal Battle' [2005] (16) SMCLN 5

Halstead, R., and Magee, S., 'Australian Takeovers Panel Defeated in Court' [2005] (20) SMCLN 5

Hannigan, B., 'The Reform of the Ultra Vires Rule' [1987] JBL 173

Hannigan, B., 'Altering the Articles to Allow for Compulsory Transfer: Dragging Minority Shareholders to a Reluctant Exit' [2007] JBL 471

Hare, C., 'Forum Non Conveniens in Europe: Game Over or Time for "Reflexion"?' [2006] JBL 157

Hargovan, A., and Harris, J., 'Piercing the Corporate Veil in Canada: A Comparative Analysis' (2007) 28 Co Law 58

Harris, J., 'Need for a Central Administration Search Facility' (2006) 27 Co Law 321

Harris, J., 'International Regulation of Hedge Funds: Can the Will Find a Way?' (2007) 28 Co Law 277

Harris, R., and Crystal, M., 'Some Reflections on the Transplantation of British Company Law in Post Ottoman Palestine' (2009) 10 Th Inq Law (forthcoming)

Harter-Bachmann, S., 'Sarbanes-Oxley Act: Have the Americans Set Capital Market Standards?' (2006) 27 Co Law 35

Hartley, T., 'The European Union and the Systematic Dismantling of the Common Law Conflict of Laws' (2005) 54 ICLQ 813

Haynes, A., 'Market Abuse: An Analysis of its Nature and Regulation' (2007) 28 Co Law 323

Hebert, S., 'Corporate Governance: French Style' [2004] JBL 656

Hemraj, M.B., 'Company Directors: The Defence of Business Judgement Rule' (2003) 24 Co Law 218

Henning, J.J., 'Limited Partnerships and Limited Liability Partnerships' (2000) 21 Co Law 165

Henning, J.J., 'Company Law for the New Millennium: Think Small First' (2003) 24 Co Law 353

Henning, J.J., 'The Enduring South African Close Corporation: 21 Years of Simply "Thinking Small First" Successfully' (2007) 28 Co Law 253

Henshaw, A., 'International Insolvency: Whose Law to be Preferred?' [1997] (July) Ins Law 5

Herrera-Davila, S., 'Companies Act has Brought Legal Measures' (1981) 2 Co Law 139

Herzel, L., and Colling, D.E., 'The Chinese Wall Revisited' (1983) 4 Co Law 14

Hitchens, L., 'Directorships: How Many is Too Many?' [2000] CFILR 359

Ho, L.C, 'Pari Passu Distribution and Post Petition Disposition: A Rationalisation of *Re Tain Construction*' (2003) 19 IL & P 155

Ho, L.C., 'Anti-Suit Injunctions and Cross Border Insolvency: A Restatement' (2003) 52 ICLQ 697

Ho, L.C., 'On Pari Passu, Equality and Hotchpot in Cross Border Insolvency' [2003] LMCLQ 95

Ho, L.C., 'The Principle against Divestiture in Insolvency Revisited: *Fraser v Oystertec*' [2004] JIBLR 54

Ho, L.C., 'Navigating the Common Law Approach to Cross Border Insolvency' (2006) 22 IL & P 217

Homan, M., 'Cross Border Insolvency in 15 Minutes' [2002] 15 Ins Intell 60

Hood, P., 'Salomon's Case and the Single "Business Organisation"' [2001] JBL 58

Hopt, K., 'Company Law in the European Union: Harmonisation and/or Subsidiarity?' (1999) 1 ICCLJ 41

Hopt, K.J., 'Modern Company and Capital Market Problems: Improving European Corporate Governance after Enron' (2003) 3 JCLS 221

Howell, C., 'The Company White Paper: A Descriptive Overview' (2005) 26 Co Law 203

Hughes Parry, D., 'Economic Theories in English Case Law' (1931) 47 LQR 183

Hunter, M., 'The Nature and Functions of a Rescue Culture' [1999] JBL 491

Hurst, T.R., 'Post-Enron Examination of Corporate Governance Problems in the Investment Company Industry' (2006) 27 Co Law 41

Hurst, T.R., 'Hedge Funds in the 21st Century: Do the Benefits Outweigh Potential Dangers to the Financial Markets?' (2007) 28 Co Law 228

Ireland, P., 'Property and Contract in Contemporary Corporate Theory' (2003) 23 Leg Studs 453

Israel, S., 'The EEIG: A Major Step Forward for Community Law' (1988) 9 Co Law 14

Israels, C.L., 'Implications and Limitations of the *Deep Rock* Doctrine' (1942) 42 Col L Rev 376

Jacobs, E., 'Conceptual Contrasts: Comparative Approaches to Company Law Reform' (1990) 11 Co Law 215

Jaehne, C., and Henning, J.J., 'The European Court of Justice and the Future of the German Private Company (GmbH)' (2007) 28 Co Law 33

Jayasuriya, D., 'Sri Lanka's New Companies Act: An Overview' (2008) 29 Co Law 250

Johnston, A., 'The European Takeover Directive: Ruined by Protectionism or Respecting Diversity?' (2004) 25 Co Law 270

Johnston, A., 'Takeover Regulation: Historical and Theoretical Perspectives on the City Code' (2007) 66 CLJ 422

Jones, B., 'The Law Determining Directors' Duties' [2005] 18 Ins Intell 29

Jones, J.L., 'Big Bang and the Stock Exchange' (1986) 7 Co Law 99

Jordan, C., 'Hong Kong Looks to Cast Off Company Law Past' [1997] IFLRev 29

Jordan, D., 'Companies Act Section 151: The Nightmare is Nearly Over' (2002) The Lawyer (4 November) 13

Kahn, K.I.F., 'Caribbean: The Demise of the Doctrine of Ultra Vires: Suggested Reforms within Common Market Structures' (1985) 6 Co Law 141

Kahn-Freund, O., 'Some Reflections on Company Law Reform' (1944) 7 MLR 54

Kahn-Freund, O., 'Final Report of the Commission of Inquiry into the Working and Administration of Present Company Law in Ghana' (1962) 25 MLR 78

Kahn-Freund, O., 'The Uses and Misuses of Comparative Law' (1974) 37 MLR 1

Keay, A., 'The Advent of a National Scheme to Protect the Entitlements of Employees in Australia' [2000] Ins Law 137

Keay, A., 'The Duty of Directors to Take Account of Creditors' Interests: Has it Any Role to Play?' [2002] JBL 379

Keay, A., 'Directors' Duties to Creditors: Contractarian Concerns Relating to Efficiency and Over-protection of Creditors' (2003) 66 MLR 665

Keay, A., 'Formulating a Framework for Directors' Duties to Creditors: An Entity Maximisation Approach' [2005] CLJ 614

Keay, A., 'Directors' Duties: Do Recent Canadian Developments Require a Rethink in the UK on the Issue of Directors' Duties to Consider Creditors' Interests?' [2005] 18 Ins Intell 65

Keay, A., 'Section 172(1) of the Companies Act 2006: An Interpretation and Assessment' (2007) 28 Co Law 106

Keay, A., Boraine, A., and Burdette, D., 'Preferential Debts in Corporate Insolvency: A Comparative Study' (2001) Int Insolv Rev 167

Keay, A., and Loughrey, J., 'Something Old, Something New, Something Borrowed: An Analysis of the New Derivative Action under the Companies Act 2006' (2008) 124 LQR 469

Keay, A., and Walton, P., 'The Preferential Debts Regime in Liquidation Law: In the Public Interest?' [1999] CFILR 84

Keay, A., and Walton, P., 'Preferential Debts: An Empirical Study' [1999] Ins Law 112

Keegan, S., 'The European Economic Interest Grouping' [1991] JBL 457

Kennett, W., 'Forum Non Conveniens in Europe' [1995] CLJ 552

Kent, P., 'The London Approach' (1993) 33 B of Eng Quart Bull 110

Kershaw, D., 'Evading Enron: Taking Principles Too Seriously in Accounting Regulation' (2005) 68 MLR 594

Kinley, D., 'Lawyers, Corporations and International Human Rights Law' (2004) 25 Co Law 298

Knight, C.J.S., '*Owusu* and *Turner*: The Shark in the Water?' [2008] CLJ 288

Krause, N., and Qin, C., 'An Overview of China's New Company Law' (2007) 28 Co Law 316

Kubler, F., 'A Comparative Approach to Capital Maintenance: Germany' (2004) 15 EBLR 1031

La Porta, R., 'Corporate Ownership around the World' [1999] 54 Jo of Fin 471

La Porta, R., 'Investor Protection and Corporate Valuation' (2002) 57 Jo of Fin 1147

La Porta, R., et al., 'Law and Finance' (1998) 106 Jo of Pol Econ 1113

La Porta, R., et al., 'Investor Protection and Corporate Governance' (2000) 58 Jo of Fin Econ 3

Lasok, K.P.E., and Grace, E., 'The True and Fair View' (1989) 10 Co Law 13

Lau, A., 'Proposals for Chinese Company Law Reform' (2006) 27 Co Law 376

Lawson, M., 'The Reform of the Law Relating to Security Interests in Property' [1989] JBL 287

Lawton, P., 'Modelling the Chinese Family Firm and Minority Shareholder Protection: The Hong Kong Experience' [2007] 49 Manag Law 249

Lazarides, M.T., 'Acquiring Companies: The Problems of Ownership and Control' (1983) 4 Co Law 66

Leacock, S.J., 'Company Law Reform in Jamaica' [1975] JBL 252

Lee, G., and Bannister, J., 'Taming the Beast: Reforms to Ch 11 of the US Bankruptcy Code Take Effect' [2005] 21 SMCLN 1

Lee, P.-W., 'Regulating Directors' Duties with Civil Penalties: Taking a Leaf from Australia's Book' [2006] 36 CLWR 1

Lele, P., and Siems, M.M., 'Shareholder Protection: A Leximetric Approach' (2007) 7 JCLS 17

Leleux, P., 'Corporate Law in the US and the EEC: Can the European Community Learn from the US?' (1967) 5 CMLRev 133

Lewis, D., 'Corporate Redomicile' (1995) 16 Co Law 295

Leyden, A., 'Section 150 of the Companies Act 1990: Some Recent Developments' (2006) 9 Trin Coll L Rev 147

Li, A.Y.S., and Ho, S.S.M., 'Rebuilding Market Confidence: China's Revised Company Law' (2006) 27 Co Law 311

Li, A.Y.S., and Ho, S.S.M., 'Proposals for Chinese Company Law Reform' (2006) 27 Co Law 376

Lidbetter, A., 'Overseas Companies: Jurisdiction' [1990] JBL 137

Lightman, G., 'Recent Developments in Insolvency Law: A Judicial View' [2005] 19 SMCLN 1

Linklater, L., 'Reshaping Criminal Sanctions in Company Law' (2003) 24 Co Law 1

Linnane, H., 'Delinquent Directors and Others: The Irish Approach' (1995) 16 Co Law 26

Linnane, H., 'Directors' Duties to Creditors: The Adoption of *Kinsella* into Irish Law' (1995) 16 Co Law 319

Lobban, M., 'Corporate Identity and Limited Liability in France and England 1825–1867' [1996] 25 Anglo-Am L Rev 397

Lowe, A.V., 'Extraterritorial Jurisdiction: The British Practice' [1988] RabelsZ 163

Lower, M., 'Limited Liability for Small, Closely-Held Businesses' (2000) 22 Liv L Rev 89

Lowry, J., 'The International Approach to Insider Trading: The Council of Europe Convention' [1990] JBL 460

Lowry, J., 'Poison Pills in US Corporations: A Re-examination' [1992] JBL 337

Lowry, J., 'Eliminating Obstacles to Freedom of Establishment: The Competitive Edge of UK Company Law' [2004] CLJ 331

Lucas, S., and Maltsev, Y., 'The Development of Corporate Law in the Former Soviet Republics' (1996) 45 ICLQ 365

Lunt, M.G., 'The Extraterritorial Effects of the Sarbanes-Oxley Act 2002' [2006] JBL 247

Lynch-Fannon, I., 'The Corporate Social Responsibility Movement and Law's Empire: Is there a Conflict?' (2007) 58 NILQ 1

Macdonald, I., and Moujalli, D., 'A Very English Concept: The Receiver Appointed Out of Court' [2001] 14 Ins Intell 76.

Macmillan, F., 'Regulating Multinational Enterprises' (2003) 24 Co Law 355

MacNeill, I., 'Shareholders' Pre-Emptive Rights' [2002] JBL 78

MacNeill, I., and Lau, A., 'International Corporate Regulation: Listing Rules and Overseas Companies' (2001) 50 ICLQ 787

Mann, F.A. 'Untitled Note' (1976) 92 LQR 165

Mann, F.A., 'The Effect in England of the Compulsory Acquisition by a Foreign State of the Shares in a Foreign Company' (1986) 102 LQR 191

Mann, F.A., 'International Organisations as National Corporations' (1991) 107 LQR 357

Manne, H., 'Mergers and the Market for Corporate Control' (1965) 73 Jo of Pol Econ 110

Manson, E., 'The Evolution of the Private Company' (1910) 26 LQR 11

Markesinis, B., 'Foreign Law Inspiring National Law: Lessons from *Greatorex* v *Greatorex*' [2002] CLJ 386

Markova, O., 'Limited Liability Company Law in Russia' (1998) 9 ICCLR 334

Marshall, J., 'Where Does a Hedge Fund Have its Centre of Main Interests?' [2007] (Winter) Recovery 9

Marston, G., 'The Arab Monetary Fund: Legal Person or Creature from Outer Space?' [1991] CLJ 218

Marston, G., 'The Personality of the Foreign State in English Law' [1997] CLJ 374

Maynard, P., 'Harmonsation of Companies Laws in the Caribbean' [1982] JBL 421

Mayss, A., 'The Status of the AMF in English Law' (1990) 7 Co Law 140

McBeth, A., 'A Look at Corporate Code of Conduct Legislation' [2004] 33 CLWR 222

McCahery, J., and Vermeulen, E., 'Does the European Company Prevent the Delaware Effect?' [2005] ELJ 785

McCormack, G., 'Self-Incrimination in the Corporate Context' [1993] JBL 425

McCormack, G., 'The House of Fraser Inspectors Report' (1994) 15 Co Law 40

McCormack, G., 'Conflicts of Interest, Chinese Walls and Investment Management' (1999) 1 ICCLJ 5

McCormack, G., 'The Law Commission and Company Security Interests – A Climb Down?' (2005) 18 Sweet & Maxwell's Company Law Newsletter 1

McCormack, G., 'Super-priority New Financing and Corporate Rescue' [2007] JBL 701

McCormack, G., 'Control and Corporate Rescue' (2007) 56 ICLQ 515

McCorquodale, R., and Simons, P., 'Responsibility beyond Borders: State Responsibility for Extraterritorial Violations by Corporations of International Human Rights Law' (2007) 70 MLR 598

McGee, A., 'The "True and Fair View" Debate: A Study in the Legal Regulation of Accounting' (1991) 54 MLR 874

McQueen, R., 'Why High Court Judges Make Poor Historians: The Corporations Act Case and Earlier Attempts to Establish a National System of Company Regulation in Australia' (1990) 19 Fed L Rev 245

McQueen, R., 'Company Law as Imperialism' (1995) 5 Aust Jo of Corp Law 187

McQueen, R., 'The Flowers of Progress: Corporations Law in the Colonies' (2008) 17 Griff L Rev 383

McVea, H., '"Heard it Through the Grapevine": Chinese Walls and Former Client Confidentiality in Law Firms' [2000] CLJ 370

McVea, H., 'Hedge Funds and the New Regulatory Agenda' (2007) 27 Leg Studs 709

Meier-Boeschenstein, O.C., 'Joint Stock Companies' [1994] JBL 212

Meisel, F., 'Worldwide Freezing Orders: The Dadourian Guidelines' (2007) 26 CJQ 176

Melis, A., 'Corporate Governance Failures: To What Extent is Parmalat a Particularly Italian Case?' (2005) 13 Corp Gov: An International Review 478

Mevorach, I., 'Centralising Insolvencies of Pan-European Corporate Groups: A Creditor's Dream or Nightmare?' [2006] JBL 468

Micheler, E., 'The Impact of the *Centros* Case on Europe's Company Laws' (2000) 21 Co Law 179

Micheler, E., 'Farewell Quasi-negotiability? Legal Title and Transfer of Shares in a Paperless World' [2002] JBL 358

Micheler, E., 'Recognition of Companies Incorporated in other EU Member States' (2003) 52 ICLQ 521

Micheler, E., 'English and German Securities Law: A Thesis in Doctrinal Path Dependence' (2007) 123 LQR 251

Miles, L., and He, M., 'Protecting the Rights and Interests of Minority Shareholders in Listed Companies in China: Challenges for the Future' [2005] 16 ICCLR 275

Miles, L., 'The Cultural Aspects of Corporate Governance Reform in South Korea' [2007] JBL 851

Miller, J.G., 'Bankruptcy and Foreign Revenue Claims' [1991] JBL 144

Milman, D., 'The Romalpa Case: Guidance from Ireland?' (1978) 122 SJ 172

Milman, D., 'Foreign Companies Compliance with Company Law' (1979) 123 SJ 560

Milman, D., 'Registration of Charges Created by Overseas Companies' (1981) 125 SJ 294

Milman, D., 'Freezing Orders and Foreigners' (1985) 6 Co Law 184

Milman, D., 'Le Quesne: Finding Fact or Fault?' (1989) 10 Co Law 113

Milman, D., 'The Courts and the Companies Acts: The Judicial Contribution to Company Law' [1990] LMCLQ 401

Milman, D., 'Strategies for Regulating Managerial Performance in the "Twilight Zone" [2004] JBL 493

Milman, D., 'Two Cases of Interest for Company Directors Operating in the "Twilight Zone"' [2008] 21 Ins Intell 25

Milman, D., and Evans, A., 'Corporate Officers and the Outsider Protection Regime' (1985) 6 Co Law 68

Milman, D., and Singh, D., 'The Evolution of the Share Freezing Order in UK Company Law' (1992) 13 Co Law 51

Milman, D., 'Companies Have Rights' [2000] (3) SMCLN 1

Mitchell, C., 'Lifting the Corporate Veil in the English Courts: An Empirical Study' [1999] 3 CFILR 15

Mitchell, R., and Stockdale, M., 'Your Answers May not be Used in Evidence Against You' (2002) 23 Co Law 232

Mitchell, V., 'Company Law Reviews in Australia and the UK' (1999) 20 Co Law 98

Mokal, R.J., 'Priority as Pathology: The Pari Passu Myth' [2001] CLJ 581

Mokal. R.J., and Ho, L.C., 'The Pari Passu Principle in English Ancillary Proceedings' (2005) 21 IL & P 207

Moloney, N., 'Financial Market Regulation in the Post-financial Services Action Plan Era' (2006) 55 ICLQ 982

Moore, M.T., '"A Temple Built on Faulty Foundations": Piercing the Corporate Veil and the Legacy of *Salomon v Salomon*' [2006] JBL 180

Moore, S., 'Chapter 15 – A New Era for COMI Disputes?' (2007) 23 IL & P 178

Moore, S., 'COMI Migration: The Future' [2009] 22 Ins Intell 9

Morgan, T., 'He that is Without sin Among You – Let Him First Cast a Stone' (2003) 24 Co Law 194

Morris, P., and Stevenson, J., 'The Jersey Limited Liability Partnership: A New Legal Vehicle for Professional Practice' (1997) 60 MLR 538

Morse, C.G.J., 'Retention of Title in English Private International Law' [1993] JBL 168

Morse, G., 'Mutual Recognition of Companies in England and the EEC' [1972] JBL 195

Morse, G., 'The Introduction of Treasury Shares into English Law and Practice' [2004] JBL 303

Morse, G., 'Regulating Takeovers: The Regulators and the Courts – Quis Custodiet Ipsos Custodes' (2007) 22 NZULR 622

Moss, G., 'Cross Frontier Cooperation in Insolvency: Assistance from the Courts in England and the US' [1999] Ins Law 146

Moss, G., 'Protected Cell Companies" Insolvency Issues' [2001] 14 Ins Intell 73

Moss, G., 'Cooperation Between Courts' [2003] 16 Ins Intell 47

Moss, G., 'Asking the Right Questions? Highs and Lows of the ECJ Judgment in the *Eurofood* Case' [2006] 19 Ins Intell 97

Moss, G., 'Common Law Judicial Assistance Comes of Age' [2006] 19 Ins Intell 123

Moss, G., 'Bear Necessities: Chapter 15 Goes on Appeal' [2007] 21 Ins Intell 27

Moss, G., 'Modified Universalism and the Quest for the Golden Thread' [2008] 22 Ins Intell 118

Moss, G., and Paulus, C., 'The European Insolvency Regulation: The Case for Urgent Reform' [2006] 19 Ins Intell 1

Muchlinski, P., 'The Bhopal Case: Controlling Ultrahazardous Industrial Activities Undertaken by Foreign Investors' (1987) 50 MLR 545

Muchlinski, P., 'Corporations in International Litigation: Problems of Jurisdiction and the UK Asbestos Cases' (2001) 50 ICLQ 1

Muchlinski, P., 'Holding Multinationals to Account: Recent Developments in English Litigation and the Company Law Review' (2002) 23 Co Law 168

Murray, M., 'The Collapse and Liquidation of the HIH Insurance Group in Australia' [2002] Ins Law 223

Mwenda, K.K., 'Liability of Company Directors for Wrongful Trading and Fraudulent Trading: the Case of Zambia' (2008) 8 Ox Uni Comm LJ 93

Nadelmann, K.H., 'Bankruptcy and Treaties' (1944) 93 Univ Penn L Rev 58

Naruisch, T. and Liepe, F., 'Latest Developments in the German Law on Public Companies by the Act on Corporate Integrity and Modernisation of the Right of Resolution-Annulment (UMAG) – Shareholder Activism and Directors' Liability Reloaded' [2007] JBL 225

Naylor, J.M., 'The Use of Criminal Sanctions by UK and US Authorities for Insider Dealing: How Can the Two Systems Learn from Each Other?' (1990) 11 Co Law 53 and 83

Noack, U., 'Modern Communications Methods and Company Law' (1998) 9 EBLR 100

Nolan, R.C., 'Less Equal than Others: Maxwell and Subordinated Unsecured Obligations' [1995] JBL 485

Obadina, D.A., 'Irregular, Intra Vires Corporate Transactions and the Protection of Third Parties in the UK and Commonwealth: The Case for Reform' (1997) 18 Co Law 45 and 76

Ogowewo, T., 'The Application of the Residence Test in the City Code's Jurisdictional Rule' (2002) 23 Co Law 216

Okeke, L.O., 'Nigeria: The Resurrection of Dead Preincorporation Contracts' (2000) 21 Co Law 320

Omar, P., 'Private International Law Rules in Insolvency: The British Model' [1998] (April) Ins Law 7

Omar, P., 'France: Company Law Reform: Another French Revolution' (1998) 19 Co Law 62

Omar, P., 'France: The 1998 Company Law Reform Programme' (1999) 20 Co Law 310

Omar, P., 'Cross-Border Cooperation in Australian Corporate Insolvency Law' [1999] Ins Law 69

Omar, P., 'New Initiatives on Cross Border Insolvency in Europe' [2000] Ins Law 211

Omar, P., 'Insolvency Law Initiatives in Developing Economies: The OHADA Uniform Law' [2000] Ins Law 257

Omar, P., 'The UNCITRAL Insolvency Initiative: A Five-year Review' [2002] Ins Law 228

Omar, P., 'Centros Redux: Conflict at the Heart of European Company Law' [2002] 13 ICCLR 445

Omar, P., 'Cooperation between Courts: The Common Law Legacy' [2003] Ins Law 74

Omar, P., '*Centros, Uberseering* and Beyond: A European Recipe for Corporate Migration' [2005] 16 ICCLR 17

Omar, P., 'Cross Border Insolvency Law in the UK: An Embarrassment of Riches' (2006) 22 IL & P 132

Omar, P., 'Addressing the Reform of the Insolvency Regulation: Wishlists or Fancies?' [2007] 20 Ins Intell 7

O'Neill, A., 'Corporate Reputation in the House of Lords' (2007) 28 Co Law 75

O'Neill, A., 'Relieving Directors: The Irish Approach' (2007) 28 Co Law 116

O' Neill, A., 'Part 40 of the UK Companies Act 2006: Disqualification Orders Go Global' (2007) 18 ICCLR 166

Osunbor, O.A., 'A Critical Appraisal of the "Interests of Justice" as an Exception to the Rule in *Foss v Harbottle*' (1987) 36 ICLQ 1

Ottolenghi, S., 'From Peeping behind the Corporate Veil to Ignoring it Completely' (1990) 53 MLR 338

Parsons, R.W., 'Uniform Company Law in Australia' [1962] JBL 235

Pasban, M.R., 'A Review of Directors Liabilities of an Insolvent Company in the US and England' [2001] JBL 33

Pasban, M.R., Campbell, C., and Birds, J., 'Protection of Corporate Directors in UK and US' (1997) 26 Anglo-Am L Rev 461

Patterson, M., and Reiffen, D., 'The Effect of the Bubble Act on the Market for Joint Stock Shares' (1990) 50 Jo of Econ Hist 163

Pekmezovic, A., 'Determinants of Corporate Ownership: The Question of Legal Origin' [2007] ICCLR 97

Pen Kent, 'The London Approach: Distressed Debt Trading' (1994) 33 Bank of Eng Quart 110

Pennington, R.R., 'Report of the Company Law Committee' (1962) 25 MLR 703

Perry, A.J., 'Effective Legal Systems and Foreign Direct Investment: In Search of the Evidence' (2000) 49 ICLQ 779

Perry, A.J., 'The Relationship between Legal Systems and Economic Development: Integrating Economic and Cultural Approaches' (2002) 29 Jo of Law and Soc 282

Perry-Kessaris, A., 'Finding and Facing Facts about Legal Systems and FDI in South Asia' (2003) 23 Leg Studs 649

Pettet, B., 'Limited Liability: A Principle for the 21st Century' [1995] CLP 124

Pettet, B., 'The Stirring of Corporate Social Conscience: From Cakes and Ale to Community Programmes' (1997) 50 CLP 279

Pettet, B., 'Towards a Competitive Company Law' (1998) 19 Co Law 134

Pettet, B., 'Company Law and Corporate Markets Law: European Integration' (2004) 57 CLP 393.

Picciotto, S., 'Rights, Responsibilities and Regulation of International Business' (2003) 42 Col Jo of Transnat Law 131

Pistor, K., 'The Standardization of Law and its Effect Upon Developing Economies' (2002) 50 Am Jo of Comp Law 97

Pistor, K. et al., 'Innovation in Corporate Law' (2003) 31 Jo of Comp Econ 676

Pistor, K. et al., 'The Evolution of Corporate Law: A Cross Country Comparison' (2003) 23 Univ of Penn Jo of Int Econ Law 791

Plant, S., 'The Administration of Railtrack plc: Law in the Making' (2002) 18 IL & P 18

Poser, N., 'Chinese Wall or Emperor's New Clothes?' (1988) 9 Co Law 119 and 165

Prentice, D., 'Creditors' Interests and Directors' Duties' (1990) 10 OJLS 265

Prime, T., and Scanlan, G., 'Limited Partnership Reform: The Entity, the Fiduciary Duties and the Execution of Deeds' (2007) 28 Co Law 262

Procaccia, U., 'Designing a New Corporate Code for Israel' (1987) 35 Am Jo of Comp Law 581

Pulle, A.I., 'The New Company Law of Indonesia' (1996) 17 Co Law 122

Purvis, J., 'Barbados: New Companies Act Helps Island Develop as Tax and Financial Haven' (1983) 4 Co Law 280

Qureshi, K., and Sprange, T., 'Preserving the Status Quo' (2007) 157 NLJ 1958

Rajak, H., 'Judicial Control: Corporations and the Decline of Ultra Vires' [1995] 26 Camb L Rev 9

Rajak, H., 'The Harmonisation of Insolvency Proceedings in the EU' [2000] CFILR 180

Rajak, H., and Henning, J., 'Business Rescue for South Africa' (1999) 116 SALJ 262

Rammeloo, S.G., 'Jurisdiction Clauses in Transnational Company Relationships' [1994] 1 MJ of Euro and Comp Law 426

Rammeloo, S.G., 'The 14th EC Company Law Directive on the Cross Border Transfer of the Registered Office of Limited Liability Companies: Now or Never?' (2008) 15 MJ of Euro and Comp Law 359

Ramsay, I., 'Corporate Law in the Age of Statutes' (1992) 14 Syd L Rev 474

Rappaport, I., 'Freedom of Establishment: A New Perspective' [2000] JBL 628

Rapinet, C., 'ECJ Resolves Parmalat Jurisdictional Battle under ECRIP' [2006] (10) SMCLN 1

Reisberg, A., 'Israel: Promoting the Use of Derivative Actions' (2003) 24 Co Law 250

Rice, D.G., 'Foreign Companies in Great Britain' [1962] JBL 155

Rider, B., 'New Draft Companies Act is Published' (1983) 4 Co Law 47

Rinze, J., 'Konzernrecht: The Law of Groups of Companies in Germany' (1993) 14 Co Law 143

Robertson, D.E., '*Unberseering*: Nailing the Coffin on Sitztheorie?' (2003) 24 Co Law 184

Robertson, D.W., 'Forum Non Conveniens in America and England: A Rather Fantastic Fiction' (1987) 103 LQR 398

Roe, M.J., 'Chaos and Evolution in Law and Economics' (1996) 109 HLR 641

Roe, M.J, 'Delaware's Competition' (2003) 117 Harv LR 588

Rogerson, P., 'English Courts' Jurisdiction over Companies: How Important is Service of the Claim Form in England?' [2000] 3 CFILR 272

Romano, R., 'Law as a Product: Some Pieces of the Incorporation Puzzle' (1985) 1 Jo of Law, Econ and Org 225

Rose, R., 'Main and Territorial Proceedings under the EC Regulation' (2006) 22 IL & P 225

Roth, W.-H., 'Casenote on Centros' (2000) 37 CMLRev 147

Roth, W.-H., 'From *Centros* to *Ueberseering*: Free Movement of Companies, Private International Law and Community Law' (2003) 52 ICLQ 177

Ruskola, T., 'Conceptualising Corporations and Kinship: Comparative Law and Development Theory in a Chinese Perspective' (2000) 52 Stan L Rev 1599

Rutabanzibwa, A.P., 'What is Golden in the Golden Share? Company Law Implications of Privatisation' (1996) 17 Co Law 40

Rutherford, T., 'Frozen Over' (2006) 156 NLJ 837

Rutledge, C.P., 'Mind the Gap: Can Company Law Keep Pace with Technology?' (2000) 21 Co Law 62

Rutstein, M., 'The Proposal by a Foreign Liquidator for a Company Voluntary Arrangement' [1999] 12 Ins Intell 57

Sanders, F., 'Case C112/05. EC v Germany: The Volkswagen Case and Art 56 EC – A Proper Result Yet Also a Missed Opportunity' (2008) 14 Col Jo of Euro Law 359

Sanders, P., 'The European Company' [1968] JBL 184

Sanders, P., 'The Reform of Dutch Company Law' [1973] JBL 194

Santuari, A., 'The Joint Stock Company in 19th Century England and France: *King v Dodd* and the Code de Commerce' (1993) 14 Jo of Leg Hist 39

Santuari, A., 'English Corporations and French Associations: Their Influence on American Business Organisations During the First Half of the 19th Century' (1996) 17 Co Law 281

Schaub, A., 'The Lamfalussy Process Four Years On' [2005] 13 Jo of Fin Reg and Comp 110

Schmidt, J., 'SE and SCE: Two New European Company Forms – and More to Come!' (2006) 27 Co Law 99

Schmidt, J., 'German Company Law Reform: Makeover for the GmbH, a New Mini GmbH and Important News for the AG' (2007) 18 ICCLR 306

Schmitthoff, C., 'The Implications of Company Law Reform' [1960] JBL 151

Schmitthoff, C., 'Daily Mail Loses in European Court' [1988] JBL 454

Schulte, R., 'Corporate Groups and the Equitable Subordination of Claims on Insolvency' (1997) 18 Co Law 2

Sealy, L.S., 'The Disclosure Philosophy and Company Law Reform' (1981) 2 Co Law 51

Sealy, L.S., 'Overseas Companies which have Established a Place of Business in Great Britain' (1985) 6 Co Law 231

Sealy, L.S., 'The Bell Tolls for Ultra Vires' (1986) 7 Co Law 90

Sealy, L.S., 'The Rule in *Foss v Harbottle*: The Australian Experience' (1989) 10 Co Law 52

Sealy, L.S., 'Cross-Border Insolvency Regulations 2006 in Force' [2006] 7 SMCLN 1

Segal, N., 'Corporate Recovery and Rescue: Mastering the Key Strategies Necessary for Successful Cross Border Workouts' [2000] 13 Ins Intell 17

Shearman, J., 'Corporate Governance: An Overview of the German Aufsichtsrat' [1995] JBL 517

Shearman, J., 'Controlling Directors the German Way' (1997) 18 Co Law 123

Sherman, H., 'Corporate Governance Ratings' [2004] 12 Corp Gov 5

Sheikh, S., 'Limited Partnerships Act 1907: Time for Reform' (2002) 23 Co Law 179

Sheikh, S., 'A Modern Regulatory Framework for European Company Law' (2003) 24 Co Law 362

Shillig, M., 'The Development of a New Concept of Creditor Protection for German GmbHs' (2006) 27 Co Law 348

Siems, M., 'Convergence, Competition, *Centros* and Conflicts of Law: European Company Law in the 21st Century' (2002) 27 ELR 47

Siems, M.M., 'What Does Not Work in Comparing Securities Laws: A Critique on La Porta et al.'s Methodology' [2005] 15 ICCLR 300

Sifris, M., and Trichardt, A., 'The Spectre of *Houldsworth* in the Antipodes' (2006) 27 Co Law 155

Slaughter, C.M., 'Corporate Social Responsibility: A New Perspective' (1997) 18 Co Law 313

Smart, P., 'Corporate Domicile and Multiple Incorporation in Private International' Law [1990] JBL 126

Smart, P., 'Safeguarding Assets in International Litigation: The Insolvency Option' (1996) 112 LQR 397

Smart, P., 'Companies Legislation in Hong Kong: Present and Future' (1997) 18 Co Law 34

Smart, P., 'English Courts and International Insolvency' (1998) 114 LQR 46

Smart, P., 'Cross Border Insolvency and Judicial Discretion' [1999] Ins Law 12

Smart, P., 'The Rule Against Foreign Revenue Laws' (2000) 116 LQR 360

Smart, P., and Booth, C., 'Cross Border Insolvency and the Discharge of Debts' (2004) 20 IL & P 147

Smith, M.P., 'Shareholder Activism by Institutonal Investors: Evidence from CalPERS' (1996) 51 Jo of Fin 227

Stanic, A., 'Fat Cats Beware' (2007) 157 NLJ 396

Stapledon, G.P., 'Company Law Reform: Producing A User-friendly Statute' [1999] 3 CFILR 114

Stevens, R., 'Restitution or Property? Priority and Title to Shares in the Conflict of Laws' (1996) 59 MLR 741

Stevens, J., 'The Lex Situs of Shares' [1999] CFILR 138

Stock, K., 'Australian Developments in the Law of Retention of Title' [2002] 15 Ins Intell 1

Surya, B.M., 'The Harmonisation of Caribbean Company Law' (1982) 3 Co Law 44

Svernlow, C., and Dozet, T.L., 'Special Report Proposes Lowering Share Capital in Swedish Private Companies' (2008) 19 ICCLR 379

Tansinda, F., 'EC 11th Company Law Directive and Overseas Companies' (1997) 18 Co Law 98

Taylor, J., 'Commercial Fraud and Public Men in Victorian Britain' (2005) 78 Hist Res 230

Thomas, M., 'Open-Ended Investment Companies: A Hybrid Form of Investment' (1998) 19 Co Law 26

Tijo, H., 'Singapore: Companies (Amendment) Act 2005' (2006) 21 BJIBFL 316

Tomasic, R., 'Corporate Rescue, Governance and Risk-Taking in Northern Rock – Parts 1 and 2' (2008) 29 Co Law 297, (2008) 29 Co Law 330

Tovrov, J., 'Chapter 15 – Opportunities and Pitfalls' (2006) 22 IL & P 17

Tridimas, T., 'Casenote on Centros' (1999) 48 ICLQ 708

Trower, W., 'Recognition and Enforcement of Foreign Insolvency Proceedings in the UK' [2004] 17 Ins Intell 136

Tully, S., 'The 200 Review of the OECD Guidelines for Multinational Enterprises' (2001) 50 ICLQ 394

Tunc, A., 'A French Lawyer Looks at British Company Law' (1982) 45 MLR 1

Vanmeenen, M., 'Corporate Rescue in Belgium: Judges Monitor Insolvency Risks by Means of Commercial Investigation – "an Ounce of Prevention is a Pound of Cure" ' (2006) 27 Co Law 381

Vasseur, M., 'A Company of the European Type' [1964] JBL 358 and [1965] JBL 73

Verrill, L., 'UNCITRAL: Model Law on Cross Border Insolvency' (2006) 22 IL & P 155

von Nessen, P., Goo, S.H., and Low, C.K., 'The Statutory Derivative Action: Now Showing Near You' [2008] JBL 627

Vossestein, G.-J., 'Transfer of Registered Office: The European Commission's Decision Not to Submit a Proposal for a Directive' (2008) 4 Utrecht Law Review 53

Walker, G., 'Sub Prime Loans, Inter Bank Markets and Financial Support' (2008) 29 Co Law 22

Walters, A., 'Judicial Assistance in Cross Border Insolvency at Common Law' (2007) 28 Co Law 73

Walters, A. 'Statutory Redistribution of Floating Charge Assets: Victory (again) to Revenue and Customs' (2008) 29 Co Law 129

Walters, A. and Sarchet, A., 'Protected Cell Companies' (1997) 18 Co Law 219

Walters, A., Williams, I.G., and Marsh, H.M., 'Service of Process in the United States under Insolvency Rule 12.12' [2006] 19 Ins Intell 58

Wan, W.Y., 'Singapore's Insider Trading Prohibition and its Application to Takeover Transactions' (2007) 28 Co Law 120

Watson, A., 'Legal Transplants and Law Reform' (1976) 92 LQR 79

Watson, A., 'Comparative Law and Legal Change' [1978] 37 CLJ 313

Watson, S.M., 'Directors' Duties in New Zealand' [1998] JBL 495

Wedderburn, W., 'The Social Responsibility of Companies' (1985) 15 Melb Univ L Rev 4

Welch, J., 'The Draft Fifth Directive: A False Dawn?' (1983) 8 ELR 83

Werlauff, E., 'The Development of Community Company Law' (1992) 17 ELR 207

Werlauff, E., 'Main Seat Criterion in a New Disguise: An Acceptable Version of the Classic Main Seat Criterion?' (2001) 12 EBLR 2

Wessels, B., 'Recent and Pending Changes in Business Law in The Netherlands' (1998) 9 EBLR 2

Wheeler, S., 'Works Councils: Towards Stakeholding?' (1997) 24 JLS 44

Whincop, M., '*Gambotto v WCP Ltd*: An Economic Analysis of Alterations to Articles and Expropriation Articles' (1995) 23 ABLR 276

Whincop, M., 'Painting the Corporate Cathedral: The Protection of Entitlements in Corporate Law' (1999) 19 OJLS 19

Whincup, M., 'Inequitable Incorporation: The Abuse of a Privilege' (1981) 2 Co Law 158

Williams, R., 'Bona Fide in the Interest of Certainty' [2007] CLJ 500

Wilson G., and Wilson S., 'Responsible Risk Takers: Notions of Directorial Responsibility – Past Present and Future' (2001) 1 JCLS 211

Winter, R.K., 'The Race for the Top Revisited: A Comment on Eisenberg' (1989) 89 Col L Rev 1526

Wood, P., 'World Corporate Law: Mapping the Real Differences' (2003) 24 Co Law 34

Wooldridge, F., 'The Private Company in French Law' [1970] JBL 317

Wooldridge, F., 'The Definition of a Group of Companies in European Law' [1982] JBL 272

Wooldridge, F., 'The Application of the First Directive Regime of Nullity of Unregistered Companies' (1990) 11 Co Law 62

Wooldridge, F., 'Groups of Companies under Italian Law' (2004) 25 Co Law 93

Wooldridge, F., 'The European Company: The Successful Conclusion of Protracted Negotiations' (2004) 25 Co Law 121

Wooldridge, F., 'The Tenth Company Law Directive on Cross Border Mergers' (2006) 27 Co Law 309

Wooldridge, F., 'Affiliated Companies under the Belgian Companies Code' (2007) 28 Co Law 154

Wooldridge, F., 'The Supervisory Boards of Large Dutch Companies' (2007) 28 Co Law 312

Wooldridge, F., 'Proposed Reforms of the German GmbH' (2007) 28 Co Law 381

Woon, W., 'A Cosmic Saga: Note' (1983) 25 Mal L Rev 399

Worthington, S., 'Shares and Shareholders: Property, Power and Entitlement' (2001) 22 Co Law 258 and 307

Wotherspoon, K., 'Insider Dealing – The New Law: Part V of the Criminal Justice Act 1993' (1994) 57 MLR 419

Wouters, J., 'European Company Law: Quo Vadis?' (2000) 37 CMLRev 257

Wymeersch, E., 'Company Law in Turmoil and the Way to "Global Company Practice" ' [2003] 3 JCLS 283

Wymeersch, E., 'Is a Directive on Corporate Mobility Needed?' (2007) 8 EBOLR 161

Xanthaki, H., 'The Establishment of Foreign Companies in France' (1996) 17 Co Law 28

Xanthaki, H., '*Centros*: Is this Really the End for the Theory of the Siege Reel?' (2001) 22 Co Law 2

Yavasi, M., 'Turkey: Unlimited Companies in Turkish Company Law' (2000) 21 Co Law 225

Zaphirou, G.A., 'Approximation of Company Law in the Common Market' [1968] JBL 280

Zink, T., and Vazquez, F., 'US Bankruptcy Code – Chapter 15: The Early Returns' [2007] 20 Ins Intell 17

OFFICIAL REPORTS

Loreburn Committee (1906) (Cd 3052)

Greene Committee (1926) (Cmd 2657)

Cohen Committee (1945) (Cmd 6659)

Gedge Committee (1954) Report of the Committee on Shares of No Par Value (Cmnd 9112)

Jenkins Committee (1962) (Cmnd 1749)

Cork Committee (1982) (Cmnd 8558)

Committee on Financial Aspects of Corporate Governance (1992) (Gee)

Gower, C.B., *A Review of Investor Protection (Part I)* (1984) (Cmnd 9125)

Company Law Review (1998–2001) (UK) Final Report (URN 01/942)

Company Law Review Group: First Report 2001 (Ireland)

Company Law Review Group: Second Report (2007) (Ireland)

Cromme Code (2001) (Germany)

Annual Report on OECD Guidelines for MNEs (2004)

Dickerson Report (Canada) – Dickerson, R.W.V., Howard J.L., and Getz, L., 'Proposals for a New Business Corporations Law for Canada' (1971) (Information Canada)

Law Commission Report, LC no. 296, 'Company Security Interests' (2005) (Cm 6654)

Marini Report (1996) (France)

Index